2008

A Bittersweet Journey

A Bittersweet Journey

Whit Stennett

The Basford Press

The Basford Press
6 Basford Road, Firswood, Manchester, M16 0GE
Tel: 0161 860 6733 Fax: 0161 860 6281

A CIP catalogue record is available for this book from the British Library

ISBN: 978-0-9556543-0-5

Designed and edited by Andy Searle

Photographs courtesy of Kenneth Jarvis and Gareth Hurst

Printed and bound in Great Britain
by Cromwell Press, Trowbridge, Wiltshire

To my father Joseph William Stennett, who passed away in in 1946, and my mother Maud Elizabeth Stennett, who was called to higher service in 1999

CONTENTS

ACKNOWLEDGEMENTS

I would like to thank the following people who, whilst attending my mother's funeral in Jamaica during 1999, first suggested that I wrote my autobiography:

Ivylyn Morgan, Louise Palmer, Andella Henry, Marjorie Hodges-Moulton, Lil Pitterson, Gauntlett Fairweather, Pastor Alvin Francis, Deacon Gideon "Dada" Green, Evadney Tait, Beryl Tait, Deacon Aldin Robinson, my sisters Lurline Moodie, Lorna Clarke, Icylyn Essor, Evelyn Jenkins, the late George Ward, and the late Joy Eccleston-Parchment.

I owe a great deal to my aunt Edna Williams, my cousin Mildred Wallace, Amanda Williams, Teena Redway, Joseph "Joe Reid" McKenzie, Ephraim "Jack Ruby" Dawson and Eric McInnes. These people, and of course there are many others who have not been mentioned (and it is not deliberate), have not only been blessed with longevity but they also have the mental capacity to sustain the oral tradition from which I was able to draw on in the writing of my book. I would also like to thank Linford Sweeney, whose interest in genealogy has put into perspective the importance of Jamaican oral tradition, which I have never taken for granted.

To those who reminded me about the details of my cricketing career from the day that I started playing under the mango trees at our "yard" in Discovery Bay with an orange ball and a coconut bunker bat; then onto playing for my school and the village team. I particularly want to say thanks to Crampy Williams, Hernandez Gayle, Caleb Marshall and the late Arnold "Banky" Sullivan. A great deal of thanks also goes to Syd Lewis for details of when I played cricket in Kingston.

Thanks for the memories of my cricketing exploits in England must go to the late Carl Garner, Euton Christian, John Stephens, Roy Gavin and Johnnie St John. They have all proven their worth in bringing mc up to spccd - thanks for the memories guys!

I would also like to thank Glyn Davis, from my playing days with the Post Office, for presenting me with a portrait entitled "The Lloyds at Lancs" at one of my mayorial functions at Lancashire County Cricket Club in 2004.

To Carl Palmer, former journalist with the Manchester Evening News and many other publications, thanks for your quiet words of advice - you always find the time to help others.

To Paulette Simpson, Jamaica National Building Society, your depth of generosity cannot be measured.

Thanks to all the people who were involved in the STEP Project, in particular Les Chambers, Charles Lauder, Wallen Matthie, the late Jay Hamilton, the late Ossie Smith, Alti Daniel, Louise Dunn, Rita Grizzle, Reverend Robert Boulter, Hyacinth Cooper, David Wiseman, Sandra Walker, Sam Toure and Henry Bonsu.

Thanks to the generosity and kindness of people and organisations in the Manchester Caribbean community, including members of the Jamaica Society, the West Indian Sports and Social Club, the Star of Manchester Lodge No 6 and Esther Chapter No 5; and to the people of Trafford, for their confidence, support and the opportunity to represent their needs and aspirations.

Special thanks to the following people who served on my Mayor's Fundraising Committee (2003-2004): Hyacinth Lawson, Joyce Spencer, Dorribell Williams, Myrtle Smith, Vera Reid, Dorothy Richards, Victoria McLeod, Cherry Levy, Alan Vernon (by the way, he is the best bonfire organiser in the Borough of Trafford and always turns up at election counts wearing the biggest yellow rosette) Pam Dixon and Pearl Morgan.

Special thanks to Sharon Campbell, who had the unenviable task of typing my manuscript and putting up with my handwriting without any complaints.

I am indebted to Andy Searle for bringing to bear his vast experience in publishing and in the process leaving no stones unturned in helping me to realise my dream. He has given me the confidence to rise to the challenge suggested by my friends in Jamaica in 1999. Andy, like the dedicated wicket keeper that he is, makes a very good team-mate. Nuff respect, Andy!

I would like to take this opportunity to say thanks to my wife Gwen for her love, encouragement and patience. I know that at times it must have been frustrating for her when at two o'clock in the morning I would wake up, turn the lights on and start to jot things down on paper. She has never complained. My daughters, Patricia and Angela, and my eldest grand-daughter, Nikesha, have always been encouraging as every time they visit their question is always: "How's the book coming on daddy?" Thanks, girls! My other two grand-daughters, Shanique and Imogen, both want to know when I am going to be famous. Watch this space, girls!

I would also like to thank Reverend Robert Boulter for his generosity in helping to get this book published.

Above all is my gratitude to God for giving me the courage and faith to persist when the going got tough.

God bless you all. Whit Stennett, October 2007

PREFACE

All things being equal I have had a good life and the title of my book was originally intended to be "Perseverance will make you conquer". The words from a Jamaican mento of the 1950's entitled "Dig Dig Water Boy". It was the first record that I have ever bought.

I am not sure why I did not stay with that title but be that as it may my story is an honest account of my life. A story of a boy born and brought up in a small fishing village in Jamaica from parents of meagre means and who through hard work and determination took opportunities as they became available and eventually became a Mayor in the Metropolitan Borough of Trafford. A testimony that with the right attitude, and belief in self, anyone from a humble background can make a success of their lives. It is a story about love for families, and friends, love for even those people who may have despised me. It is a story about the people who were there for me and who helped in making me what I am . Above all it is a story about having faith in God.

CHAPTER ONE

A Defining Moment

A DEFINING moment in my life came literally as 'a bolt out of the blue'. I was 13 years old and on the 8th August 1948 I was struck by lightning.

At the time I was living with my brother and four sisters in Dry Harbour, then a small sleepy but idyllic fishing village in the North Coast Parish of Saint Ann in the County of Middlesex, Jamaica, now extensively developed as a tourist resort and shipping port for the St Ann Bauxite Company. Dry Harbour is reputed to be the first place in Jamaica that Christopher Columbus set foot on land when he arrived on the 4th May 1494, hence the present name, Discovery Bay, to commemorate the event.

Along with some of my friends I went to an afternoon rally to celebrate what was a great event at the time; the installation of electricity in the Congregational Church, which was also at the time used as the school from Monday to Friday.

Some 130 people were in the Church waiting for the concert to start. It was like any other August evening, a cloudless sky, with a cool balmy breeze blowing in from the sea. A group of seven boys were standing under the window of the west side of the building when suddenly I noticed a great ball of fire, about the size of a large grapefruit, entering through the opposite window on the east side of the building travelling at tremendous speed. From where I was standing I calculated that this ball of fire would exit through the window where we were standing. Caught up within the confusion of fright and flight I instinctively ducked only to hear an almighty bang, the shattering of glass, and an instant smell of sulphur. There was pandemonium all around and in the process of drifting from consciousness to unconsciousness at one stage I vividly recall seeing my body lying on the ground and I was hovering in the air above it.

Another experience I had was being in a country that was not Jamaica. It was only when I came to England in 1959 and joined the Territorial Army in 1961 and went on the annual two week camp at Salisbury and, having gone to Newquay in Cornwall, I realised that it was the place where I was on the day when I was struck in Jamaica.

What was also interesting was, as I walked around Newquay, quietly reflecting on my experience of 1948, I met a man who enquired if I was from

Jamaica. Having responded in the affirmative he mentioned that as a young Rating in the Royal Navy, serving on the HMS Vidal, which was stationed in Bermuda, the first time he visited Jamaica was in August of 1948. Thirteen years after meeting this man in Newquay, the incident in Jamaica gave rise to me revisiting my childhood and putting things into perspective. Based on my Christian upbringing, if what happened to me had anything to do with miracles, this process of evaluation was made even more interesting especially as when I was born I was a premature baby and except for Ma Shatty Morrison, the 'Nana' - that was the name that people in rural Jamaica referred to midwives- nobody expected me to live.

Ma Shatty not only assured my mother and my father and other family members that I would live for a very long time, she also prophesised that the mole on my left palm signified that I would either be a teacher or a preacher, and would eventually travel abroad and be like Marcus Garvey. As to the mole on my left heel she claimed that I would play cricket and be like George Headley!

I was not the only one to be struck by the lightning amongst the group of us who stood at the window. With myself there was Glaister 'Bennie' Stewart who is now retired from The Post Office and lives in London, his brother Norman 'Buggie' Stewart, a successful businessman who still lives in Jamaica, Llewlyn 'Bugs' Faulcher, who lives in New York, Frank Cover who had a successful career in Banking and is now retired and lives in Miami, Florida, and Wendell 'Crampy' Williams, acclaimed as one of the best house painters in St Ann, now retired and a local Historian - what Crampy doesn't know it has not happened yet.

Five people got injured Bennie, Buggie, Dudley Kelly, a local tailor living in Jack Lodge at the time; he has since passed away and Vincent Walwyn from Kingston; he had the contract to paint and decorate the Columbus Inn Hotel that was being constructed at the time, and myself. There were so many differing and unexplained aspects to the incident. Firstly, Frank, Crampy and Bugs, who were part of the group were not affected, and Dudley Kelly and Vincent Walwyn, who were in the Church, were not sitting near each other. Secondly, when the lightening exited, the accepted theory is that the ball of fire went to the back of the building where the water tank stood and burst through the concrete, which resulted in water gushing from the tank. And thirdly, none of those who were affected had any damage to their clothes. We were all rushed to the Saint Ann's Bay Hospital some 14 miles away from Discovery Bay.

I was still very dazed when I was placed in the vehicle; I remember my mother holding my hands and crying. There was also this reassuring voice inside me saying "be brave I am with you". It was at that stage I said, "Mother, don't cry I am going to be okay" and then slipped again into unconsciousness. It was many years after recalling the incident when mother told me that when Frank Cover came up to the house to inform her of what had taken place, although she had put on a brave face, it was difficult to come to terms with as my dad had passed on two years previously, yet that was the measure of Mother who had the strength to accept situations. It is one of the lessons that I have learnt very well.

In 2004 I had the privilege to visit Jamaica in my capacity as the Worshipful the Mayor of the Borough of Trafford, and being mindful of the importance of giving something back to the community that nurtured me, I took some wheelchairs and other medical equipment, donated by people from the Trafford and Manchester communities and presented them to the Saint Ann's Bay Hospital. At the end of the presentation ceremony, Arthur Clemetson, one of my contemporaries and President of The Discovery Bay Community Association, in his vote of thanks reminded those present that my generosity of spirit and my ability to be concerned for others even when I am exposed to personal conflicts are some of the reasons that has given rise to my achievements. He used the example of my consoling my mother in 1948 and my subsequent stay in St Ann's Bay Hospital.

On the way to the hospital I had regained consciousness and though I was suffering severe pains I was able to listen to the music drifting over the Caribbean from Miami. The song that was being played was "There is a tree by the meadow with a stream floating by, and carved upon that tree is the words 'I'll love you till I die'". If I ever get the opportunity to go on Desert Island Discs that will definitely be one that I would want playing.

Of the five of us that were admitted to the hospital three were treated and sent home. Vin Walwyn and I were detained. I was given a bed on the veranda, which was comfortable, and as I was severely burnt only a sheet was placed over me. Little over five minutes after medication was given it resulted in vomiting which was quite unpleasant in terms of the length of time that it had taken and the stench which could best be described as a mixture of burning rubber and vinegar; I must confess that I felt much better afterwards and to replace the fluid that I had lost I was given a large mug of milk.

Although I have always liked drinking milk this particular evening I had no desire for it even if it meant saving my life, and I was still having pains all over my body and at best all I wanted to do was rest. Fortunately or otherwise this was not to be when a boy, maybe two years older than I, came up beside my bed gesticulating that he wanted to drink the milk. I realised then that he was dumb and so to stop him from what I felt was too much pressure on his part I took the mug and emptied its contents over the side of the veranda; I often ask myself where my charity was.

If I felt that my action was one that had put paid to the insistence of my dumb friend I was completely wrong because within ten minutes he hotfooted it back to my bed, this time with a nurse in tow gesticulating to her that I had tipped the milk over the side of the veranda. Having realised what I had done she shooed the youngster away and with an angelic smile she looked at me and said "Goodnight Mr Lightning". I often thought that it would be an ideal topic for a romantic film!

As I lay in bed and tried to sleep, given that I was still in pain although not as severe as when I was admitted, it became rather difficult as I found myself revisiting John Bunyan's Pilgrim's Progress. My first read of this story was in 1946 when I was presented with a copy for being the most outstanding boy in School in deportment, sports, school work, and punctuality; I was eleven years old. In the process of revisiting the book my young mind was able to have a better understanding of what Bunyan tried to convey to his readers. For example, I pictured Vanity Fair as the Discovery Bay Church where people had dressed to attend the Rally, my mother holding my hands, the driver of the station wagon as the music from the radio, the young nurse who I learned was Nurse Pitter; all had their relevance and wider significance to my understanding. I named by dumb friend "Mr Speechless Parrot". I have always maintained that even in times of great adversity and tragedy humour has its place. I cannot remember when I did fall asleep but what I did remember were the times of great singing with gusto at our Christian endeavour meetings - 'who would true valour see' - it has since become one of my favourite hymns.

Waking early has never been a problem for me; the family custom was up by 5 o'clock, wash, dress, followed by prayer; the adage that 'the family that prays together stays together' is something that I have tried to preserve and have encouraged with my children, who have their own families to do the same.

I was anxious to hear what the doctor had to say to me as he did his rounds on the day following the accident. The blisters and the weals on my body were more visible and it was only then that I had the chance to see the extent of the impact of the lightning to my body. I accepted the situation and decided that, at best, I was still alive and I was going to try as hard as ever to get better and go home to my family and friends. My spirits lifted as I watched a stream of doctor birds flying from amongst the trees, extracting pollen from the flowers in bloom. Altogether it was a beautiful day, and I was determined to enjoy it.

Following a thorough examination Doctor Palmer confirmed that the burns were not life-threatening, but by the same rule I would need to remain in hospital for a week or longer depending on how I responded to treatment. Hardly had the doctors and nurses finished their round when the speechless parrot came up to my bed. I started to feel uncomfortable, and as it would be the second time that I would have seen him since my arrival my first encounter made me feel difficult. In my little world there was no place for a "chat chat person", the order of the day was to 'see and blind, hear and deaf, and dumb also'; In other words, mind your own business. Like myself I assumed that he had the same reservations. Too right he did because in his palm was an orange which he tossed from hand to hand like a spin bowler would on approaching the wicket before he bowls. He made sign language to me which I realised was enquiring if I played cricket. I bowed and he placed the orange on the floor; this time with a batting stance first like a right handed batsman, and secondly like a left handed batsman. I nodded at his left hand stance, he then came close to the bed and stretched his hand which I shook as other patients looked at what had happened and started to laugh. The previous incident, as far as I was concerned, was now dead and buried. I immediately started to feel better both in mind, spirit and body; proof that forgiveness is the central plank by which one must tread towards the healing process; throughout my life I have made every effort to embrace the ideal.

Having satisfied himself that he was accepted he waved goodbye and in less than 15 minutes he was back, this time with two nightshirts that I merely had to slip into like a dressing gown. I chose the blue one, my favourite colour, signifying my Aquarian status. We walked into the main ward to see my friend, Vin Walwyn, who was reading a bible. He took time off to inform me of what the doctor had told him; it was similar to me and we both agreed that we would be making efforts towards a speedy recovery. He had a deadline to work towards in as far as his painting contract was concerned; I wanted to be back with my friends. As it happened my young friend would be leaving the following day; he signed, which I knew was that he was there to have his tonsils removed and when he was leaving he brought his mother to see me and it turned out they lived a few miles outside of Saint Ann's Bay. Until I left Jamaica he helped his mother in running a stall in the market selling fruit and vegetables. What I learnt from him is that every person has a place in God's empire, a fact that was borne out to me by Ernal Stevens from Saint Mary, Jamaica, who lived in Manchester, England and who wrestled under the sobriquet of 'Honey Boy Zimba'. When he told me about the unique qualities of a wrestler that he had met who was both deaf and dumb, it helped me realise that people like them help to reinforce the importance of breaking barriers down that stand in the way of progress.

The determination to attain a level of fitness and a feeling of well-being warranting being discharged was continually being tested by a wide cross-section of people who were interested to find out information of what had taken place. In essence people were curious, which was reflected in the questions that they asked and over the years I have come to appreciate what Edmund Burke said: "The first and simplest emotion which we discover in the human mind is curiosity". On questions Charles Steinmetz said, "No man really becomes a fool until he stops asking questions".

I recall in 1971 being in Wythenshawe Hospital for an Haemorrhoidectomy, and after relating what happened to me in August 1948 in Jamaica I was asked, "Mr Stennett, did you die?" My response was, "Nurse, do you think that it is a ghost that is speaking to you?" More about ghosts in other chapters of this book.

I was as excited as a youngster opening his Christmas presents when I told the doctor who was doing his rounds that I was feeling fine and wanted to go home. I was still having niggling pains in my leg about which I deliberately refused to mention. As far as I was concerned, given that I was well looked after, I wanted out, especially knowing that Vin Walwyn was being discharged that same day. In addition I wanted to give my mother, whom I knew would be visiting in two days time, a surprise.

It was about 11.30am in the morning after all the formalities that we were officially discharged; having got dressed I realised that my shoes were missing; I found out later that in the confusion they were left in the vehicle that took me to the hospital. For me it was not a big deal walking barefoot and did not pose a problem because wisdom has dictated that having no feet is a total disaster, having no shoes is hardly an inconvenience. I remember canvassing with the Honourable Beverley Hughes, Labour Member of Parliament for Stretford and Urmston and saying that she would win "the election walking barefooted"; that was confidence personified.

Vin Walwyn sent a telegram to the Company that was building the hotel requesting transport to pick us up; after about an hour he received a reply that the transport would be arriving at 3pm. In between waiting he took the opportunity to enlighten a group of people sitting under the shade of an almond tree about aspects of his Seventh Day Adventist beliefs. Three O'clock came and went with no transport, four o'clock no transport. By then our boats were completely burnt in that we were fully discharged from the hospital. Come 6 o'clock we decided to walk the fourteen miles to Discovery Bay on the assumption that trucks from the Western Parishes travelling from Kingston would give us a lift. Our first stop was at Priory about a mile and a half from the hospital where we had something to eat. Whilst we were in the shop a truck passed by and I felt reassured that it would not be long before we would be picked up. As we proceeded on our journey I realised that the pains in my leg were getting more acute and I should have spent another day or two in hospital. I also observed Vin Walwyn's pace was getting slower and no doubt he was also having reservations about taking his discharge. I consoled myself that like the Children of Israel I had left Egypt and nothing was going to stop me reaching my Promised Land, Discovery Bay.

Except for the stars in the skies the night was pitch black and with a gentle wind blowing from the hills, wafting a mixture of the blossoms of plants and the scent of ripened fruits that titillated the nostrils, and from time to time the occasional frog or crab darting across the road, the night was still which on reflection resonated within me. "I see skies of blue, and clouds of white, the bright blessed day, the dark sacred night, and I think to myself, what a wonderful world" - Louis 'Satchmo' Armstrong.

We were now moving just a little above snail pace as we passed Laughlands, Cranbrook and Big River, in keeping with our pace our conversation was gradually being silenced. We had completed roughly six miles of the journey when apprehension started to build within me as we passed Big River and entered onto the stretch of road on the way to Salem. As kids the oral tradition perpetuated several stories about duppies, rolling calves, three foot horses, and other ghostly phenomenons that constantly traversed this section of road. Looking back I saw two lights piercing through the darkness, coming towards us; there was no sound to indicate that it was a motor vehicle and my instant reaction was that it was a rolling calf. One of their features is the strong array of light from their eyes. As the lights came closer we heard voices which turned out to be three men on bicycles; one had no lights and they were workmen who had just finished their shift at the Landovery Sugar Estate. We flagged them down and told them who we were and they placed us on their handlebars and the running commentary kicked in as to what exactly had happened to us; they had already heard about the incident with them living at Runaway Bay, only four miles away from Discovery Bay. For them seeing us in the flesh and talking to us assured them of a place in local history. I cannot recall seeing or hearing anything that could be linked with the spirit world; suffice it to say that it put paid to my fear of the darkness and the great comfort that I get from hearing the song which is Liverpool Football Club's theme song, "When you walk through the storm, hold your head up high, and don't be afraid of the dark".

We were dropped off at Runaway Bay Square, expressing appreciation to our earthly saviours who were William Edwards, Ernal Meredith and Reynard Shaw. Filled with renewed vigour we continued on our journey to Discovery Bay. We travelled over a mile when there was the sound of a vehicle with bright headlights approaching; the driver responded to our wave and the short explanation of who we were saw one of the sidemen alighting from the truck and lifting me on board. Vin Walwyn was also helped on board, it was clear that we both were still struggling with some measure of discomfort. It was now sheer determination that was keeping us going. Like the men on the bikes the two sidemen on the truck started their own commentaries and we were quite happy to oblige. I was particularly struck with the younger of the two men, who at the end of every question would say "Bwoy oonu lucky God is 'good'".

It was about 9 O'clock when we reached Discovery Bay and the street was deserted. There was a light on at the Police Station and in the accommodation upstairs, the shop which now houses a branch of the St Ann Parish Library. I shouted upstairs to Lance McCarthy, who came down to greet me and volunteered to walk up the hill to my house. I bade Vin Walwyn goodnight, promising him that I would come to see him regarding doing studies about the Adventist Religion and he disappeared into the darkness on his way home.

A light was still on in our house; it being holidays staying up late was the norm. My grand-Aunt Granny Edith was sitting on the veranda, Scamp, our dog, ran down the steps of the veranda and started to make much of me. On entering the living room my mother and sisters all hugged me and started crying, but their tears were of joy.

I have never been a big eater but that night I could have eaten a horse and was not afraid to express my feelings and my desire for food. Granny Edith was from the old school which dictated that a man should eat to live as opposed to the other way round and within a jiffy she had prepared a meal which we all enjoyed.

In keeping with the family tradition the last activity of the evening, a Chapter from the Bible followed by prayer and then to bed. That night my eldest sister, Carmen, chose Psalms 121, "I will lift up mine eyes unto the hills from whence cometh my help". I went to bed feeling confident that whatever happened I was at home and tomorrow would be another day.

Words of my arrival spread like wildfire throughout the village and by mid-morning the yard was literally full, in a sense it was an example of how rural Jamaican Communities, or for that matter the real people, who had a sense of their history and their values that they created and made efforts to maintain and reflect that we are our brothers' keepers.

Every conceivable theory was discussed, not only regarding what had given rise to the accident, but what would be the best course of action that needed to be applied in my restoration to full fitness. One suggestion was that my demise was due to a rebellious streak; or behaviour that I had taken on, even to the point where I started absenting myself from Sunday School and Church. On this note I would like to put the record straight and say what had exactly happened.

On Monday 29th July, eight days prior to the lightning strike, I had played my first cricket match for the Senior Team Discovery Bay versus Thicketts at their home ground. On the morning of the match there was a lady from another village, Content. Her name was Auntie Lett and she was a revivalist Prophetess who would go around warning of forthcoming disasters. Most of the time her prophesies came to pass and some people viewed her with suspicion; others held her in high esteem. I was part of that group who was not quite sure of what to believe, in other words keeping an open mind was and is always an option that has been important to me. However, on the morning when she warned, as always people of all ages gathered round to more or less discuss as to what would be affected. My input to the discussion was to establish as to why this lady has never gone to the well-to-do members of the community gates, to warn them. In addition I also implied that God seemed to pick and choose who he allowed to die; for instance, taking away my dad who was a good man and leaving people who were bad. What I said did not go down too well with a lady who was one of the leading lights in the community and a member of the Church that I attended. I was in no way disrespectful to her and all the people who were there on the morning testified to that. The lady finished by saying that I was a Heathen; that being said she went up to my house and told my mother that I was getting too big for my boots and that was enough to cause my mother to hide my cricket clothes, adding, "No cricket for you today; you are staying in the yard". My ego was deflated but I was not going to take my mother's ultimatum lying down, or for that matter sitting down on the veranda or under the mango trees crying. I needed a lawyer to plead my case and George Henry (we called him "Mass Georgie") was the man, but I was now grounded so to get Georgie I shouted Crampy who lived not far away. One cannot stop a man from shouting even when he is in prison! Quick as a flash, Crampy was at my house and I explained the situation.

I was rather relieved when "Mass Georgie" arrived and the outcome was my clothes were given back to me after promising my mother that I would be good. Incidentally, Georgie was one of the umpires for that match; more about Georgie as a man and an umpire later. As it happened the match proved to be the litmus test in sorting out the men from the boys.

I was in exalted company that day playing for and against men such as the Bowie Brothers, Lloyd "Bugsie" Day, Marshy Marshall, Dickie Campbell, James Marshall, Grand Uncle of the Jamaican and West Indies Player, Xavier Marshall, all seasoned players playing at Parish level and in competitions such as the Nethersole Cup, West Indies Sugar Company and Crum Ewing Competitions. Some of these players were also attracting the eyes of the selectors for Jamaica. The next step was playing for the West Indies, above and beyond all considerations. They took their cricket seriously, for us it was a plank that provided 'an escape route or rite of passage' for a better future.

Thicketts batted first and posted 189 on the board. All credit to 'Bugsie' Day who bowled that day like a man inspired; I bowled two overs and got a wicket, I also took a catch in the slips. My spirits soared like a kite with the encouragement and acknowledgements coming from team mates and spectators. So far my selection was justified. Walking into bat last man in with twelve runs to win, facing Isaiah Paisley; a mean and fearsome fast bowler, could only be described as walking into hell naked. As I approached the wicket L.B. Welsh, a Constable stationed at Discovery Bay Police Station, met me and said to me, "Don't try to hit him, get in line, keep your eye on the ball and dead bat him and when I shout run to me like hell". I took leg stump guard and the umpire shouted out 'five more balls to come and the bowler is the devil hell Isaiah Paisley'. In those days we played eight ball overs, there were five men in the slips, a silly mid on, a silly mid off, a fine leg, and short backward square leg except for the wicket-keeper who was standing back. I could literally feel the breath of the fielders blowing on to my body. To say that I was scared is not an understatement. I was scared like hell; this is what facing fast bowling is all about; fearing that you are going to get hit. This being said, I was not prepared to give any indication to the bowler, fielder or wicket-keeper that I felt afraid. I was thirteen years and eight months old but I knew that I had the patience, the ability and the determination to be a cricketer. What I expected from Isaiah Paisley was the Yorker, instead he bowled one of the most vicious bouncers that I have ever seen; in the process of taking evasive action the ball hit the outside edge of the bat, ballooned over the slip cordon for four. The Discovery Bay supporters went wild, shouting "David has come to slay Goliath"; by this time Paisley was facing up to me saying, "You little bang belly bwoy, you come to mash up my business". In Jamaican lingo the word 'mash' means 'smash', so when 'mash up' is being used it means beyond repair. Rather than responding to him I hissed my teeth at him, which was rather rude on my partm, after all he was twice my age and respect was due.

The crowd, realising that there was an impasse between us, shouted out to him, 'take time bowling to the youth it is only a game'. Walking back to his mark he shouted back to them, 'he has a bat in his hand, he is a man and a cricketer'. I knew that I had rattled him and was now prepared to throw caution to the wind and take him on. The next ball was short outside off stump, it had "come on Whit" written all over it and being a left-handed batsman I applied all the strength in my body and hooked it for four. It was the side with the shortest boundary and by now with the field spread out I expected the worst. The next ball was pitched up; I dead batted it and was off like a rabbit.

In true Caribbean style I was lifted shoulder high off the pitch, the ovation, the back-slapping was tremendous and it was quite an experience to savour. I was now a local star, but even at that young age, in keeping with the way that my parents brought me up, I was not going to allow things to get to my head; it is a lesson that I have learnt well.

Paisley was the first of the Thicketts players to congratulate me on my performance. I remembered him saying to me, "Sten you are a young cricketer but if you want to get anything out of the game take my simple advice, keep away from the wimmin, not too much food, not too much rum, not too much music, just a little at a time". Some of the best advice I have ever been given and as I got older I saw so many sportspeople who have fallen by the wayside as a result of over-indulgence with the things that Paisley warned me about.

Caught up in the euphoria and excitement of my performance I stayed out late that night celebrating with my friends and as a result I missed going to church the following morning, which could be seen as a confirmation of what Aunt Pooda said, that I was getting too big for my boots. I am sure that she heard of my performance but that did not cut any ice with her; deep down I knew that she meant me well but saw my assertiveness and determination to defend what I believe in as rebellious. Her status in the community would have given rise to some people believing her; hence it was not difficult to make the argument that my being struck by lightning was a sign from God warning me of my wicked ways. I think that more harm is done not by the things that one does but by the negative views or sometimes spiteful things people do to perpetuate the action.

Getting better and to be able to play my cricket, go swimming, shooting birds and all the things that boys do, especially during holidays, became important to me. Central to my predicament was my star rating as a cricketer and a swimmer - and my contemporaries have all always alluded that I was the best swimmer in school - had heightened my celebrity status and everybody and anybody who had a term of reference wanted to be with me. I was now public property and a symbolic representative for the community. Wendell "Jack" Barrett, the local correspondent for the Jamaica Gleaner, did a story on me which was published and of course this added to the interest outside of my own community. Looking back I think that this interest was fuelled by the fact that the oral tradition would have established that trees and animals have been killed by lightning but no human being has ever been struck before in Discovery Bay, and five at the same time was indeed a miracle.

All different kinds of advice were given to hasten the healing process. For a start both Miss Zetel and Miss Doris, neighbours of ours, pooh poohed the idea that my mother should use the lotion that the doctor had prescribed for healing and clearing my body of the burns. I cannot remember my mother telling me of the doctor's explanation as to why there was a wound almost the size of a halfpenny at the soft tissue of my body just above my hip; Miss Zetel, Miss Doris and my uncle in law, Gus Edwards, all agreed that it was the spot that the lightning exited from my body. Be that as it may, the external herbal potions put to my body were honey, fish oil, and sempervivum Juice.

I must confess that the taste was horrible but it was effective and within four months, except for where it was supposed that the lightning exited from my body, the burn marks had disappeared. It was not until September 1974 when this lump was completely erased from my body. In a sense I was rather disappointed in that I attached some kind of importance to it as a badge of courage.

In the period of abstaining from my outdoor activities I devoted most of my time to reading and was quite pleased with myself when the results of the First Jamaica Local Examinations that I sat in the July of that year arrived, confirming that I passed with Distinction in English and History. In reading the Bible I found the Book of Psalms, The Book of Proverbs and The Book of Revelations quite inspiring. I also read Edward Fitzgerald's "The Rubaiyatt of Omar Khayyam", but when I came across a copy of The National Geographic Magazine with an article on Lightning and their behaviours, it was mind-boggling. My newly acquired knowledge on the complexities of hurricanes, waterfalls, waterspouts, earthquakes and lightning, which I had experienced, made it much easier for me to engage with adults and ask a number of questions on matters that were confusing my young mind.

From reading The National Geographic Magazine, and with my religious or Christian upbringing, it was quite clear in my mind that whilst man had the knowledge to trace the source of the various weather patterns he had no control in preventing disasters. Central to some of my questions were why God allowed them to happen and where he is when they are taking place. I was also interested to know if those people, some of whom were semi-illiterate, who warned people of impending disasters, had any special gifts from God. On this particular question it was only Captain Leslie from Old Folly who agreed that some people who had a high forehead and a dropping ear had a seventh sense that can tell the brain when something out of the ordinary is going to happen. Well, as I have alluded I have always kept an open mind with an understanding that events and time will be a convincing factor.

This convincing factor was brought to my attention by The Reverend Dr David Wheeler, who was my Chaplain when I was the Worshipful the Mayor of the Borough of Trafford 2003/2004, who came to see me during my writing of this book and referred me to an article in the Manchester Evening News of Friday 18th February 2005 under the heading, "Tsunami Survival Secret Found".

As the continual search for widening my knowledge base was being realised so was the improvement to my health. I was now fully aware as to why I was created and that each person is different from the other, no one else has the same future, gifts or talents, as human beings we are unique. Having reached that understanding I made the decision that each day, whatever the circumstances, I would strive to do better than the day before. Through adversity I arrived at a point in my young life that I had grown up and with both elder brothers being away from home I had earned the right and knew the responsibilities that go with the right to be dubbed 'man of the yard'.

A week before I went back to school in September I received a letter from my eldest brother who was in America not only congratulating me on my speedy recovery but for passing my first exam. He signed with the words 'Persevere to the end'. I was made a monitor within a week of school re-opening.

CHAPTER TWO

Following the Tradition

THE FIRST school that I attended was Aunt V Bell "Quattie-a-week" School at Old Folly. A 'Quattie' was the then Jamaican colloquial term for a penny and a half penny. Established with the support of the churches in the early 1890s, these schools were the fore-runners for the basic schools which are still popular now.

Admitting pupils from about the age of four until they reached seven, when they entered into the then free Elementary School system where they remained until they were fifteen, these schools were largely run by women who represented that rising group of civic-minded free blacks and brown-skinned people who saw education and the teaching profession as an avenue for social mobility and the creating and maintenance of their status in the community.

In addition to teaching the rudiments of the three R's, Aunt V placed great importance on a more than copious diet of bible stories, a strict code of conduct on time-keeping, cleanliness, respect for others, and the importance of fresh air and exercise. In essence she was the epitome of a role model and mentor with the kindness and humility that went with it. Other than a weakness to cope with sums or figures, to which the oral tradition have always perpetuated that the Stennetts and figures have never travelled on the same boat, I could hold my own with the other subjects. I enjoyed the bible stories, especially those from the Old Testament, such as Noah and the Ark, Joseph being sold by his brothers, Moses leading the children of Israel out from bondage in Egypt, and David killing Goliath with a stone. Of the New Testament stories I enjoyed Christ's birth in the stable, the Three Wise Men and Jesus turning water into wine. Time-keeping, cleanliness and respect for others were values that were instilled at home; as for fresh air and exercise which involved skipping rope, Chevy chase, rounders, hop-scotch, playing cricket with home-made bats and oranges for balls, I could not have enough of those and I was in seventh heaven participating. Boys and girls always took part and one of my rivals at sport was Daphne 'Tiny' Green; I always had to dig deep into the tank to beat her as she was so good.

As I grew up I was able to put into context how that early exposure to bible stories and sports viewed into a colonial, social and political context that sustained the argument underlining 'Liberation Theology' and 'Muscular Christianity'.

Whilst not impeding my progress, I had to fight against the then prevailing taboo of being left handed, and the constant pressure for me to talk as often as I possibly could to expose my pronounced lisp which my compatriots, especially girls, found rather funny and amusing. My dad was left handed and he coped but maybe I wanted to please my teachers and in the process I developed a strategy to use both hands when it pleased me. One thing that I decided to do was to bowl right handed and bat left handed, and in my time I have switched from batting left handed to right hand and have bowled a few left arm googlies; In most cases they prove annoying to the opposition.

As for my lisp, I have spent time correcting it and my friend Samuel "Rex" Gordon from Content who lives in Manchester, England, has always reminded me that during my teenage years when the use of the word "Rass", the personification of Jamaican Speech in the presence of an Officer of the Law, could result in arrest and a fine from Court, that I could use it and get away with it because of my lisp. I could make the case that I did not correct it as well as I may have thought. Be that as it may I am convinced that there has never been a better sight than to behold a left handed batsman walking to the crease. Over the years I have mastered the art of 'talking the talk and walking the walk'; I learnt so much at the "Quattie-a-week" School that when I went to big school as we called it in those days, I was placed in Third Class, the highest class in Lower Division.

My first headmaster was Teacher W.W. Williams from Manchester. A very good leg break bowler and an excellent player of the piano, whenever we were playing cricket he was always on hand to support us. He encouraged me to be a leg break bowler always saying "Bowl with Guile Stennett". It was from him that I learnt to appreciate Boogie Woogie, Rag-time, and Swing music. He lived at the Manse just above the school, which at the time was run under the auspices of the Congregational Church.

He spent more time playing the piano than he did in school teaching; and he got the local band practising in the Manse much to the annoyance of some of the members of the church. The situation was resolved when my dad intervened, reminding those who were incensed that people may have well enjoyed themselves because no one knew what lay ahead if Hitler won the war. The Germans were in Caribbean waters, or for that matter in Dry Harbour, as conveyed in the lyrics of the following song written by W.W. Williams:

A Bittersweet Journey

Four fishers folk went out one night to catch some Red Mouth Grunt
The moon was shining in the sky and did not disturb their punt
When suddenly out of nowhere a funny boat appear
It had no lights perhaps no gear and it did make the fishers fear.

Then one fisher shout Bwoy mek wi cut wi line and row fi shore fah dis a
submarine
Yu larn fi, row you larn fi pray when you si one submarine
The four fishermen were Elkanah Williams, Jacob Leslie, Michael Williams and
Ronald Seivewright

Following the incident men from the village formed themselves into groups and armed with machetes and sticks took it in turns to patrol the beach area against German invaders. Prior to the Hurricane of 1951, amongst a group of visitors to Discovery Bay, was a man from Germany who met a group of us at the beach and informed us that during the war he served on one of the German U Boats following the ships transporting sugar from Jamaica to Liverpool, and on one occasion surfaced in the harbour. It was quite moving when he met face to face with Michael, Jacob, and Elkanah; Ronald was away at the time. It was then peace time and it was clear that no-one showed any kind of animosity and for me it showed that people have the capacity to forgive.

When I was born in 1935, Marcus Garvey, one of Jamaica's national heroes who was also born at Priory near St Ann's Bay, left Jamaica for England to set up the London Headquarters for The United Negro Improvement Association (UNIA). That very year George Headley, playing for the West Indies against England at Sabina Park in Kingston in the Fourth Test made 270 not out. West Indies won the match by an innings and 161 runs. The oral traditional has also highlighted three local events that are worthy of mention happening in 1935. First was the pumpkin that PA C planted at Old Road near Runaway Bay. It grew so large that a man who had reported one of his sows missing, after searching for many days without success eventually found her inside the pumpkin with ten little piglets. Then there was Captain Leslie from Old Folly who caught a turtle that weighed eight hundred pounds and it took twenty men to carry it to his yard and when it was killed people five miles out of Dry Harbour came to buy the flesh; four gallons of oil was extracted from its liver.

That same year Seppy Gordon, a left handed batsman, playing for the Dry Harbour Cricket Club at the site not far from where the Saint Ann Bauxite Sports Ground now stands against a United Fruit Company team from Kingston, hit the longest six off the then Leslie Hylton, the Jamaica and West Indies fast bowler, who was hanged in 1955 for murdering his wife. My dad, bowling fast left arm round the wicket with a packed leg side, had figures of five overs, two maidens, three runs, two wickets. The match was interrupted by a swarm of bees that settled at the Tamarind tree over which Seppy had hit the six. The match resumed when Uncle Fred Clarke, my mother's Uncle, removed the bees. That was the last time my dad played in a competitive match; he later told me he had to make way for younger and better players.

The relevance of these events in terms of my own experiences and aspirations has firstly been explained by Michael Manley, a former Jamaican Prime Minister, who when writing in his book "A History of West Indies Cricket" made the interesting correlation between Marcus Garvey as a social reformer and George Headley as a cricketer. He wrote about Garvey in the context of a Caribbean society in the 1920's and 30's that needed a voice that could articulate the plight of the majority African-Caribbean population and the extent to which the onus was on them to make a positive link between black pride, black rights, black self-worth, and self esteem. On self-confidence Garvey said "A man with no confidence in self is twice defeated in the race of life. With confidence you have won even before you have started".

Manley alluded to Headley in terms of the impact that he had on the aspiring middle class who were half black and were happy to align themselves with personalities who would help them to have a better understanding of their own self-awareness. In their quest in the pursuing of a national identity the white upper classes felt proud of George Hedley. I remember going to Trent Bridge, Nottingham in 1976 to watch England against West Indies in the first Test match when Viv Richards made 232 runs. In the process of hitting the bowlers all over the park I heard a voice behind shouting "drop lashes in dem backside Viv". I recognised the Barbadian accent alright and when I looked around the man said to me, "You think I am an English man, I am a Bajan", ample proof of Caribbean identification.

According to Manley it was the majority black masses that attached so much importance to Headley. He wrote, "When he walked to the wicket, brisk, self-assured, and took guard in his quaintly old-fashioned 'two-eyed' stance, he became the focus for the longing of an entire people for proof. Proof of their own self worth, their own capacity".

I had heard so much about PA C and his pumpkin that I wanted desperately to meet him in the flesh. It is something about being a child that I like to check things over for myself and where he cultivated it was off the beaten track from the main road. My elder brother, Noel, had met him before and PA C was very black, with more grey in his beard and on his head than black, he laughed with a twinkle in his eye showing a full row of white teeth. I liked him and his first question to me was if I played cricket and whether I was good at bowling, fielding or batting; having responded in the affirmative he said, "Bwoy yu is like yu Uncle Joshie bowl right hand, bat left hand and could feel anyway, yes bwoy Joshi was boss wid cricket". His next question was, "Tell me some'ting you head quick like fi Joshi?"; my brother answered this question again in the affirmative. PA C said, "Joshi could never do sums". That being said he pointed up to a hill and "the little bwoy who say I can will climb to the hill top, the little bwoy who say I can't will at the bottom stop". I did not ask him about his pumpkin; he gave us a water melon to take home and as he placed it on the cotta on my head he said "Ting's don't come easy". A cotta is made mainly from grass, from the bark of a banana tree or from a piece of cloth in a shape that is placed on the head, making it more convenient to carry loads. I left PA C knowing in my young mind that climbing hills is important, which reminds me of the time when I was doing The Youth and Community Course at Manchester Polytechnic and went to the Lake District for two weeks as part of the course requirement. This involved outdoor activities such as canoeing, trivial pursuits, and mountain climbing. It was in June, during the hay fever season, when the group that I was with had to do some climbing at Grasmere. My chest was wheezing, my eyes and nose running; altogether I felt rather lousy but decided I was going to do it even if it was going to kill me. As I slowly made my way up the side of the mountain some people were passing me at a rather rapid pace but I kept reminding myself of what PA C said about the little boy. Half way up I saw some members of the group coming back saying, "Whit I have had enough I can't make it to the top". I persevered and when I finally reached the top there were loud cheers and it sounded good to the ears but it put into perspective the adage "That one can take many paths to reach the top of the mountain but when you get there the view is all the same".

Captain Leslie, walking with head held erect, chest out, was the true embodiment of a captain. I would have guessed that he was dubbed Captain as a result of him being in charge of Captain Blagrove's yacht anchored in the Bay at Dry Harbour. Captain Blagrove was one of the English landed gentry who history has recorded his family settling in Jamaica in the 1600's. They came with Penn and Venables.

As a local boat builder and fisherman, Captain Leslie was acknowledged and recognised as the best of his generation. His knowledge of the tides and currents around Dry Harbour, Rio Bueno, and Runaway Bay, in addition to his seafaring skills, was aptly rewarded when in 1941 along with his half-brother and my Uncle-in-Law, Elkanah Williams, and Ronald Seivewright, one of PA C's sons, they were bestowed with the honour of Order of the

British Empire (OBE) for Bravery, saving the life of Randall Johnson from drowning in atrocious weather conditions, and this act of making the impossible possible is still being talked about in Discovery Bay.

Their medals were presented to them in the Dry Harbour Congregational Church, which was dressed with the Union Jack and other ceremonial decorations by Captain Peter Blagrove K.C.M.G. who represented King George VI.

I was only six years old at the time but I remember feeling a sense of pride for these local heroes. The same way that I felt in 1998 some fifty-seven years after when I travelled up to London to receive the Member of the British Empire Medal from Her Royal Highness Queen Elizabeth the Second at Buckingham Palace for services to the African-Caribbean Community in Greater Manchester.

Seppy Gordon was typical of the majority of cricketers that I have come to know over the years; modest about their achievements and whether consciously or unconsciously not knowing how much people admire them, as far as I can remember Seppy would be at every practice or competitive match; his hands trembling. In the course of maturation I realised that he had Parkinson's Disease. His explanation about hitting sixes was that anyone can do it providing they have eyesight, balance and timing. In his words, "Get de ball on de driving shaft it gone". I have hit many sixes in my time but I honestly believe that the nearest I ever got to perfect Seppy's instruction was when I played in the South Lancashire Cricket League for Post Office Engineers in a match at Brooksbottom, hitting the ball right over some tall trees; that ball has never been recovered.

One of my abiding memories of Seppy was of his objection to players who because of their ability would never turn out to practice and expected to be chosen for matches. His expressed feeling was that practice is "paying first to play later"; this philosophy applies to life in general.

I remember my father, Joseph William Stennett, as a quiet unassuming man, a good listener, height about five feet seven inches, athletic in build with a firm and confident walk. He was born on the 10th September 1895 at Old Folly, Dry Harbour, the very year that Alexander Bedward, the founder of the Jamaica Native Baptist Free Church, told over one thousand of his followers at Mona that "the white wall has oppressed us for a long time; now is the time for us to oppress the white wall". Amongst some of Bedward's followers was an Aunt of my father, Aunt Dorcas, who migrated to Costa Rica in 1900 where she got involved with the Marcus Garvey movement. 1895 was also the year that Slade Lucas took a cricket team from England to the Caribbean; it was the first touring side that played in Barbados, British Guinea, Jamaica and Trinidad.

My father was very proud of his African heritage; this pride was fuelled by his father, Samuel Stennett, who traced his ancestors as part of the Ashanti Tribe from Ghana. He claimed that he was from Royal Lineage hence everybody in Dry Harbour called him "Old Prince"; some of the older members of my family still refer to me as Prince.

The accepted version of my grandfather and presence in Dry Harbour is that his parents were members of the Baptist movement involved with thousands of others in the Montego Bay slave uprising of 1831 led by Daddy Sharpe, a leading figure in the Baptist Church; after the hostilities some Stennetts left St James for Saint Ann.

The Sharpe-led rebellion was the major factor in Britain granting freedom to over 500,000 people. Sam Sharpe is one of Jamaica's national heroes.

My grandfather could read and write and held classes under a Naseberry Tree teaching others. He was a fisherman and stonemason who worked on the construction of the Dry Harbour Police Station in 1894. He enjoyed gardening, his sporting interest was canoe racing with other fishermen and the oral tradition is that he got hit on the head playing cricket; he that incident put paid to his playing and instead he became a "beyond the boundary" critic.

My memory of my grandfather was a man, the same height as my father five foot seven, rather squat, wide nostrils and a pronounced forehead. Whenever he came to our home he always had a copy of the Jamaican Gleaner which he read under an Ackee Tree in the yard. He was always enquiring as to what we had done at school, sometimes looking at our slates. At church he would always be in the back pew with his bible, sometimes hissing his teeth during the sermon. He had a beautiful tenor voice which was always in tune with the singing of the congregation. The community grapevine portrayed him as a ladies man by linking their attractions to him on the grounds that both he and my father wrote hymns. The title of Samuel Stennett's "On Jordan's Stormy Banks I stand" sung to the tune of "Varina"; this hymn was sung at my mother's funeral in December 1999. "Return my soul enjoy the Rest", sung to the tune of "Brookfield", was according to the local community written by my father. My understanding is that both men have never acknowledged writing these hymns; the community at the time felt otherwise basing their belief on the fact that the Stennetts did not like to show off.

My grandfather hated injustice and was never afraid to speak up for the underdog hence his falling out with the English Minister and some of the members of the church committee who refused the daughter of a member of the congregation from practising on the organ. I understand from my father that a meeting was called for people to air their views; when it was my grandfathers turn to speak he started reciting, "though I speak with the tongues of men and angels and have no charity I am like sounding brass and tingling cymbal". By this time his jacket was off, along with his shoes and socks, when the Minister said, "Brother Stennett what are you doing". My grandfather replied, "Parson I am here to speak my mind and tell the truth, the naked truth, which is that some of you are from a generation of vipers and no one can stop me coming to church. It is God's church, and I know that one day a Stennett will rise up to lead this church". The Stennett he spoke about was my brother, Egbert, who served as a Deacon for over fifty years and in 2004, as part of our family reunion, I laid a plaque in the church to commemorate his memory.

In a discussion with my brother Egbert before he died he said that our grandfather bore no grudges against the minister or some members who stopped the young woman from playing the organ, if anything he felt that the black members on the committee were afraid to speak out simply because they felt that their own self interest would be jeopardized. It is as a man, dedicated to his community, that Samuel Stennett is being remembered by a generation that is rapidly declining. The present site at Old Folly where the New Testament Church of God stands was given to them by him.

He is also remembered for phrases which are evergreen and which strike resonant chords within me. On death he said, "When one dies if they are not buried for love, they must be buried for scent." On thriftiness, "To buy house and land you must learn to save money to buy chicken". On being streetwise, "Barefoot man can laugh when he can tell big man on horseback that his horse is stink". On the art of listening, "Close your eye to listen is far better than having your eyes open and cannot see". On the importance of starting from the bottom up, "You can't give a man a fountain pen to cut down a banana tree".

My father went to Costa Rica when he was sixteen years old to join his eldest brother, Laban, and his Aunt Dorcas, who were both involved with Marcus Garvey's movement in the fighting of the cause for a better way of life for the thousands of people from the various Caribbean Islands who migrated to the country where they found employment on the sugar and banana plantations. My father told me that in addition to the deplorable conditions under which they had to work and live is the extent to which highwaymen and bogus banks divested workers of their hard earned cash. He said that other than Garvey there was no one to articulate the plight of people who the majority were subjects of his King George of England; the conditions and the resistance to them were the reasons for him becoming a Garveyite.

After two years, from being a labourer on the banana plantations in Costa Rica, he went to Panama where he got a job as a timekeeper on the canal where black workers were referred to as 'silver workers' and paid less than the 'gold workers' who were white; this was part and parcel of the "American Jim Crow" psychology of that period.

If there was anything that my dad learnt from being involved with Garvey's United Negro Improvement Association it was the ability to organise people around a common cause with the large Caribbean group representing so many islands; he spent all his spare time organising cricket and domino matches, outings and dances, his employers recognised that it worked for the morale of their workforce and encouraged him in what he was doing. He said that he spent more time organising these events than he did timekeeping and people were enjoying it. One of his claims to fame regarding cricket in the Canal Zone is meeting Sir Pelham "Plum" Warner, recognised as the father of Caribbean cricket in the context of his speaking out against the racist policies of The West Indian Cricket Establishment that kept black players from participating at the highest level. The year was 1938 and Sir Pelham, who took a team on a tour of South America, stopped off in Panama where the West Indian Community had a dinner in his honour. My father was by then working in Cuba and had gone to the funeral of his Aunt Dorcas.

He used to say that his meeting with Sir Pelham made him realise that the game of cricket could only have originated in England and that to understand how the true Englishmen thinks one needs to understand cricket, adding that for him, a true Garveyite, Africa could only ever be a great nation if they learnt how to play cricket. C.L.R. James' "Beyond a Boundary" to a large extent has expanded on my father's argument and as I grew older I was able to understand why his cricketing compatriots called him 'Voce', because of fast left arm over or around the wicket similar to Bill Voce of Nottinghamshire. As a youngster my brother Noel, as part of the family tradition, called him 'Force' when we played cricket under the mango trees.

I learnt a great deal about my community, the people living in the community, and myself, by sitting under trees in Jamaica. For instance, my first school classes were held under two trees, a Guined Tree and a Tamarind Tree. At my Elementary School classes were held under a Guango, an almond, a pear, and the famous Red Seed Tree. Of course, when it was raining we all had to huddle together in very confined spaces; the Guango Trees at the cricket ground provided all the information about the rules of the game, how to set a wicket for spin or fast bowling and about the feats of past players.

The Sea Grape and Silk Cotton Trees at the Fisherman's Beach provided all the shade, not only for fisher folks to repair their fishing gear and to cook or roast fish. On reflection any journalist, television producer, or film-maker could get enough material to make several documentaries. Every subject under the sun was discussed under these trees; this tradition is forever being perpetuated. I have always said to folks with all honesty that I did not learn about the birds and the bees at biology classes. I learnt about them either crouching in the slips playing cricket or listening to the fisher folks, the same is true of sociology, psychology, or any of the sciences dealing with people. Of course the processes of maturation and an application to academic pursuits has placed things into wider perspectives, but as I have alluded I have always been fascinated with trees and in 1995 when I did a series of workshops for The Jewish National Fund on Bury New Road in Manchester, at the end of the project I was presented with a Certificate of Appreciation from the organisation acknowledging the planting of trees in the British park in the Judean Hills near Jerusalem in my name; it was quite a humbling experience and I am hoping one day to travel to Jerusalem to see the trees.

Had I not cut down a limb from my fathers favourite Angel Flower Tree to make a cricket bat chances are that I would never have had the opportunity to learn so much more of the family tradition from my father within a comparatively short time. Having owned up to cutting down the tree he gave me a hiding, which I felt was unfair because he was the one who taught my brothers and myself all the skills that were necessary to survive within our world; so in retaliation I chopped down one of his roses and part of his Bougainvillea trees. We were both on the war path but instead of giving me another hiding he stripped, naked, hid all my clothes and locked me in the bedroom.

No sooner had he locked me away than I opened the bedroom window and went down to the part of our land where we had a full length cricket pitch and started playing stark naked; I often think that I was the first cricketer to play naked. It was the first and only time that my father had ever laid hands on me; neither has he ever done the same to any of my brothers or sisters. It was not his style, or for that matter any male member of the Samuel Stennett clan. From time to time my wife, Gwen, reminds my children and her friends that "Whitty never use the strap"; as Stennetts, the men of course, we believe that the look and a warning as to the folly of one's ways can cause dire consequences. Not so the Stennett women, even those who are married to one; a back hander will suffice when the strap is not handy, but that particular day my father broke the tradition, which required an explanation.

He told me that as a young man my grandfather had the sad experience of seeing one of his old female relatives dying, and going through the travails of death she talked about going back to Africa to join those who had gone before. At one stage she asked her relatives to turn her on her belly and feebly she pulled down her clothes to reveal a series of marks on her shoulders saying "Cudjo kill fi dis". As it happened an overseer on the sugar cane plantation that she worked made sexual advances to her. Cudjoe intervened and they were both flogged. Cudjoe bided his time and when it became convenient he dealt a massive blow to the overseer's head with a stone. Cudjoe ran off and was never seen again. The accepted explanation regarding Cudjoe is that he fled to Maroon Town. My granddad made a pledge that from that experience he hated men who beat women or children.

In the days that followed there was more in-depth information that was passed on. Except for my sister, Lynn, who was two years old at the time, it was like a renaissance as he talked about his experiences growing up in the days when Dry Harbour was a thriving sea port for the shipping of logwood and copra to the United States. It was on one of those boats that his younger brother, Joshi, joined as a carpenter and he eventually settled in New York where he found work on the railroads as a Dining Room Attendant, and studying at the same time he finally qualified as a Dentist. I could see that my father was quite proud of his brother's achievement and he said that I was like Joshi, quiet but very strong-willed to get what he wanted; I decided there and then that I wanted to be like my Uncle Joshi.

On the importance of thriftiness he told us his determination to save enough money to buy the property on which we lived and where he once worked as a Labourer, adding that the Brown's Town Benefit Building Society which was established in 1896, a year after he was born, was where he saved when he lived and worked abroad. I joined the Society in 1952; in 1970 the Society became The Jamaica National Building Society of which I am still a member.

What started as an immediate family history class gradually finished up as an extended family and friends, one with each additional member of the group bringing additional information. It was a meeting of minds that put into context the importance of "each one teach one". It was during these sessions that I heard about people like Mary Seacole, the Jamaican Nurse, Cuffey the Runaway Slave, Tussaint from Haiti, Booker T Washington, the American educator, Learie Constantine, the West Indian Cricketer, Jack Johnson and Joe Louis, boxers, Jesse Owens, the American Athlete, and Claude McKay, the Jamaican-born Poet. In the group discussionn were two other people and my father, who saw George Headley at Sabina Park in 1935 making his 270 runs against England. There was pride mixed with emotion as they gave their ball by ball commentary to their enthusiastic audiences. It was during this time that I learnt that George Headley was born in Panama to a Jamaican mother and Barbadian Father. My own sense of pride, mixed with emotion and elation, was kindled in 1958 when at Sabina Park I witnessed Sir Garfield Sobers and Conrad Hunte making 365 and 260 not out respectively, beating Pakistan by an innings and 174 runs.

Considering the age that my father died I know that if he was around in 1958 he would have been at Sabina Park with me, but by the same rule in keeping with the tradition of our love for the game his spirit was there.

That week during the cutting down of the tree incident another window into my fathers past and my future opened when three canoes, at the time they were the largest in Dry Harbour, left for Montego Bay to purchase wire for making fish pots. The Second World War had only finished a year previously and things were still being rationed and Montego Bay, some forty four miles or, as the fisher folks would say, knots from Dry Harbour. I have always been impressed with the self-confidence and independence of people who make their livelihood on the sea or on the river. However, on one boat was Captain Leslie, Brother Collins and Eustace Stennett; on another was Elkanah Williams, Michael Williams, and Jacob Leslie, and on the final boat was Cayman Evans, my Uncle-in-law Gus Edwards, my father and myself. My brother Noel was afraid of being sea sick so he did not join us.

It was around five in the morning when we left, each boat in line with each other, making it much easier to have a tow line for fishing. I was in the bow of our boat, Cayman Evans naming me as Captain. We were just about passing the American Air force Base at Braco, the site on which Breezes Resort now stands, when Captain Leslie caught a Barracuda, up until that time I was always hearing about the struggle that is involved when one catches a Barracuda. I was to witness it that morning; it took nearly an hour to finally get it in the boat. Catching a Barracuda puts into context my analogy "that when I was in Jamaica I fish for food and fun". Within minutes of landing the Barracuda it was scaled and cut into slices and the customary silver threepenny piece placed in the flesh, which means if the coin turns black or green it indicates the meat is poisonous as sometimes fishes eat copperas grass. It was not the case with that one, but if catching it was fun what followed after was quite frightening for me because as a result of throwing the entrails of the Barracuda overboard the blood attracted sharks. The older fishermen took it in their stride; for me it became part of a learning curve as Gus Edwards enlightened me on the various species of sharks. Those following us that morning even for their size were sand sharks, which are not dangerous, but in as far as I was concerned a shark is a shark; more on them in regards to my own personal encounter.

Our first stop on the way was at a small fishing village, Salt Marsh, between Falmouth and Montego Bay; like all fishing villages the folks were friendly and here I was to discover that youngsters my own age were much better swimmers than I was and their own experiences with barracudas, sharks, stingrays, and porpoises were quite interesting to hear. None of them that I spoke to had ever been to Montego Bay even though they lived not very far away.

Leaving Salt Marsh, we came across a group of porpoises, their skins glistening in the bright sunlight as they playfully leapt out of the water into the air and back into the water; in the distant hills standing majestically was the Greenwood Great House, built by the famous family of the Barrett's of Wimpole Street in the late 1780's when sugar was King. Next was the Rose Hall Great House, built in the 1700's by John Palmer, hence the well known story 'The White Witch of Rose Hall' and the ghost of Annie Palmer, even from the distance that I was on the morning that the stories I heard of the antics of the ghost, I was quite scared. I was twenty years old when I paid my first visit both to Greenwood and Rose Hall and was very impressed, not only with the architecture of these two great houses but also the extent of the planting of sugar cane and the production of sugar and its by-products such as Rum and Molasses.

Largely oppressed people from Africa became one of the firm foundations on which Britain built an empire on which "The sun never set" and, deeply interwoven in the fabric of building Jamaica, were British values embracing culture, in the form of literature, which from my visit to Greenwood Great House highlighted that some of the works of Elizabeth Barrett Browning, who was related to the Barretts, was written in that house. Cricket has always been synonymous with sugar, and in tradition Rose Hall had its own team and one spectator confided in me that whilst watching a match there he saw a bowler-hatted man on horseback watching. When he asked his friend to look at how near the horse was to the umpire both horse and man disappeared. Such stories add to the folklore of Annie Palmer, The White Witch.

Arriving in Montego Bay late morning is one of the things that I will never forget and over the years I have come to appreciate and agree with Samuel Eliot Morrison, Christopher Columbus's biographer, who wrote that on seeing Jamaica for the first time Columbus said, "The fairest island that eyes have beheld, mountainous and the land seems to touch the sky, all full of valleys and fields and plains". Once ashore my father, who was the Chairman of the Fishermen's Guild, made his way to the depot where the fishing tackle was stored at the time. ACS Combs, a veteran of the West Indian Regiment and a leading figure in the Trades Union Movement, was the most well-known personality in Montego Bay, fighting for a better way of life for the underprovided. His presence only for a brief moment at the depot where the fishing tackle was being distributed became one of the highlights of my visit as people greeted him shouting out, "Father Coombs, see what you can do for me". There was no doubting in my youthful mind that there is something that makes working with people rewarding and to be a teacher as my mother wanted me to be would be good for me.

After receiving our quota of gear, we went back to the fisherman's beach where preparations were made for cooking, hoping to make the journey back to Dry Harbour late in the evening. It was my first visit to Montego Bay and I was determined that my father and other members of the group who had been before show me around. I remember being taken to Sam Sharpe Square where there was a group of people listening to a man talking about Sharpe. I noticed that some people in the crowd were crying while others bowed their heads, almost in reverence, to the great man. I left with a feeling of pride and went on to the Dome, another landmark in the history of Jamaica's second city.

Unlike the fisher folks of Dry Harbour those in Montego Bay were equally friendly but appeared to be more hardy; some of their back yards being on the beach. One of the families we made friends with were the Gitchies, and in 1958 I swam in the Kingston Annual Cross, the Harbour Swimming Competition sponsored by Pepsi. One of the competitors representing St James was a Gitchie from Montego Bay.

It was around seven in the evening when we left Montego Bay for Dry Harbour; it was a full moon and in the morning I was able to see the hills and the sky in cheek and jowl almost kissing each other. The night sky provided a canopy that placed into perspective psalms that speak so eloquently of "The heavens declaring the glory of god and the firmaments showed his handy works". It was on this occasion that I got to know more about Cayman Evans, who in actual fact left the Cayman Islands for Jamaica to seek a better way of life. The Cayman Islands are about 80 miles (130km) west of Jamaica and was a dependency of Jamaica from 1863 until 1962 when Jamaica became an independent country. Cayman Evans was very praiseworthy of my seamanship, seeing that up to that point I was not sea sick. This last thing I remember is my father making sure that I was safely tucked in the bow of the canoe, a crocus bag shielding my face from the moonlight.

Whatever conversation that occurred during the rest of the journey I did not know until I woke up on the Saturday morning knowing more about myself, my father and some of his friends, about another part of my country and the wonderful works of nature.

My mother's antecedents differ from that of my father in the light that she is more racially mixed than my father. Amongst her relatives on her mother's side are Irish, Scots and Jews. Her father's side are of African descent. She was born at Farm Town about three miles from Discovery Bay on the 12th March 1901 to Louise Clarke and Edmund Jones, a staunch family of upwardly mobile half-whites, semi-browns and free blacks, who became a bridge of convenience between the majority black working class population and the minority but privileged ruling classes.

My mother told me of walking with her mother and other relatives from Farm Town to the Anglican Church in Rio Bueno every Sunday, where she played the organ. All this changed when she met my father and the then prevailing social order or custom of consent, courtship, and marriage, saw her leaving Farm Town to live in Dry Harbour, which is now Discovery Bay.

She became a member of the Dry Harbour Congregational Church, called in those days The Independent Church, and all of us except my youngest sister, Lyn were christened in that church. My mother relinquished her membership in 1940 and joined the New Testament Church of God at Old Folly. She told me that she had too much of the starched front and uppity type kind of theology that failed to preach Christ crucified and Christ sanctified. My brothers stayed with the Congregational Church, which in some ways has still held on to some of its straight-laced brand of theology. Whenever I am in Jamaica I still visit the Church and the expressed feeling by some of the younger generation is that it is the Posh Church of Discovery Bay.

As part of the Stennett family reunion held in 2004 a plaque was unveiled in the New Testament Church of God in memory of my mother being the longest serving secretary in the history of the Church. Like my father and his family, my mother and her family saw sports, music and the arts as necessary tools that can be applied in sensitising people of their potential that can be utilised to achieve their goals. Both sides of family play sports and music and I can remember as a young boy going to my mother's family home at Ginger Hall where there was an organ, a bass and a violin. There was always music and singing in that I remember the family singing songs like 'Max Whelton Brays', 'On the Old Front Porch', 'When Irish Eyes are Smiling', 'Old Black Joe'and 'Tales of Hoffman'; they truly were happy days.

Similar to their love of music, sports and arts both sides of the family had members who served in the army, the police force and served in both world wars. Some died abroad in active service for King and Country. The observing of Empire Day in my time, which was always on the 20th May, celebrated the birthday of Queen Victoria. This annual event provided the opportunity for men, some who were severely disabled as a result of injuries received in combat, to parade with their ribbons and medals on their chest singing at the top of their voices songs such as 'Rule Britannia' and 'Land of Hope and Glory'.

Two of these men who meant so much to me were Stephen Carter, who lost an eye in Palestine during the 1914-18 war. Occasionally he would get agitated, cursing everybody in sight and threatening to write to King George VI when anyone offended him; some people felt that his oddball behaviour was attention-seeking. I remember him saying to a group of people that everybody is fighting whether we are rich or poor, black or white, and the world owes nobody anything.

Jimbo Hyton was the other person, a very intelligent man who believed that education was the only way out for poor boys and that travelling helped to build a knowledge base. His leg was amputated below the knee and I have seen him writhing in agony as a result of pains in his ankle and lower leg, of which he had none. I learnt that these were phantom pains. His philosophy on war was that it was necessary to stop bad people being more evil and greedy people wanting more.

When I started getting interested in girls I remember telling a girl from Browns Town that when my father was alive he was the Prime Minister and my mother held all the other ministerial positions. The very fact that they say love is blind prevented her from asking me to further explain what I meant and rather than asking me to clarify what I meant she went and asked Crampy's sister, Doris, who told her that my father was a good breadwinner but my mother held the purse strings, which reminds me of attending a conference in 1991 at the Central Hall on Oldham Street, Manchester. The conference was held under the auspices of The Race Unit of The Anglican Diocese in Manchester, and an off the cuff remark that I made about living with three women did not go down well with one of the women in my group, and like my experience in Jamaica instead of seeking an explanation which I would have gladly given she went behind my back telling other people that I was a male chauvinist. Mrs Louise Da-Cacodia, a well respected member of the community saved the day for me when she explained that I did not say that I was I was living with three wives but I was living with my wife and two daughters.

When I went to visit my mother in Jamaica and told her she reminded me that it has always been part of the Stennett tradition to speak in parables, which reinforces what I have and will always say that in this world there are people who will leave the positive aspects of any circumstances and hold on to cheap throwaways that perpetuate ignorance and misunderstandings.

41

The link that binded my friendship with George Blissett could only be broken by death, for me his spirit lives on. I remember him telling me that speaking in parables is the art of being without offence or alarmist and telling people about the past or what could well happen in the future. He was absolutely right because between my cutting down of the tree two days after All Fools' Day 1946 until the 31st May of the same year that my father died, he did so much by words and action, which in the process of time I arrived at the conclusion that he must have had a premonition of his early passing and was sensitising us of the realities of making our way without him.

I remember him saying to me two days after we came back from buying the fishing gear in Montego Bay that when he leaves to take his rest he wanted to be buried under the Pear Tree from where he would be able to see us playing cricket and look out to the sea. Three days after he had said this to me we were all sitting on the veranda looking at a waterspout on the horizon when he complained of a pain in his chest and asked that we go to get his sister, Sarah. My elder brother, Noel, and myself mounted the donkey and away we went. On our way Noel casually said to me, "Father is not going to make it"; he was then sixteen years old and apprenticed to a tailor, Harry Brown, in Farm Town. My brother was always a quiet person, a private man more like and to hear him say that was rather numbing for me. However, he continued by saying that he was doing well at his vocation and that it would not be long before he would be able to start making his own way.

It was dusk when we arrived at Helicon where Aunt Sarah, we called her Aunt Guvvie, lived; having told her what had taken place her husband, Gus Edwards, said, "That is the same way his brother Joshi went". I was later to learn that heart disease is common with the Stennetts and so it is for this reason that I informed my family of the hereditary trait that is so much akin to us as a family. By doing so one is able to adjust to a lifestyle that is in keeping with the enjoying of a better quality of life. On the way back to our house I did not utter a word; I was deep in thought in terms of the challenges that I had to face - I would not stop playing cricket or stop going to school whatever the circumstances would be.

My father was in bed when we returned and appeared much better than when we left; as expected our neighbours Miss Zetel and Miss Doris were at his bedside and they assured us that it was not a stroke and neither was there anything to suggest that it was a blood clot to the brain. Along with my Aunt Guvvie the consensus of opinion was that his heart may have 'skipped a beat' and if that was the case the doctor would have to be called depending on his condition the following day. I was rather relieved on knowing that his condition was stable and that night it was Noel who read the bible before praying and retiring to bed. He chose Psalms 27 that starts, 'The Lord is my light and my salvation whom shall I fear'. The only thing that was missing was that before retiring to bed, my father always closed the back and front doors, sometimes either whistling or humming his favourite hymn, 'O Jesus I have promised to serve thee to the end'. My mother closed the doors that night singing 'Peace Perfect Peace' and for most of the night I was kept awake reliving the times that we had together as a family, the good ones, the in-betweens and the bad ones, of his own personal triumphs over adversities, and his cautious daring in treading into the unknown. My reflective mood was broken by a slight drizzle of rain playing a musical pit-a-pat as it hit the zinc roof and the panes of glass on the windows of our room. It is part of the Jamaican folklore to 'read' or in other words to attach significance to almost everything or anything, such as dancing eyes, sneezing, itchy feet, owls screeching at night, breaking of a drinking glass, the sound of thunder during dry weather, so when the rain started drizzling it gave rise to feelings of anxieties, especially under the circumstance which we were all experiencing, so my brother got out of the bed to see how my father was and he came back to say that he was asleep and looked okay.

As was the custom in our house we were up at five and my sister, Lurline, read from Psalms Chapter One, 'Blessed is the man that walketh not in the Counsel of the ungodly'. Prayers having been said, we made our way down to the beach; my mother stayed at home with my father and the five minutes walk down to the beach that morning lacked the usual fun and gaiety that was a part of our early morning ritual. It was more like doing a ten mile walk up a steep hill with a very heavy load on the head. One of the many things that I remember on those occasions was that it did not matter what time of the day that I went to the beach with my father, he would always insist that before I go into the water I should use my big toe to test the temperature of the water. He referred to the act as 'killing the cold'. The moral of 'killing the cow' can be equated to 'fools rush in where angels fear to tread'; what my father meant was that before I get too deeply involved with anyone or in a situation I should use caution. I have made every effort to live to that maxim and was only caught out once when I threw caution to the wind so as to prove a point that had no scientific, psychological or physiological bearing whatsoever - more will be revealed in later chapters of this book.

Arriving back from the beach that morning, which was Friday 24th May 1946, father was sitting up in bed having his usual fruit breakfast. He had shaved himself, an indication that he had not had a stroke. Even so, he was still complaining of pains in his chest travelling down his arms. He was overruled on the decision to summon the doctor and my mother told me that from the day they met he had never had an occasion to see a doctor or dentist. He did not smoke or drink alcohol and along with his friends, they would go into the bushes to gather roots and bark from trees into which they made their tonic. This practice still goes on in Jamaica.

On concluding his examination the doctor advised that he needed to go into hospital and as I understand it my father was not happy with the prospect and he told the doctor that he wanted to die with his family around him. That was the measure of the man in terms of his commitment to his family. Within a week of being admitted to hospital he died from a heart attack.

In Jamaica, where temperatures are approximately 90 degrees Fahrenheit, and where, at the time, except for Kingston, there were no available facilities to preserve the body of a deceased person, burials take place within twenty four hours. Typical at the time was that coffins were built whilst graves were being dug and in those circumstances grievances and misunderstandings are put to one side and communities come together to genuinely engage in acts of kindness in keeping with the paying of respects and support during bereavements. In other words, crying together when we were sad and laughing together when we were happy were fundamental to the building of a sustainable and caring community from the cradle to the grave.

Some people frequently use the term that in the midst of life there is death, an addition to that is that in the midst of death there is also life. I have no objections in agreeing with both statements in that they mean different things to different people. Amongst many of the outpourings of sympathies and empathies expressed during my period of bereavement when we huddled as a family around my father's grave and the act of 'dust to dust, ashes to ashes' was being performed, I overheard a lady say, "How is Miss Maud going to manage with all these children?" I vividly remember looking at her and in the deep recesses of my mind I said, 'If my brothers and sisters cannot manage I, Whit, must manage'. Looking back, to me it was a challenge and I would definitely take it on. My friend, George Blissett, has always said, 'Make sure your enemies don't see you naked'.

In keeping with my father's wishes he was buried under his favourite pear tree with a vantage view of the sea and our little cricket ground under the mango trees, and like his father in following with the tradition of making their own quotations which gained community currency in my village and to which I constantly evaluate as circumstances arise. I felt that at the time of his passing there was an overriding ambition on his part to expose us to a number of situations that would not only get the best out of us but also let us understand that life has its ups and downs and that 'ability without stickability' had left a number of people on the starting line.

His definition of characters did not always link with the words that he described, the onus was always placed on their actions; for instance, an infidel was a person who he knew did not know better. On leaving the yard he would leave the gate open, whereby stray animals would wander in to destroy his flower and vegetable garden. A God damn infidel is the person who should know better and do the same, a scoundrel was a person who would borrow a book from you and not return it. My father enjoyed looking after his garden and reading.

On flowers he said that they make women smile; regarding reading he said when you give a man a book to read he keeps his knowledge to himself, when you give a woman a book to read the village want another book to read, on sports or for that matter cricket he said cricket can take you anywhere, but always carry your books with you; on prayer he said that it is through prayer that we learn how to be humble and patient.

Even before the moulding of the grave on the morning of Saturday 1st June 1946 and the laying of wreaths followed by the hymn 'Till we meet at Jesus Feet', I started to ask myself if there really is life after death. I still do and in some way draw comfort from the fact that as a result of my religious upbringing man has a unique place within the universe and as such we are a reflection that highlights how we respond to the challenges of society. In his own style my father followed in the tradition of his father preparing me for some of the challenges that I had to face and deal with.

CHAPTER THREE

Many Rivers to Cross

IN JAMAICAN terminology, "My father did not even start to turn cold in his grave" when I was confronted with the daunting prospect of crossing the Rubicon by no other person than Alex, who worked with Charles 'Son' Stewart, a prosperous businessman and philanthropist at the time. Alex would have been around five years older than I was; he had a bull-like neck that tapered down into shoulders and an upper body that announces strength personified. For some unknown reason nature did not bless him with a handsome face but be that as it may, from the time that he arrived in Dry Harbour I have never bothered him and when he had some spare time he would play cricket with us. He learnt to swim whilst he was there and I remember once when a group of us went swimming Bugs Faulcher sea licked him, a sea lick is diving into the water, flipping one or both feet whilst submerged and hitting someone and Alex claimed it was me. It wasn't and the matter closed; our code of conduct in those days was what happened at sea was left at sea. If he carried a grudge I did not know it as things seemed to carry on in a normal way.

As it happened the men who made my father's coffin borrowed lumber from the contractor who was refurbishing, or rather rebuilding, the Church cum School which was damaged by the hurricane in 1944 to make a work bench, so immediately after the funeral I changed into my working clothes and started taking the lumber back to the Church. There was no one around when I took the first piece of lumber and placed it where I was instructed to, on taking the second piece down I noticed that other pieces were laid in a different position from where the first piece was laid, which meant I had to rearrange the whole lot. There was no one around that I could blame or even enquire as to what was going on.

Walking back to my house, which was not far from the Church, I saw Alex hiding behind a shed and the penny dropped. Knowing that I would be facing a showdown, more than likely he saw the opportunity for getting his own back for what happened when we had been swimming. I prepared myself for the worse but by the same rule I did not want to give him any indication that I feared him. I was in my own little world trying to come to terms with my grief and as such confrontation of any sort was not the situation that I wanted to be involved in.

Fortunately, on my third trip people who had attended the funeral passed by and there was no sight of Alex. I remember a woman giving me a bottle of cream soda which I hid under some lumber on the understanding that on my last trip I would go to the Post Office and take it home to drink. This was not to be for on the final trip I saw the empty bottle on the wall with Alex firing at it with his sling shot; this action reminded me of the Jamaican proverb where the frog told the boy who was throwing stones at him that what is a joke to him, the boy, is death to him the frog. I kept my composure and proceeded to the Post Office, the two letters that I received I placed securely in my trouser waist with my shirt hanging over them. I had a three penny bun in my right hand. My tormentor was in his glory poking his fist under my nose and asking me to smell his grandfather's gunpowder and demanding that I share my bun with him; I was not going to back down and neither was I going to let him have any of the bun as I have already said, I was not in no mood for confrontation. As I moved away from him he called me a "Fatherless Bang Belly Boy". I stood my ground, stared in his face and said to him, "Go to hell you are damn following", meaning that he was not from that village.

He went into a mad rage and like a wild bull he rushed into me with the intention of grabbing me and possibly wrestling me to the ground. I side-stepped and let loose an uppercut that travelled the forty four miles from Montego Bay, hitting him flush on the button, his head going back in the process. Quickly I shifted the bun into my left hand and caught him with a right to the jaw and jab to his face only to hear ,"Beautiful". It was from one of the Deacons at my Church, Abraham 'Brammie' Morales.

Alex was sobbing and threatening to kill me and went for a bit of board with a nail sticking out of it but as he bent down for it Sylvester 'Racketeer' Leech placed his foot on it and said 'No stick or stone, give the youth a fair fight'. Alex's lump of wood was his weapon of mass destruction.

I have always said that what people say and what people do are always different. The incident on that day reinforced it because the first person to denounce me that morning, calling me a ruffian, was the very lady, Miss Lily Hyman, who at the graveside in what could be accepted as genuine concern in enquiring about our welfare, without even making an effort to ascertain as to what had given cause to my actions saw me in the light of an aggressor. Looking at the damage that my fist had done to Alex's face that day made me feel quite uncomfortable, and to add insult to injury I was branded a ruffian but truth will always win out and by knowing the truth it will always set you free. Mr Brammie and "Racketeer" Leach were more than worthy advocates in my defence.

Sensing that Alex was embarking on something that would not have a fruitful outcome they hid themselves in the Church from where, without him knowing, they could observe his activities. Realising that I was ashamed of what I had done both men sat me down and reassured me that they had seen what had happened from when I had made the first trip and I should never feel ashamed of myself to stand up to a bully. The Second World War had only ended twelve months previously and, like the First World War to which many of our relatives and friends from the village had served overseas in the British Armed Forces, they said it had to happen because Germany wanted to have her own way and Britain had to step in to stop Germany. Mr Brammie said if I did not stand up for myself I would finish up being a beating stick. "Racketeer" Leach ascribed my boxing prowess to that of Kid Gavilan, the Cuban Welterweight, and although I have always admired Alan 'Fire' Alexander doing his sparring at the beach and, over the years I have become very interested in boxing as a spectator, the comment on the morning did nothing for me, especially in light that my fists had done so much. I did not have to use them again in a way which was justified until thirty five years later.

Having gone to the beach to get himself cleaned up Alex had to pass the Church to go to where he worked. Both men called him and requested we shake hands, which we did and he went his way and I went home. I told my brother, Noel, and in the process of showing him the bruises on my knuckles asked him not to breathe a word to anyone. We were now into the beginning of the Mango and as is customary, boys will be boys, Alex came to get mangoes from us and it has never been my style to bear grudges but like life there were other hurdles to surmount.

On our way to Church the following morning we were told that amongst two of the boats that went missing the previous night as a result of joy riders, one was belonging to my father. These joy riders were mostly the upwardly mobile middle classes from Browns Town and Alexandria who would come down at night to have fun by the beach. They had very little idea of manning a boat and panicked if they felt that they were losing control, whereby they would scramble for shore leaving the boats to drift away. Depending on the current sometimes the boats would be found at Old Folly, where it was easy to row them back to the beach at Top Bay. If the current took them past Old Folly they would more than likely be lost forever. This was what happened to those two boats, to find them at Old Folly that morning was hoping against hope.

At Church the Preacher based his sermon on Jonah and the whale, although I was very much acquainted with the story from my Quattie-a-Week School days, that morning the Preacher added a great deal more excitement to the episode and although the reality of the situation was that the loss of my father and the loss of the boat would create a financial burden on my mother, I viewed the sermon in the light of what happened to Jonah as a great sea adventure of which one day I would like to be part of.

The seriousness of my loss did not have an impact on me until after my brother and I started talking on our way home from Church; it was not just talking for talking sake, it was an in-depth discussion picking up from where we had left off on the night which our father took ill and he said that he would not make it. We were now faced with the reality and adjustments that would have to be made to come to terms with all eventualities. To begin with our eldest brother, Egbert, was away in the United States on the Farm Workers Programme, which meant that he was not in a position to be involved in the practical day to day application of things in Jamaica that were relevant to our survival.

We were now only three days into mourning and it was even more crucial that as the two males in our immediate family we had to show that we had the resolve to stand up to the struggles, both short and long term.

Other than selling the produce from the land such as Pimento and Citrus and sometimes timber, which after each hurricane destroyed the trees, and when the ships arrived from England and docked at Rio Bueno for sugar my father worked as a winch man; fishing was his main occupation and even bad weather created its own occupational hazards which, without proper planning, lack of cash created its own fears and anxieties, especially in a society that has no welfare benefits.

My Uncle-in-law, Gus Edwards, who fished with my father, would most certainly want to carry on but my brother would have to help out, quite a daunting prospect and to put it bluntly a very frightening one, for the sole reason his boat had all the credentials looking at it to be called a boat, it had a major flaw and that was it had no buoyancy to keep it steady on the water and he always placed a heavy stone in its bow. Only he had the knack of doing it because more than once I have seen the boat capsizing, throwing him into the water. No wonder before he went fishing he would always sing "Nearer my God to thee". I called the boat Roly Roly, not to his face of course. Looking back I think that his sense of balance was learnt in Cuba where he did a lot of boxing. Just in case one travels to Jamaica and goes sailing in Discovery Bay, chances are that you might still be able to see some of the heavy stones that he used to balance Roly Roly. Now you know why joy riders have never attempted to meddle with it.

My brother and myself decided that we would need to have a boat of our own and the only way we could do that was to make a personal approach to Mr Mattheson, who was in charge of the Home Castle Properties near Keith, a member of the land-owning aristocracy. Mr Mattheson understood the importance of cricket in helping to bridge the gap between those who were privileged and had a voice and those who were underprivileged and had no voice.

A Bittersweet Journey

One of my contemporaries from Content, Dan Dunbar, said that Mr Mattheson had the knack to use a cricket bat and a cricket ball to lead one from total darkness into perpetual light; it is a statement that could never be debunked. Home Castle had in those days one of the best cricket grounds in the Parish of Saint Ann and on the Wednesday evening when we got to the ground there was a practice game on and both my brother and I were asked to participate. We were now much closer to meeting and talking to him and were determined to create a good impression. I think that I did that and gained a lot of confidence when I stopped balls going to the boundary and heard cheers and hand claps with the words 'well fielded son'.

At the end of the match we told him why we had come to see him and following the conversation in terms of our future, he assured us that all we had to do was to contact Knibbs, who was one of the Supervisors on the property, to show us where the silk cotton trees that were used for making boats in those days were and we could choose one for free. The going prices at the time was thirty shillings for a twenty four or thirty foot long tree, a lot of money in those days. As we returned our thanks he reminded us that whatever we did we must continue to play cricket. It was almost dark when we stopped on our way home and told our Uncle-in-law of the progress that we had made in acquiring a tree for the making of a boat. He was as excited as we were and promised that he would go and see Knibbs the following day and make the necessary arrangements for all three of us to go and choose a tree on the Friday.

He was mindful that on the Sunday it would be nine days since my father's passing, and custom dictated that there would be the final rites when families and friends meet at the house to read passages from the Bible, sing hymns, pray, eat and wish the spirit a safe journey to its resting place. It was an opportune moment to inform those present that come the following Wednesday we would be going to the woods to cut a tree for the making of our boat. The response which was expected from volunteers was overwhelming, everybody wanted to do something for Uncle Baba; except for the teachers, Police Officers, the Minister and those who came from outside who called my father Mr Stennett, he was Uncle Baba to everybody else. I remember him telling me that as we make our way in life we must be prepared to take others with us, if we don't our journey can be dull and unrewarding. I have tried to follow the principle and see the merit in having others share the journey with me.

My brother and I were central to the proceedings on the day the cotton tree was cut down. According to Jamaican folklore, during the time of the Arawaks, who where the first inhabitants of the country, they not only used the trunk of the silk cotton tree to make their dug out canoes but they also

50

buried their dead under the tree, which meant that before anyone attempted to cut a silk cotton tree down they must offer something to appease the spirit, such as opening a bottle of rum and killing a young cockerel, spilling both around the roots. My brother began as he was the eldest; he killed the cockerel and I opened the rum and we both performed the ritual to loud handclaps from over fifty people who had come to help on the day. In less than an hour the tree was down to the tumultuous roar of timber. I am sure that the spirits joined in with a feeling of gratitude for the way that we catered to their needs, like the building of King Solomon's Temple where a large proportion of the timber, stones and other materials were prepared in the forest and transported to the site where the temple was being erected and then fitted into place. The same pattern existed in my time when the bulk of the work would be done in the bushes.

Unknown to us Mr Mattheson was being kept informed of our project and when the boat was ready to be taken to the beach for its final completion he sent one of his carts to transport it. All together it was an act of kindness that put into perspective that the Englishman's word is his bond and as far as I am concerned the recognition or acceptance of that statement is largely due to the historical experience between Britain and the Caribbean, and the extent to which sport, or for that matter cricket, which was more popular then, reinforced that concept.

There was no shortage of labour in the completion of our boat. We were now into the midsummer holidays and things generally were returning to normal; money was short or sometimes non-existent, but with so many fruit trees, pumpkins, vegetables and bananas and a more than generous supply of fish from extended family members, we could more than keep the wolf and her cubs from our door, but then when one is content to think that when there is peace and safety around the corner there is sudden destruction.

This was to reflect itself one morning when I went to get the donkey to prepare for taking water from a spring which was about two miles from home. It was dead and I could not control myself; there was anger, bitterness, grief, and all other negative human emotions literally leaking out of me to the point where I remember vividly asking God what had we done and why he was picking on us. Things became even more unbearable when Andrew "The Farrier" came and opened the donkey, which on his examination revealed that it had eaten a grasshopper which poisoned its system. It addition to paying Andrew ten shillings and sixpence for his fees, I had to travel the two miles to fetch the water, which I carried on my head; others had to do the same and in time I came to value the experience as a part of growing up in the community.

****

One of the realities of living in Jamaica is its link with hurricanes, hence the country's proverb "June too soon, July standby, August you must prepare, September remember, October all over". Fortunately, in 1946 we did not have a hurricane; the boat was launched in August of that year just in time for the annual Hamlet and Yellow Tail Fish Season. It was a lovely boat, thirty feet long and four feet wide, we named it Kananah, the name of one of Marcus Garvey's ships of The Black Star Line. However, my predicament at the time was as a result of the aftermath of the August 1944 hurricane that almost completely destroyed our house, my father's boat, all his fishing pots, and lumber and fruit trees on the land. I was only nine years old at the time, Britain was still at war and in Jamaica we were subjected to rationing of all commodities that had to be imported from abroad.

As a youngster the storm created more fun, adventure and an extended midsummer holiday from school. We used the wrecked canoes for racing each other out to and beyond the reef that broke the great waves. It was in one of these makeshift boats that I had my first experience with a shark. It was late evening, the beach was deserted save for my brother, Noel, and a friend, Peter Williams, who was much older than us. He and my brother went out in his boat to lay a pot, I followed on my boat and on our way back to shore I heard my brother shouting "Shark, Whitty, Shark".

I looked around and could see the fin of the shark out of the water swimming towards me, I could hear Peter shouting "stay on, stay on, don't jump off" as he started rowing to me. In the confusion I jumped into the water and could feel the nose of the shark on my body; to me it was like two boys playing in the water. By then Peter and my brother had got hold of me and had pulled me into their boat. As it turned out it was a nurse shark that according to Peter may have lost one of its young ones and felt that I was one of them, a good story. That incident was one of the best kept secrets in the community; Peter left after to work at King's House in Kingston and whenever we met there was always that sense of camaraderie. My brother would often jokingly ask if I thought that I was Jonah. I often wondered what Steven Spielberg would have done with my story which certainly would have superseded Jaws.

There were no insurance policies to compensate for the damage and loss caused by the hurricane and to compound the crisis which was island-wide was that, with Britain still being engaged in the Second World War, any aid from the Colonial Office would be a long drawn-out process; the only alternative was to remortgage the property, which my parents did.

My mother told me that even old money that was set aside to buy a sewing machine for my brother and to pay towards my tuition and boarding fees at

Cornwall College in Montego Bay had to be used towards the repairs of the house, replacing furniture and clothes for the entire family. Of the items that could not be replaced were books, family photographs, and other memorabilia.

Over the years I came to the realisation that my parents accepted the fact that the past was something that they had no control over. Their sole responsibility was to consolidate the present and make preparation for the future. Central to that was their determination that come hell or high water foreclosure would never be a part of our experience. The sacrifices that were being made to face the challenges became more onerous and lengthy as a result of my father dying intestate and the processes of administration had to take their full course.

If nothing else, what I learnt during this particular period of my life was not to be hijacked by obstacles, and to be able to understand that disasters and times of triumph and achievement are part of the sum total of life. Logic also dictated that struggles and sacrifices are fleeting moments that can be endured or enjoyed, hence Bob Marley's "De rain dey fall but de dutty tough, de pot dey bwill but de food nuh nuff" strikes a significant cord that echoed our shared family understanding that individually, and collectively, times of comfort and times of conflict is a human condition which applies to every one, but what is important is the extent by which the individual can muster the courage to sincerely believe that even in the face of adversity and when it is almost impossible to see the light at the end of the tunnel, there must be the light of hope and that sense of optimism that can be clouded but can never be extinguished.

I was fortunate during this period of inconvenience to have as my headmaster John McIntosh Whitely. He came out of retirement to run the school and whereas it was to Teacher Williams that I owe my interest in Jazz Music and the skill of bowling leg breaks, it was Teacher Whitely who ignited my appreciation for the contributions of the Greeks to world civilization in terms of literature, arts, sports and war, and the contributions of Normal Washington Manley, Founder of the People's National Party (PNP) in Jamaica, a former Prime Minister and one of Jamaica's National Heroes. Teacher Whitely also had an appreciation for good handwriting; he said "that reading maketh a man, but writing maketh an exact man". Locating himself in Homer's Iliad he made the exploits of Hector and Achilles, Odysseus and the Cyclops, Apollo and Zeus seem so surreal in that I was able to make the connections with some of the characters and the circumstances under which they occurred, for example, Jason sailing with the Argonauts, Zeus the Ruler of Nature, and Apollo, the Sun God; also there were villages in my parish such as Helicon, Delphi, and Arcadia that made the stories more relevant.

Teacher Whitely left no stones unturned when he related the history of Norman Washington Manley as a sportsman where he excelled at cricket, football and athletics; his record of 10 seconds flat over 100 yards as a student at Jamaica College competing in the Jamaica Interscholastic Athletic Championships lasted for over 41 years, his winning The Rhodes Scholarship to attend Oxford University where he read Law, and his joining the 1914-1918 war where as a result of holding out against German firepower which killed his brother, Roy, he was awarded the Military Medal.

For Teacher, other than Marcus Garvey, Manley was the most influential leader in Jamaica and one of the best barristers in the Caribbean. The lines between the Greeks and Manley in terms of sport, politics and education in as far as Teacher's perception were concerned became more apparent to me, especially as far as what Manley's, "We are going to build a new Jamaica", meant my understanding of the slogan was pushing for changes for a better future.

For me, starting to build a new Jamaica meant more concentration on my school work, more time playing cricket and, of course, making sure that I did not renege on the chores that were in keeping with the smooth running of operations within the family environment. One of the things that I did whilst working in England was to speak to a wide cross-section of both voluntary and statutory groups on aspects of motivation and mentoring. One of the most frequent questions that is asked is how I find time to do so many things, my answer to them is about the ability to manage time effectively. I learnt that in those early days and I have come to agree with Benjamin Franklin who said, "Dost thou love life? Then do not squander time for that is the stuff of life".

I did love life and I still do and part of my make up is about taking calculated risk, so in keeping with some of the adventures of my Greek mythology heroes I decided that I wanted to find out for myself whether some of the folklore that abounded in and around the community had a kind of validity. To embark on the mission I first had to find the people who were willing to make the journey. I believe that the true Leader is one who can help others to do things that make them feel good about themselves, in other words people who have the ability to take others with them.

My first assignment was twofold. Firstly, to see the mermaid that according to local legend lived in Cave Hall, which is now the Green Grotto Cave. The tale is if that if one saw her combing her hair she would throw away the comb and whoever retrieved it the mermaid would dream to that person and tell him or her where there is a hidden jar with golden coins.

Secondly, I wanted to find out, according to the folklore, that there were Arawak Indians who survived the Spanish Occupation and who were still living in the caves. The Arawak, also known as Tainos, were the first inhabitants of Jamaica; they were originally from Venezuela, and sailed from there in their dug out canoes, arriving in Jamaica around AD1000. They called the Island Xaymaca, which means 'Lands of Wood and Water'. History has recorded that the Arawaks not only lived in caves but they also buried their dead in them.

Against such a backdrop it is understandable why the oral tradition perpetuated the mysteries surrounding the caves. Present day logic has put into perspective the importance of folklore and history and positive PR and marketing enhances tourism in Jamaica.

It was early on a Saturday morning when Bugs Faulcher, Vannbert 'Vannie' Alexander and I entered the cave. For light we had bundles of sticks tied neatly together, the first quarter of a mile was well explored as a result of people gathering bat manure for their gardens and the seeds from the Breadnut Tree, which is grounded and when cooked makes quite an appetising dish. As we pursued further into the bowels of the cavern there was the occasional sliver of sunlight shining through crevices of rocks from above, except for that we were enveloped in darkness as the flicker of light from torches revealed a series of markings etched on the walls of the cave. Below us was a stream and the water was as clear as it was still; up to that stage no sign of a mermaid or the sound of anything living or dead other than our own whispered voices could be heard. The eeriness was broken when Vannie used a stick and touched one of the stalagmites. The sound emanating from it was musical. If nothing else it lifted the spirits and acted as a reminder that the inner man wanted looking after; in other words hunger dictated that the exploration was coming to an end. Slowly and for most of the way we came out of the cave almost the way we had gone in, daring not to turn our backs to be in keeping with what the old sages advised; that by turning one's back for any length of time the ghost of an Arawak is likely to follow you home.

The community grapevine relating to our adventure was one that I expected in terms of the risks that we had undertaken and the consequences of those risks. Based on the legends that had been planted in the minds of the people in the community over many years, some people hinted that within a matter of days one or all three of us would experience some kind of unpleasantness. That very night I had a dream that I was locked in the cave, when I told Teacher Whitely he said it was mind over matter and that cowards die many times before their deaths.

Weeks passed and nothing untoward had overtaken any of us. I was now ready for my next assignment. This time it was to see the golden dining table with six chairs that surfaces every Good Friday at the lagoon adjacent to the Green Grotto Caves. The story surrounding this table is that once when it surfaced in the early 1900s Captain Blagrove's father, one of the wealthiest of the land-owning plantocrats, sent a boat out to the lake where the men tied ropes to the table and chairs which they then attached to over a hundred of his cows hoping that they would pull the table and chairs ashore. To the surprise of all the bystanders the table submerged, pulling all the cattle down with it and from that day no one has ever gone near the lake on a Good Friday on the understanding that whoever sees the table the brightness of the gold would render them sightless forever.

One of the age old customs in Discovery Bay which was still practised when I migrated to England in 1960 is the annual Good Friday Baptism Service at the beach conducted by the Grateful Hill Baptist Church from Helicon. After the service people went on to their own churches for the Good Friday Service. Like the first expedition secrecy was paramount, but like every well planned activity things occasionally go wrong! This time Vannie dropped out as a result of being hit by a cricket ball whilst fielding too close at silly mid-off. As far as Bugs Faulcher and myself were concerned, we had no intention of waiting for another Good Friday; we arrived at the lagoon at about twenty minutes to twelve and hid under the Mangrove Trees that surrounded the lake. It seemed like an eternity as we anxiously waited for the table to surface. Each time the wind rose, which created ripples in the distance, our expectations heightened; from the position of the sun in the sky we knew that it was well past twelve o'clock. The water was tranquil and irresistible as we divested ourselves of our clothes and slid off the Mangrove Trees into the water. I was surprised at the tameness of the coots swimming around and as I dived under the water I realised that although they floated so easily on the surface their little feet were working at some speed underwater. What I learnt from that experience is that in life when things seem to be going quite smoothly there is a lot of effort inside to keep things going.

There were no golden table or chairs to be seen other than one of the largest eels I have ever seen, and, to add insult to injury, when I dived into the water after submerging to about two metres, it was pitch black and the water was ice cold; when I surfaced I was chattering in the bright sun shine. We dressed hastily and on our way back we hardly said a word to each other. Within a matter of four days I was down with a severe cold accompanied with fever, headaches and vomiting. My grand aunt, Granny Edith, nursed me back to fitness; in between she tried to ascertain where I had been on Good Friday when I had slipped out of Church and did not return. But, as they say, mum's the word and I was confident in my mind that neither Vannie or Bugs would divulge any information regarding the adventure, which was kept a secret until 1950, when Harold Peat, the man responsible for starting the development of Discovery Bay as a tourist resort, brought a team of underwater experts to probe the lake, that we made it know that we had swam in it. Like the body of water at Loch Ness in Scotland, the lake at Discovery Bay continued to be a source of speculation in terms that it is bottomless and is likened to other lakes worldwide.

Like Cave Hall and Lagoon, Traveller's Cave, which bounds our land to the west, also has its own legend which is linked with the Arawaks occupation. It was also the place that a man travelling from one of the Western parishes to Kingston took shelter from bad weather and eventually died, hence the name Traveller's Cave.

It was from the Cave that, along with Michael Williams and my father, I took shelter from the 1944 Hurricane; as far as I can remember it was the first time that I have ever gone and I was quite amazed at not only how spacious it was inside but the way it was laid out. It left no doubt in my mind that it was inhabited by the Arawaks. Undaunted by the severe bouts of fever and colds that I picked up when I dived into the lagoon, I decided that it was time to explore Traveller's Cave. The pretext that I used to get Crampy to accompany me was that two of our goats who were about to have kids had gone missing. Walking down a flight of rugged stone steps we came into what could be described as a living room and from there two other smaller compartments. We followed the sheath of light that shone through overgrown bushes, wild orchids, wild pine and ferns that brought us to a single hole that revealed a large pool of water with two of the largest groupers that I have ever seen. There were also lobsters and other fishes swimming, or rather basking, in the water at peace with themselves.

Until the construction of the Queen's Highway in the fifties, that part of the coast between what is now Portside Villa and Old Folly had a headland that jutted out into the sea, Dinah Rock, which when the tide was low revealed a gaping hole that ran under the road; how deep and how far it went inland nobody has ever tried to find out. I don't think there was a reason, it was just how things were in those days and as times went on the theories of historians and geologists started to make sense that Jamaica, like other Caribbean Islands, evolved from a large volcano that erupted out of the sea some million year ago and in its wake left a myriad of caves and sink holes. Emerging from the other side of the cave we came across a skull and bones, and stone carvings neatly laid out, needless to say I did not find any goats, but reflecting on this experience I understood where Teacher Whitely was coming from in locating himself within an ancient civilisation that fuses history into mythology, and from his position as a trusted mentor he captured my young mind, which I was to appreciate in the process of growing up that there is a correlation between fiction and reality and that for centuries writers have made efforts to create characters that are symbolic to the human condition and the human experience within a historic time frame. So, for example, whereas

I could stay in Jamaica and visualise Zeus and his father Apollo commanding a place within Greek civilisation, the Greek student could or should be able to make the link with Huracan, the name that the Caribs, a man-eating tribe from the same Venezuelan coast as the Arawaks, gave to Hurricanes that slakes the Caribbean from time to time. According to the Caribs Huracan was a God who created havoc when anyone displeased him.

My exploration, or rather adventure, in the lagoon and the caves started with coming to terms with matters of economic, social, historical, and leisure-seeking circumstances. For me these activities became foundations for the inventing of myself; in the process I knew that without God I would not be able to make it through the valley of the shadow of death, but I also knew that there were still a lot of rivers to cross.

CHAPTER FOUR

Every dog has its day

IN FEBRUARY 1950 I was voted Captain for the Discovery Bay Elementary School Cricket Team to participate in the Moulton-Barrett Cup Competition for schools in the Parish of Saint Ann. It was the first time that the school was entered in the competition, which was quite prestigious. Youngsters who do well would more than likely be encouraged to play for the Parish and maybe for Jamaica. In essence it was the induction to the game from where opportunities, limited as they were at the time in rural Jamaica, could be had for advancement to better things and to be voted as Captain for my team was both an honour and an achievement.

The lack of, and the high cost of, transportation dictated that schools participating in the competition were zoned approximately four or five miles from each other, which made it easier to walk to play our matches. Discovery Bay was zoned with Waltham Abbey, Runaway Bay and Hoolebury. Each team played each other twice on a points system, three points for a win, two points for a draw and an automatic three points if a team failed to turn up, although this never happened as we all loved cricket too much; it was easier to miss going to Church or school than to miss a cricket match. Vannie Alexander always said 'to miss a cricket match is to commit sacrilege'. It is a testimony to the extent to which cricket was in my blood.

The standard of cricket was very high and as newcomers to the competition one of the things I was quick on picking up was that one or two schools played boys who had already left Elementary School, although our school had never resorted to that tactic. Teacher Sudlow, my head teacher at the time, would never have entertained it anyway. As a team we believed and lived out the old saying that, "The fairer one plays the fairer one wins". Equally important, I have never encouraged any member of my team to be involved in "mouthing", in other words 'sledging', as far as we were concerned we played hard, we enjoyed what we were doing and let the bat and the ball do the talking and the spectators responded with their spontaneous and off the cuff banter that at times caused young minds to drift and as a result lose their concentration, whereby they dropped catches, failed to save boundaries or, worse, got hit by bouncers. When that happened in my capacity as captain I would tell the errant player, "you have fallen for mimicry"; I am sure they got the message, be that as it may without that kind of spectator participation.

For me as a Caribbean person the game would have no meaning, the point has been expanded by Hillary McD Beckles writing in "The Development of West Indies Cricket Volume One; The Age of Nationalism" that cricket as the popular cultural occupation of the region therefore converts spectators into artists in a dialectical and symbiotic way allowing for some of the finest expressions of music, theatrical performance and oral literature.

The first match that I captained was against Runaway Bay School, the Headmaster at the time was Teacher Titus, recognised and acknowledged as one of the leading educators in Jamaica. He was also a keen sportsman, which reflected in the high standard of his school cricket and football teams. I won the toss and elected to bat, our two openers, Alexander 'Jack' Hodges and Kipper Lynch got us off to a solid start. Jack was the first out, caught behind for 28 with 68 runs on the board. There were some useful contributions from Vincent Cover and Lloyd Case, I batted at my usual no. 6 position for 20 and we finally managed 190, for which I was quite satisfied knowing that I could depend on the firepower of Edwin Johnson, Lloyd Case, Joseph Day or myself, backed up with Egbert Wisdom bowling off breaks and Crampy Williams bowling spin.

With a batting line up of players like Guthrie, Miles, Moulton, Bloise, Geoffrey and Ross, Runaway Bay must have imagined that they were in with a good chance of winning; their aspirations were soon shattered with the speed and accuracy of Johnson and Day, the competence of Lynch behind the stumps and yours truly at first slip, who took three beautiful catches; we got Runaway Bay out for 110 runs.

It was my first victory as Captain and at the customary speech after tea it was sheer joy on my part as I paid tribute to my team for their co-operation and also thanked the opposition for a good game. My confidence was boosted not only as a Captain but also to the extent by which I was able to understand how people think and the strategies that need to be put into place that motivated them to achieve, both as an individuals and as a collective. I also discovered that as bowler I had the ability to use the Yorker effectively, which over time I developed into a fine art.

The tongue of good report relating to the victory preceded us and the traditional singing of songs in keeping with winning matches such as "Captain Stennett go before us like a great man of war" and "You are wrong to send and call us because you know that we are the lions and the lions will devour you" signalled the village, comprising all ages and gender, coming out to congratulate us with hugs, kisses, food and bunches of flowers. As I said, it was my first victory in well organised competition and it reminded me of the biblical David's reception by the people of Israel after his army defeated the Philistines in the Valley of Gath, but even in the euphoria of my victory I was aware that the same group of people who sing your praises one day will not bat an eyelid on the following day to jeer in song when you lose; the village social commentator in the guise of the mento or calypso singer would always make sure of that. For drawing a game the song would be "home once more, I left this world of sin and Jesus took me in glory be to God I'm home once more". When you are beaten, whether at home or away, they would sing "Discovery Bay boys are Pifnas". I never knew what a 'Pifna' was until Joe Day defined it as 'perfect incompetent foolhardy natural asses'. Looking back I understand why some people shunned responsibility; it is because they are afraid of failure. For me, like cricket the same applies to life, you cannot win all the time and the important thing is to be able to turn failures into successes.

The next game was playing Waltham Abbey at home. I stuck to the team that won the first game and the result was even more convincing that the first game. The team, the school and the wider community were now fully behind us and morale was in its ascendancy. For my part my brother, Noel, who was then living and working in Kingston, came to watch the match and was proud of my performance. I had match figures of seven overs, two maidens, fifteen runs and three wickets, but in the process of assessing my performance he said that he noticed after bowling my fourth over I was limping and on returning back to my mark I was massaging my calf. On explaining to him that I tended to get cramps which could well be as a result of being struck by the lightning two years previously, he recommended that I started doing weight training. Within the space of a week we had rigged up an open air gym in the back yard; for dumb bells we filled two large butter tins with sand and cement. Using a bamboo pole as the bar, the pully machine consisted of an old bucket with stone, sand and cement. All primitive but they worked and over time I reaped the benefits and it is easy to understand why in those days I referred to Noel as my doctor, my lawyer, my financial advisor, and my psychologist. Every cricketer, or for that matter every sportsperson, must have one with that combined advice if they want to succeed. I was so keen to succeed that I did not wait for advice, I went and sought it and encouraged my friends to do the same. There will always be merit in the adage of "each one telling one".

The community as a whole was in the way forward mode and as such everyone was happy to share in whatever way possible; their ideas and experiences would help to promote the well-being and the common good of the community so it was not surprising that they would glean as much information about the players from other schools participating in the competition and pass them on to us. I do not believe that this was anything new, except that for the first time the school was playing for the prestigious

Moulton-Barrett Cup. Captain Moulton-Barrett was not only related to the Barrett's of Wimpole Street, London, but he was also the Custos for the Parish of Saint Ann. The Custos is the Chief Magistrate and plays a similar role to the High Sheriff in England. Incidentally, Jamaica is the only country in the Caribbean that continues with the British tradition of Custos.

Through the grapevine I learnt that except for Boland, Coore, Williams and Botek, Hoolebury did not have a very good team but by the same rule they could come good on the day. I was never one to tempt fate and both times that we played them we played hard, that is always the objective, to play to win within the rules of the game. Never take anything or anyone for granted because cricket is a funny game. The first match against them Edwin Johnson got four for seventeen, Joe Day three for twenty seven, myself three for twenty, Kipper Lynch and Jack Hodges between them got forty and twenty four respectively. There was no stopping Discovery Bay, it was great fun both on and off the field.

The second game saw us rolling them over for twenty six. I opened the bowling and had match figures of three overs, one maiden, five runs, five wickets and that feat was repeated in June 1963 when I played for Manchester General Post Office versus Salford Transport at Swinton.

Performances like those linger for a lifetime and to add spice to the occasion in Jamaica, SAXA, an itinerant entertainer made up the following:

> *Here they come with bat and ball*
> *To give merriment to one and all*
> *Stand up for cricket the game we love*
> *For it was sent down to us by the man above.*
> *Wicketkeepers, batsmen and fielders share in the glory*
> *But all fast bowlers have the power and the glory*
> *And the right to claim the ground as their own.*

(The above was sung to the tune of 'Lo he comes with clouds ascending.)

My admiration for Saxa, and that was the only name that I and for that matter a majority of the people in the village knew him as, was that he was a very good guitar player who held dances. He being the only musician would use his mouth to emit sounds similar to the trumpet, the clarinet, and the saxophone.; he was also good at whistling. Jamaican humour dictated that of all the instruments that he imitated Saxa would be the most appropriate soubriquet, that being said he attracted a very impressive following. I was always taken in by his rendition of 'Stardust Melody', 'Sentimental Journey' and the Calypso:

Every dog has its day

Dorothy went in the sea to bathe
Cat fish come and mek a raid
Don't bawl Miss Dorothy
De cat fish bite you
On you junior come under.

To compliment his musical capabilities he was a very good dresser, white shirts, black pants, felt hat at a rakish angle on his head, shoes always shining; he looked the part. What I did not know then was that he gambled on anything, from whether it was going to rain, or at what time the bread van would arrive at a given spot. I was too young to gamble but unknown to me he saw me as someone worth placing a bet on, his faith in me almost put paid to my captaincy, but on the other hand it gave birth to my fetishism for shoes.

As it happened we were playing Waltham Abbey at their ground at Allen Hall in Farm Town; it was the sixth game of the Cup Competition and at that stage we were on level points with Runaway Bay so this game was crucial. Waltham Abbey won the toss and batted, posting eighty five runs on the board. Bowling honours went to Joe Day with four for forty, Edwin Johnson three for thirty two, Crampy two for eleven and there was a run out - I did not figure amongst the bowling but every bowler has an off day and even the angels from above cannot intercede on your behalf. Absent from the team that day was Kipper Lynch, hence Jack Hodges opened with Vincent Cover, vice captain, both capable of hitting the runs off or at least giving us an excellent start. The decision was that come what may I was first wicket down, quite an elevation - and who was I to go against the wishes of the team. Jack was the first out, caught behind for twenty seven off the bowling of Howard Clarke, a mean and hostile fast bowler who had no compunction in shaking up batsmen and had no code of ethics in relation to the fast bowlers' union. The score at that point was fifty seven and making my way to the wicket I could hear the Waltham Abbey supporters encouraging Howard to give 'us some skin', meaning shaking me up with bouncers. My Discovery Bay supporters were also rooting for me, yet above the din I could hear Saxa as it were striking up the band. What did Shakespeare say, 'Music hath charms to soothe the savage breast'. That day I was the savage and I was intent on putting Howard in his place.

In those days we played eight ball overs and watching him from behind the boundary I noticed that he tended to pitch short on the delivery of either his sixth or eighth ball. When I arrived at the wicket Vin Cover suggested that I played myself in and when he pitched short I go for my shots, it would appear as if Howard heard what I was told, or rather anticipated what I had in mind as his first ball to me, which was the sixth of the over, was rather short on off stump and I duly obliged by heaving the ball with my favourite hook shot for six runs. His next ball was well pitched up and I played it to mid off, who fielded the ball and threw to the wicketkeeper. Suddenly I could hear a large section of the Waltham Abbey spectators willing Howard Clarke to appeal. To add insult to injury, he stuttered a bit in those days and I could not believe my ears or eyes when he stuttered 'how is he' to see the umpire, Teacher Mcon Hudson who was the headmaster at his school, holding up his finger allowing the appeal. I stood my ground and felt even more resolute when Vin Cover, batting at the other end, willed me not to move.

Well, in those days, and it is still the case, when Vin Cover talks no dogs bark and I knew that to obey is better than sacrifice. Not said Teacher A Spencer Sudlow, my headmaster, who was standing at square leg, who when I turned to face him I heard his commanding and precise voice saying, 'Stennett, what is the use of the umpire?' With that I trailed off unwillingly to jeers and boos from a very hostile Waltham Abbey crowd. Leading the onslaught was my mother's favourite uncle on her mother's side, Uncle Fred's son, Leonard Clarke, the best shoemaker for miles around. Without a doubt he was an excellent shoemaker but that day he was a nasty spectator baying for my blood. We won the match and at the customary speech-making after tea I apologised for my behaviour towards the umpire; what was interesting is that to every word that I spoke Saxa's guitar strings twanged. He was in his element for what I did not know and it was to be revealed some months later.

At school on the Monday morning, Teacher Sudlow was in a sombre mood and was not sparing in his criticism of me as a captain; as far as he was concerned I had failed to live up to my role as an ambassador for the school and the community as a whole. To make amends I had to stand and apologise to the whole school and in addition write two letters, one to Waltham Abbey and one to Mr Brammie Morales, who was the president of the Parent Teachers' Association; altogether it was quite a harrowing experience and although by the very fact that the rules of the game would have dictated that the ball was dead, the umpire or umpires should have consulted and ruled in my favour. This did not happen, and realising that to err is human I decided that from that day as long as I was involved with the game I would not want to give an umpire any feeling that I was above his running of the game; that is not to say that in my time I have not enquired of umpires what has given rise to decisions that they make, but I always do this in the true spirit of the game.

The competition was structured in such a way that the finals had to be played before the summer holidays and then the Jamaica Local Examinations were in July so whether it was by accident or design, Discovery Bay found themselves in the same position as Runaway Bay with the same amount of points which meant that we had to have a play off to gain the right to play Chalky Hill in the final. It was quite daunting and for that matter very challenging in that a majority of players from both schools were in preparation for sitting various stages of the exam. I was sitting the Second Examination, failing to turn up for the match which was the Thursday before the exam on the Friday would mean forfeiting the game and Runaway Bay would play in the final. Incidentally, the match was at Runaway Bay, the very centre where we had to travel to take the exam. The only concession that the organisers made was that instead of play starting at eleven o'clock it would start at ten. From the regular and best team on the day was myself, Vin Cover, Jack Hodges, Edwin Johnson, Kipper Lynch, Crampy Williams, Lloyd Williams, Frank 'Bugsie' Williams, Rook Barrett, Shirley Williams and Noel Seivewright.

There is no doubt that there were a lot of misgivings from family members who expressed their concerns that I was playing too much cricket and not giving enough time to my studies; certainly this view was not shared neither by my mother or my teachers, who knew that I was working equally hard with my sports and school work. I knew what I had to do and had no intention of failing the exam for a second time as I have said, failure makes me more determined to succeed.

Whatever plans Runaway Bay had to upstage us was of no concern to me. True, there were newcomers to the side, they had practised and supported us all along and were more or less biding their time to prove themselves. There were even suggestions that the opposition had a track prepared to take spin; they won the toss and put us in and as usual Jack Hodges and Kipper Lynch got us off to a very good start. Kipper was the first out with fifty three to his name and the score on eighty one. Two balls later Jack was out for eighteen eighty one for two. Vin and myself made every effort to get back into contention but by then it was quite clear that the wicket was taking spin. We followed each out and when the score was on ninety five for five, it was the newcomers, Michael 'Tower' William and Lloyd Williams, ably assisted by Crampy and Rook Barrett, who gave us any sense of respectability as we were finally bowled out for one hundred and forty seven.

In my time as Captain I have never experienced a player demanding what they want to do. In life there is always a first time and that day, Crampy demanded and was granted the privilege to open the bowling with an amalgam of right arm leg spin, googlies and off spinners. He had the Runaway Bay batsmen in all sorts of trouble, finishing up with figures of eight for fifty four. His cousin, Lloyd Williams, had two for fourteen. It was a fitting win which found resonance with me when the West Indies beat

England at Lords three weeks previously by three hundred and twenty six runs. The event was placed into the annals of cricket history with the song which has gained world recognition, 'Cricket, lovely cricket, at Lord's where I saw it, with those little pals of mine, Ramadhin and Valentine'. I remembered getting up at four o'clock that morning of the 24th June 1950, it was a Saturday and I made sure that all the chores were complete before I was able to take up my position on the wall outside of the Discovery Bay Police Station to listen to the commentary by Rex Alston, John Arlott, E W Stanton, and our own Jamaican, Roy Lawrence of Radio Jamaica.

In those days, except for the landed gentry who owned radios, there was only Charles 'Son' Stewart or the Police Station that we could go to to listen to any sporting commentary, or otherwise read it in the Daily Gleaner's articles by L D 'Strebor' Roberts. When I arrived Jeff Stollmeyer, who opened the batting with Alan Rae, was already out LBW to the first ball off Johnny Wardle for twenty. Next in was Frank Worrel and by this time there was a large crowd of men, women and children gathered at the side of the Station. In such a setting and over five and a half thousand miles away I found myself enveloped into my own little world as I listened and at the same time trying to imagine what Lord's was like, and the extent to which the three W's, Weekes, Worrell, and Walcott, and of course Rae, would stay at the wicket to get a century. All the questions and the ponderings were put into some kind of reality by the commentators, especially John Arlott and Roy Lawrence. By the end of that match and those that followed I more or less had a clear picture of what Lord's, Old Trafford, Trent Bridge and the Oval were like. I was determined that I would go to England to see for myself these famous grounds, but as things were there were things that had to be taken care of and that was the final match in the Moulton Barrett Competition against Chalky Hill.

With exams out of the way our team was back to full strength and from the information that I was receiving, and of course their record was there to prove it, they were the strongest side in the competition having won the cup four times since its inception. They were well balanced in terms of batting, bowling and fielding, the names often mentioned as being outstanding were Rose, Forrest, Hay, Stennett and Hinds.

The Final was played at Archer Park in Runaway Bay and we won the toss and batted. An interesting aside or coincidence is that all during the competition I had only lost the toss once. As usual Kipper Lynch opened with Jack Hodges and gave us an excellent start with seventy seven on the board when Jack was out LBW to an inswinger from Rose for forty three. There were valuable contributions from Cover, Case, Wisdom and Barrett and I batted not out for twenty seven. We were all out for two hundred and one, the highest total we had made in the competition and we had every reason to feel confident of winning; we always did anyway.

Our supporters were in carnival mood when Johnson bowled Stennett, one of their opening batsmen, first ball for a duck. They weathered the storm and when I took Johnson off they were forty three for one. My first over was a maiden, Wisdom came in for Day with his right hand medium leg breaks and on the third ball of his first over he had Hay caught at silly mid on and the score was then seventy five for two. There were two run outs and the score was eighty three for four and in came Forrest. He was dropped by Case at first slip the first ball that I bowled to him, as they say 'Fortune favours the brave'. That day the gods were definitely on his side and I did every kind of bowling change, but it was to no avail. Forrest, like 'Old Man River', just kept 'rolling along'. There was no stopping him and he carried his bat for one hundred and three runs and we lost by six wickets. It was a good game and there was no denying that the best team won on the day. For me it was more than a sobering experience, of the ten matches in which I captained in the competition I won eight, drew one and lost one. What I learnt was that I had the strength of character to lead, either from being upfront or from behind, and beside, the ability to empathise and sympathise, to be able to listen, to share, and to engender trust and confidence. I also knew that I was a committed team man and that I had what it took to be a good cricketer.

That last game heralded the mid-summer holidays and all the fun that is associated with that period. As I recall The New Testament Church of God were having their Parish Convention at Discovery Bay that year and two of the delegates stayed at our house. Coming from the service on the Monday evening as always, Ralph, our dog, would come to meet us. There was a car approaching us and it had only one headlight and it came quite close, almost running us over; it was too late for Ralph to get out of the way and it ran him over, whereupon my other friends, who were much further behind us, heard me shouting that Ralph had been run over, jumped into the middle of the road and demanded the driver to stop, which he did.

As it happened the occupants of the car were Brigadier and Lady Sewell, who owned a large property in Trewlawney Brian Castle. They were on their way home from Cardiff Hall, another of the great houses owned by the landed gentry, where they had been playing bridge. That is what their chauffer tried to explain to us as I told him in no uncertain terms within earshot of his master and mistress how I felt about it. By this time the car was surrounded by people coming from the service and I told the driver of the car that I had sent for the police because the car should not be on the road. It was at this stage that the Brigadier alighted from the car and enquired of my name, which I gave to him. He apologised for what had happened to my dog and said that he would be getting in touch with me. His driver drove off leaving my friends and myself the agonising task of taking Ralph's carcass and throwing it into the sea. My last act of affection was to take off my shirt, which I could ill-afford to do, and tie it around his body. When I got home one of the visitors read Psalm 61 verse 2, which says that 'when my heart is overwhelmed, lead me to the rock that is higher than I'. I was clear in my mind that given the fact that I had expressed my feelings to the Brigadier and his driver, at no time was I disrespectful which could give rise to them taking me to court for bad conduct. I also knew that even if the Police were called and the vehicle was found to be defective to prosecute would mean that the Police Officers could end up being transferred to Cave Valley and the beginning of a long and painful walk to promotion; that was how things were in those days under colonial rule. On the other hand, with my supplying all my details they could be passed around to employers which could negate against me and based on what could be said was not in my favour. All that would be in the future, as far as I was concerned if the worst got out I could always go fishing. No one other than God could stop me going to the sea and people would always eat fish for which they would have to pay; at any rate I had a deep sense of satisfaction that I had said what I did and if needed I would be willing to repeat it.

On the Thursday I was playing cricket on our land when Brigadier Sewell's car drove up in the yard. The driver came out with a letter in his hand and it was addressed to Mr E W Stennett ESQ, Harbour View, Dry Harbour. By this time everyone in the yard stood around as I opened the letter and started to read aloud the contents, which were as follows:

> *Dear Master Stennett,*
> *I did promise a few evenings ago that I would be getting in touch*
> *with you. Both Lady Sewell and I are dog lovers so we know how*
> *sad it is for you losing yours, but accidents do happene and once*
> *again I sincerely hope that you accept our apology.*
> *As a token of our sincerity we hope the enclosed cheque will be*
> *used towards getting a new dog.*
> *All the best for the future.*
> *Yours sincerely, Brigadier Sewell*

There were cheers, laughter and exclamations of 'Good', 'Alright' and 'He is a man of his word', and we went back to our game of cricket and the driver finished his refreshing drink of lemonade and drove away. My mother was noted for her lemonade, made with the juice of the Seville Sweet Orange, some locals referred to it as a bitter sweet orange. In a wider context I viewed life as being bitter and being sweet but the most important thing is to find a way in which both can be blended so as to appreciate their value. On the Friday morning I took the cheque which was for One Pound Ten Shillings and placed in into my Post Office Savings Bank Account; it was the first cheque that I had ever received. The letter from the Brigadier written in his own handwriting was placed in the trunk that contained other valuable family keepsakes; sadly the trunk was destroyed with all its contents when Hurricane Gilbert demolished the family home in September 1988.

I went back to school in the September after the long summer holidays filled with renewed vigour; I was successful in the examination that I had taken in July, passing with Distinction in History, English and Scripture. Passing this exam was my message to those people who had more or less written me off that I was putting too much into cricket. That the same commitment and dedication that one put into sport the same can be applied to achieving an academic pursuit, as was often implied I knew that I wanted and was quite prepared to take on the challenges that were necessary to achieve them. The Jamaican proverb that, 'when chicken is merry the hawk is near' assumed its full meaning two weeks into the resumption of the September term in the person of none other than Lenny Clarke, the shoemaker, my mother's favourite Uncle Fred's son.

Months before the cricket match against Waltham Abbey, his school, where there was a misunderstanding between the umpire and myself, I took the hide of a goat that we had killed for the family Christmas dinner for him to make a pair of shoes for the school Christmas Breaking-up Concert. He took my foot measurement and I paid him the advance of ten shillings on the understanding that on completion I would pay him the balance of twenty five shillings. Thirty five shillings was a lot of money in those days but as I have said, he was an excellent shoemaker and to wear a pair of shoes made by Lenny Clarke meant you were socially mobile. In my case it was even more important because I had reared the goat from it being a new kid, not only that I prepared the hide myself.

The first time I went to see him to find out how he was advancing with my shoes he showed me the lathe on which they were on ready to be stitched up and to add the finishing touches; I came away feeling quite excited, picturing in my mind's eye my tall pants on the night of the concert, complete with my handmade shoes. If I was not going to be the best, I most certainly would be amongst the best, unfortunately for me Lenny Clarke was not thinking what I was thinking. It was a fortnight after my first visit that I went back to see him and the shoes were in the same position and I got the same story with a sly smile that they would be ready for the concert. As they say in Jamaica, 'promises are comfort to fools'. November visit he was nowhere to be seen and, to add insult to injury, one of the lads working with him told me that the shoes were in the back of the shop untouched. All along I refused to let my mother or any other family member or friends be aware of what I was experiencing; it has never been my style to complain to others and I believe in dealing with things myself.

The Monday before the concert, which was on the Friday, I went to see him and my patience was exhausted. Nevertheless I faced up to him and in the presence of other people in his shop, which included a District Constable, a school teacher and my favourite Grand Aunt Gran Edith, I told him that he was unreliable, untrustworthy and a shylock. The last thing I called him as I backed out of his shop was a shuffler, preparing for the third Jamaica Local Examination, my vocabulary was at its best and even if he felt annoyed and wanted to attack me with the kind of people in the shop common sense prevailed on his side; rightly so he being a pillar of society. For my part, although I felt good inside that I had personally dealt with him, it was just the beginning of sorrow because coming home from school after rehearsal on the Tuesday I walked with a girl who was about two years older than I and on reaching my gate she said, 'see you tomorrow sweet young prince'. I replied 'ok you honeycomb'. I had no idea that my mother was talking with Lenny Clarke at the top gate of our yard and it was only when I stood on the veranda of our house that I saw him riding his bike past our gate. My heart sank when I walked into the living room of our house to see another Aunt of my mother, Aunt Cis, and her grandson, Noel Seivewright. I fully realised then that from the response that I received from mother and Aunt Cis that I was due to receive some heavy manners, this was to be confirmed by Noel who came to my room to tell me that he had overheard Lenny Clarke telling my mother that I had been to his shop and cursed him and likened him to a dog.

As a youngster I have never liked soup or porridge and my mother knew that, but on this particular evening after Aunt Cis had said Grace I passed my soup to Noel saying 'Soup again'. Suddenly my mother turned around and hit me on the head with the wooden soup ladle saying, 'you eat what I provide, you are a boy and I am not going to allow you to do what you like'. When I put my hand to where the ladle landed it was moist with blood. Aunt Cis showed no sympathy towards me, if anything she added to my discomfort when she said, 'These days children need to know who is the boss and the bible say "do not spare the rod and spoil the child"'. That being said, I knew that my mother believed everything that Lenny Clarke had said to her and I think that it was rather unfair that she did not give me the opportunity to explain what had happened. Anyway, to be fair to her she did wash the blood from my hair and placed some healing oil on the bruise. That night the lesson that my mother chose for me to read from the Bible was Proverbs Chapter

Fifteen Verses One to Ten, which starts 'A soft answer turneth away wrath but grievous words stir up anger'. I went to bed that night with a heavy heart, feeling that I was more sinned against than sinning and decided that I was going to run away and join my brother, Noel, in Kingston. I had barely fallen asleep when my mother came into my room and sat on my bed, with her hand on my head she told me that she was sorry for what she had done to me and that she wished that I would not feel angry towards her. For all that I still had a bruised head deep down. I knew that she cared for me, which placed into context the lines from the song, "Can a woman's tender care cease towards the child she bear".

On my way to school the following morning I met Granny Edith making her way up to my house. She enquired as to how I was, I told her I was fine and if anything I dreaded facing my friends on the assumption that Noel might have told them what had transpired the previous evening; even my sisters did not know as they were still at rehearsals. Above all my young female admirer knew nothing about the incident so I was quite relieved but by the same rule, shoes or no shoes, I was determined to show Lenny Clarke that I was a man of mettle and not someone to be messed about, to run away to Kingston would have been the easy way out and to stand and fight was the best thing to do. How I was going to do it and make him or other detractors, by which time I was convinced that there were, called for a lot of thinking and planning. To travel three miles to Farm Town and throw stones into his shop or slash the tyres of his bicycle did enter my mind as the most logical thing to do but the consequences would be if I got caught, arrested, hauled up before the Court, and more than likely sent away to an Approved School, and that would be the end of my dreams and the number of people from my community, who recognised me as a true ambassador and role model. True enough I wanted to know what had given rise to the antagonism against me, yet by the same rule I did not want to be a martyr or crusader - I was a rebel and I had a cause.

At the end of the final rehearsal on Thursday and the arranging of the programme it suddenly dawned on me that it was in the same building many years before I was born that my Grandfather Samuel Stennett, or 'Old Prince' as he was affectionately called, took off his jacked and his shoes and like a true thespian expressed his anger at how some members of the congregation behaved negatively towards the black daughter of a member of the same church. Given that my circumstances were different there were two central themes that had a link. First, Tuesday evening of that same week Joyous Jones referred to me as a 'sweet young prince'. I just could not wait for Friday evening to arrive, to put my plan into action which I knew would be an effective one.

Granny Edith was at home when I arrived from school and she'd decided to stay until the following Monday. It was always a pleasure when she was around, a stickler for hygiene and getting you out of bed to do your chores, but with all that she was fair and had a heart of gold. At dinner she produced a box which I knew had shoes in it and she gave it to me; it was a nice Bata black shoe fit for my feet and also for a prince, my sisters and I were full of gratitude towards her, but having the shoes was in no way going to prevent me from doing what I had planned - 'a man must do what a man got to do'.

Our house was a hub of excitement and conviviality as we prepared for the concert on the Friday evening and I dare say that I was sartorial elegance in all its glory in my well-cut tailored black pants made by George Blissett, my very good friend from Mount Olivet; we called him Comrade Blissett as a result of his commitment to the People's National Party, light blue shirt and of course, my brand new shoes. To top it off I had my splash of Limacol, the fragrance that symbolised 'the freshness of a breeze in a bottle'. I was fifteen years old and was endeavouring to live out one of the many advices given by Miss Zettel Williams, "always make sure that your drawers and Merino are clean and your arm smell good". With advice like that it is impossible not to be attracted to the opposite sex and there will be more about that later on!

What my mother did not know was that underneath my tall pants I had the shortest of my khaki school pants and they could almost pass for hot pants that became the rage in the seventies; from how the programme was set like other members of the cast I had both solo and group parts, so immediately after I had done the group part I slipped off stage, took off my tall pants and shoes and gave them to Crampy for safe keeping and was on cue for the Master of Ceremonies, Vernal Fairweather, to announce me on stage. It was no concern of mine as to what was going on in the minds of the audience, who I am sure would be expecting to see me dressed as per the programme and there was utter silence as I used the stage, the enunciation and my pronounced lisp to deliver Alexander Selkirk's "I am Monarch of all I survey". The encores and shouts for more almost lifted the roof off the building and as I surveyed the faces of the audience I could see smiles and I guess a feeling of appreciation almost to the extent that for some people they had thrown a weight off their backs. I vividly recall at the end of the long standing ovation the Master of Ceremonies said, "This is a boy who will definitely be a man of tomorrow helping to build a new Jamaica". The back slaps, handshakes and comments of appreciation were overwhelming and I will always remember the comment of Andy Forbes from Helicon who said, "Boy Whitty Stennett walked on the stage barefooted and without batting an eyelash stole the show, what a man". Granny Edith was moved to tears of joy as she hugged me and whispered in my ear, "did you see Lenny's face?". That was justification enough. He was central to my problems and Granny Edith knew it and was happy at the way in which I was holding out by not suffering in silence, to all intents and purpose it was now beginning to dawn that I had won a battle more real than imagined, at least on the evening of the concert, and I sent out a message by my actions which emancipated me.

It was almost twenty eight years after that concert that I was able to have a deeper appreciation for what I had done on the evening of sixteenth of October 1968 when the African American sprinters, Tommie Smith and John Carlos, mounted the awards podium to receive their gold and bronze medals at the Mexico Olympics. Both men were shoeless and wore black armbands and a black glove on one hand and as the band played they lifted their gloved firsts skywards. Smith was later to explain that their raised arms represented the power and unity of Black America and the black socks with no shoes was symbolic of the poverty that affected so many black Americans. It is fair to say that on the evening I did not raise a clenched fish, firstly I did make several bows but they were in keeping with the applause from the audience. Nevertheless, my actions were expressions against unfairness, it was even more poignant when at the Mexico games the television showed the wives of Smith and Carlos asking each other, did you see Avery Brundage's face? Brundage at the time was the President of the Olympic Association, on one of my visits to Jamaica in 1999 when I reflected on my incident in 1950 with Lincoln Gabbidon one of my mentors, he said, "Whitty you were ahead of your time".

I knew that it would not have taken Noel Seivewright long to pass on to somebody that my mother had banged me on the head with the ladle and the reason for her doing that was because I was blowing kisses to women. Of all the persons that he chose to tell was Jacob Leslie, who kept wicket for the senior team, quite a good keeper but one of his drawbacks was that he had a speech impediment, so for instance, his pronunciation of sweet would be tweet. It would be foolish for me to deny that I had a rollicking from my mother, so I explained to him what had transpired, making sure that I did not mention Lenny Clarke and the shoe. Jacob's version of events was, "Titer Maud cat Witty tending tweet dreams to gal calling them honeycomb". The information was hardly mentioned on the village grapevine save for one sage who remarked that in my moment of expressing my affection I should have stopped at honey because the comb is sweeter, be that as it may the kind of rave notices that I was attracting as a result of my performance at the concert paled every other event into insignificance. I was rather flattered on the Sunday afternoon when Royland Higgins, who worked as a gardener at The Columbus Inn Hotel, came to see me and handed me a neatly wrapped parcel. On opening the parcel there were two books, a copy of Readers Digest and a copy of The Vicar of Wakefield by Oliver Goldsmith, written on the inside front cover of the Vicar of Wakefield was:

Dear Whitty,
I was quite thrilled with your performance on Friday, Defoe
would be pleased if he was around.
Keep up the good work.
Kindest regards.
Robert Lowell

Mr Lowell was a guest of the Hotel, the Readers Digest started the coming back together of my father's collection of books and The Vicar of Wakefield I used as one of my books for the English Literature option necessary for the Third Jamaica Local Examination. There was not an address for Robert Lowell, but in 1992 when I was selected to travel to Boston as part of the Manchester Anglican Diocesan and The Massachusetts Anglican Diocesan Link, realising that the city of Lowell was one of the places that I had visited and on further investigation discovered that Robert Lowell was a Boston-born poet who wrote 'Lord Weary's Castle' and 'Life Studies'. The Boston experience was quite an interesting one if for no other reason that it gave me the opportunity to have had an insight of an important part of British history and identity outside of Jamaica and England and the extent to which religion became a central plank in creating a visible link that recognises the importance of sports and music to American society based on the black American audience and working class Britain.

As I have said I have always admired Saxa, the itinerant entertainer, purely for h is entertainment value and nothing else. We had nothing in common; he was a grown man, I have never seen him holding a cricket bat or ball in his hand, although he was always at matches and when we were practising he would stand around and watch and applaud when someone did well. He also liked drinking white rum and occasionally he would have a go at the Crown and Anchor table, especially when there was a lot of money to be won.

Well I was to learn more about him and also why Lenny Clarke behaved the way he did against me; as part of the brown skinned middle class he was willing to perpetuate the concept of, 'If you are white you are right, if you are brown stay around, if you are black stand back'. Saxa told me that as a Garveyite he had never seen eye to eye with Lenny Clarke, and on the day when I played cricket against Waltham Abbey and hit Howard Clarke who was brown skinned for six, he laid a bet with Lenny Clarke that I would do it. Lenny's remark when I did was, "that little brute, I will make sure that he walk barefoot". Interestingly, other than one other relative of mine who was female no one else in my family on my mother's side has ever exhibited that kind of attitude towards me. By the same rule I decided that as long as I live I would never be wanting for shoes and I would never want Lenny Clarke to make me a pair. For me, throughout my life, I cannot remember a time when I owned less than thirty pairs of shoes, not only that I always made sure that they were shining and my friend George Blissett would always remark, "your shoes can be shine like Stennett, but not shiner than Stennett". Over time I came to realise that life is too short and when I was able to go into the Rum Shop in Jamaica and order my Q of white rum and share a drink with Lenny it was with a sense of relief and in an atmosphere when grudges were behind us. I can recall going home to Jamaica and over a drink he asked me if I remembered Saxa "That damn scamp," he said, " Did you know that he used his dead uncle's name and married his wife?". Both Saxa and Lenny have long gone, in life we shall have our day.

CHAPTER FIVE

The World of Work

I WENT back to school after the 1950 Christmas Holidays in January 1951, fully realising that within a matter of less than three weeks I would no longer be on the School Register as a pupil. According to the then schoolboy jargon I had 'come of age'. Being a monitor for three years there was an arrangement made with the sanction of the school board and the Teacher that I could stay on as a Supernumerary on the understanding that my fees for studying for the Third Jamaica Local Examination would be waived, in other words I was a Teacher and not being paid, all things being equal it was a very good arrangement, especially if one had aspirations as I did to see a career in Teaching as a strong possibility.

There were other realities that I had to face and deal with as effectively as was possible in terms of my aspirations and my survival. For a start to be placed in the role of a pupil teacher was in itself quite progressive but carried its own demands in terms of dress code and all the other social frills and requirements that were relevant, and in keeping with my new role in essence, money or the lack of it was the factor that would dictate the decision that I had to make. True, there were family members who wanted to help but they were in the same position as myself in terms of sacrifices they had to make about which of their siblings had to be placed in some kind of pecking order. According to their meagre resources for our part we, as a family, were still being constrained by austerity. Measures to meet the loan requirements following the aftermath of the 1944 hurricane meant there was still another three years to go before a final settlement. My eldest sister, Carmen, was learning to be a dressmaker, at best it meant that she could help to make our clothes, but with so many young women her age doing the same thing to make a living it was quite difficult. The same applied to fishing, when there was a glut everybody in the village had fish to sell, when there was a scarcity we all suffered the same fate.

My other younger sisters, Lurline, Lorna, and Icylyn were by now all studying for the Jamaica Local Examination and had their own career aspirations. Lurline wanted to be a Teacher and she eventually finished up as a Civil Servant with the Ministry of Telecommunications. Lorna wanted to work in a store and she finished up working for a manufacturing outlet in

76

Connecticut and Icylyn, who started working in the Post Office in Jamaica, migrated to England, studied nursing, went back to work in Jamaica and eventually finished up working as a Nurse in New York. In essence ambition achieved through prayer, hard work, determination and sacrifice. I used the word sacrifice for all that it means and much more in that the decision that I made to seek employment was purely on the basis that as young girls growing up there were more pressures on them to look the part than it was on me. Moreover, it was very important that the roof over our heads and the land was secure. As far as I was concerned to put a hold on my future was to make me even more determined to succeed. At that time I was a very active member of the 4H Club Movement, a farming organisation sponsored by the United States Department of Agriculture that encouraged new farming methods in rural Jamaica, aimed at young people. The emphasis was on combining the Head, the Heart, the Hand and Health to the enhancement of the individual and the community as a whole. I was a Project Leader for my Club and the new methods that I learned coupled with the old skills that I had acquired to survive in a rural fishing cum agricultural village came in very useful. These new skills ranged from judging dairy cattle, how to cull chickens without slitting their throats, the importance of rotating catch crops such as tomatoes, lettuce and cabbage. Central to my learning curve was the extent to which the movement encouraged cross gender activities and the importance of structured planning that involved basic bookkeeping techniques in terms of profit and loss. On reflection I view my involvement with the 4H Movement as one of the best entities that I have ever invested in. As I have alluded it was more than a foundation from which, along with my sports, I was able to build on for a career in public life.

During the period of trying to find solutions that would help to make the road less hazardous to travel, my eldest brother, Egbert, who I helped out with the fishing, in his capacity as Chairman of the Fisherman's Guild had a contact who worked for the Jamaican Gleaner, the Caribbean's oldest and largest media at the time, who got me an interview with the paper. This meant that I had to travel to Kingston to take a written test and an interview and if I was successful I would stay with my brother, Noel. I did not cherish the idea of leaving the country to go and live in Kingston, but so as not to upset my brothers, especially in the light that if I got the job I would be able to work during the day and take advantage of the opportunities that were more available in Kingston to attend evening classes; that was their take on the matter it certainly was not mine. For a start, well-meaning as they were, I knew that somewhere along the line my brother, Noel, would have to make some sacrifices which he could ill afford.

Nevertheless, I went to Kingston, took the test and interview, to which I was successful and was offered a job as a Junior Clerk in the Circulation Department for the princely sum of fifty shillings per week. To celebrate my success, Noel took me to the Ward Theatre to see David Niven in The Prisoner of Zenda. It was the first film that I was to see in a Cinema yet exciting as it was I just wanted to be back in the country to continue with my life. At any rate I would have to go back to make arrangements as to who would look after my vegetable and flower gardens, and more importantly the Bulkin that I bought with the thirty shillings that I received from Brigadier Sewell. I had named the Bulkin Sam Bull; it was purchased from The Minard Properties when it was only seven days old. These calves needed careful handling because at birth they showed very little sign of development, hence the reason for selling them off; it was a matter of taking a risk purchasing them. Fortunately for me, Sam Bull was the exception more than the rule with my own concoction of goats' milk, cows' milk, honey and a drop of white rum; I bottle fed him until he was able to feed on grass. He turned out to be a credit to his bovine species and when I had to sell him to a local farmer it was for a very good price and a massive profit; it was sad in a way that we had to part company but in life there comes a time when the best of friends have to part.

Whatever misgivings I had about Kingston was justified on the day before I had to travel back home. I went shopping with my brother only to discover that my wallet that had been in my back pocket was missing. I was quite upset and made it clear to my brother that I would not be taking the job with The Gleaner; I knew how disappointed he was and I assured him that I would join the Police Force and arrest all the pickpockets that I could lay my hands on. The following day I was back on my way home hoping that I would be selected to travel to Cambridge to play for the first eleven. I was rather embarrassed when I had to tell my mother and sisters that as a result of having my wallet stolen I would not be taking the job in Kingston. My mother's response was that God do everything for a wise purpose, and every disappointment is an appointment; I was to lean what my mother meant only days after when playing the match at Cambridge. Jacob Leslie, keeping wicket, dived for a ball on the leg side, fell awkwardly and hurt his shoulder. I could not believe my ears when Arnold 'Bankie' Sullivan told me to pad up and go behind the stumps. As I have said I was young and saw a future in cricket so it was important for me to try different things; it was a case of learning strengths and weaknesses to discover my dreams.

I took two catches, made a stumping, did not give away any byes, and on asking Jacob about my performance behind the stumps he said, 'you was agile like a cat'. For a man who had a speech impediment his comment was impeccable and which I accepted fully realising that my potential as an all-rounder could be further enhanced.

The custom in those days, providing that we travelled through Montego Bay to play our matches which were always Saturdays, except if it was on either Boxing Day, New Years or Easter Monday, was that we would always stop on our way in the morning to do the shopping and on the way back in the evening to enjoy the night life. One of the famous places in those days was the Jolly Roger Club on Barnet Street, patronised by every section of the Jamaican community and visitors from abroad. It was the first place in Jamaica that I had ever seen a Wurlitzer jukebox. An interesting aside to this jukebox is that you could punch the record, recognise the tune but in most cases the singer's name was obliterated. I suppose that it was a way of the Club Operator to make the place attractive. I spent all of my money, which I could ill afford, punching Nat King Cole's 'Embraceable You', I'm in the Mood for Love', Lord Kitchiner's 'Cricket Lovely Cricket', 'Mambo Number Five', and 'Perez Parado'. Common sense prevailed that I did the shopping on the way down, failing that I would be taking an empty basket home.

On the Sunday afternoon my Uncle-in-law, Elkanah Williams, came to see us, or to be exact came to see me with the tongue of a good report that Mr Brady, who was the Dining Room Captain at the Columbus Inn Hotel, needed a Busboy and he had recommended me. Hardly had Elkanah left than my cousin, Noel Seivewright, who was a Bellhop at the hotel, came to tell me what Elkanah said. I suppose then that both men realised that SS Hardship was now at my pier and it was only a matter of time and I would be sailing on her, or to put it another way, I was symbolic of Desmond Decker's 'The Israelites', which says "Shut dey bus, trousers dey tear up". I discussed the pros and cons with my mother and there were a lot of pluses; most importantly I would still be at home to look after my garden, my chickens and bull and though I would have to give up being a pupil teacher, I could attend evening lessons preparing for the Final Local Examination. That same evening I went to see Teacher Sudlow and outlined my situation. He fully understood my predicament and agreed that I should do what I thought in the long term would be best for me. My application for the hotel job was written in my best handwriting and taken by hand.

On the morning I was interviewed by Rose Pare, a Canadian woman from Quebec; she was the PA to Malcolm Fraser, General Manager, and Mrs Fraser, his wife, Assistant Manager, and Franz Brady, Dining Room Captain. It was quite an in-depth interview and there and then I was offered the job as Busboy and to perform any other duties as and when required all for the King's wages of twenty five shillings per week. I was given until three o'clock the same day to make my mind up. After going home and informing my mother I went to see my brother, Egbert, and my Uncle Walter 'Mate' Wallace, both men of the world, worldly and wise; their advice was always beneficial. Mate's advice relating to the job was centred around the biblical character, Joseph, who was sold to Potiphar, a high ranking officer in the Pharaoh's Army, and as a result of Potiphar's wife failing in her endeavours to entice Joseph to sleep with her, she made false accusations against him to her husband which resulted in him being arrested and sent to jail. Mates succinctly placed things into context by saying, 'Boy, keep your fingers clenched and your pee pee hole closed'. My brother Egbert's advice was about punctuality, diligence, honesty, and the importance of dignity in labour; in terms of it is not where one starts in life but where they finish up. Citing our Uncle Joshi as an example, who went to the United States of America, worked as a Dining Car Attendant on the railroads, studied and eventually qualified as a Dentist with a practice in Brooklyn.

Noel Seivewright and Frank Cover were smiling when I told them that I accepted the job, my reservation was about the wages which I said were too small and they obviously agreed, reminding me that they had started there and it was up to me to learn fast and in the deliverance of good service to the guests everything would fall into place and there will always be a smile on my face. In other words, the wages were small but tips will make the job worthwhile; it did not take me long to realise that there was truth in what Frank and Noel had said about learning fast, having said that there were butterflies buzzing both inside and around me and I was shaking and jelly-heeled even though I was assured by all the Dining Room and Kitchen Staff that I looked the part, dressed in my Nehru-type white jacket, black pants and black shoes, the onus was on me to do the job. The adrenalin was pumping as I approached the first table and poured the water on the table for four, I consoled myself with the fact that if I have the ability to stand up to fast bowling playing for fun, and have always given a good account of myself, my presence in the Dining Room surrounded by waiters and guests was another extension in the process of my growing up and the taking on of responsibilities that were important for my successful journey. I was pleased at the end of the evening when Rose Pare came up and said in her deep Canadian drawl, "Well done Widdy". Frank Brady was equally appreciative, even then the adrenalin was still high. My own perception is that the adrenalin is the secretion that kept me going, hardly surprising that before the week was out some members of the Dining Room staff referred to me as 'Speedy'. Ralph Rowe, the Head Bartender, called me 'Alacrity'; neither of those sobriquets stuck, except Rose Pare's 'Widdy", which lasted throughout the five seasons I worked at the hotel.

Within a fortnight of starting at the hotel I realised what they meant when I was told at the interview that I would be called upon to do other duties as was necessary for the smooth running of the establishment; in that respect other areas of work involved cleaning the silverware for tables, bell hopping, bar waiting, helping with stock-taking and filing, writing recipes, and songs that were sometimes requested by guests. It was a situation of the hotel paying for one post and getting the others free, personally I did not mind as it was excellent all round training for the future. I enjoyed writing the recipes and the songs in my best handwriting reflective of what Teacher Whitely said, 'writing maketh the man'. I must say that I was always paid well for my services. Two favourite songs that were always requested, especially by honeymooners, were 'Drive her home', which went as follows:

*When I give her the number one
She said Darling it just began
Put your lips close to mine and drive me home
Give her the number two
She said Darling this will do
Put your lips close to mine and drive me home
Give her the number three
She said Darling I am on my knee
Put your lips close to mine and drive me home
Give her the number four
She said Darling I am on the floor
Put your lips close to mine and drive me home
Give her the number five
She said Darling I am feeling alive
Put your lips close to mine and drive me home
Give her the number six
She said Darling I am feeling sick
Put your lips close to mine and drive me home
Give her the number seven
She said Darling I am in heaven
Put your lips close to mine and drive me home
Give her the number eight
She said Darling you are late
Put your lips close to mine and drive me home
Give her the number nine
She said Darling you are mine, mine
Put your lips close to mine and drive me home.*

The other song 'Ruckumbine' embraced amoral and saucy lyrics that were left to the imagination; it went like this:

The higher the hill is the greener the grass
The ....is the sweeter ....
Ruckambine Inna Me Santan Pee Ruckambine
Out of all the furniture's I wish I was a chair
Ruckambine Inna Me Santan Pee Ruckambine

I can recall one of the housemaids, Mavis, who was a born-again Christian, telling me that she was praying and fasting for me because I was writing badnis, her interpretation of sauciness for the tourist to take back to America and Canada to sing. My response to her was that it was not badnis that I was writing about, it is Sinbad and for that reason her fasting and prayers won't make much difference to what I do; in any event it was good for tourism.

Through helping with stock-taking and filing I had the opportunity to learn to use the typewriter; in fact I was encouraged both by Mrs Fraser and Rose Pare. Occasionally Malcolm Fraser would pass through the office and if it was one of his good days he would say in his Australian drawl, 'use all fingers Stennett'; until today I am still a two finger typist and would in no way make a boast that I am the best but I can certainly say that I feel comfortable amongst the rest of those people who use two fingers to type.

Another advantage that filing and stock-taking afforded was access to the various magazines and newspapers and novels that guests would leave behind; these ranged from the Boston Globe, the New York Herald Tribune and The Guardian from London. I can remember going through the sports pages of The Boston Globe when Malcolm Fraser said, "Stennett you won't find anything in a Yankee paper about cricket". Based on his response to my query as to why there is not much interest in America for cricket, especially in the light that America has a long historical connection with Britain where the game of cricket started, and as far as the West Indies were concerned the first overseas cricket tour from that area was to America and Canada. In 1886 the team was an all white team, there were similarities to the well known Australian Aboriginal side that toured England in 1868. If Malcolm Fraser felt put off by my knowledge of those early cricket statistics, which by the way I picked up through the oral tradition and which proved years later to be accurate. As a result of my own research his body language certainly did not convey that to me. It was difficult at my age to know or even understand what made Malcolm Fraser tick. He played golf, he scuba-dived, he sailed, he did horseback riding, he played shuffle board, pitched horse shoes, and during the bird shooting season he would go shooting. In addition to all that he used weights as part of his fitness programme; he was the consummate all-round sportsman. Some of the workers called him the Jaguar; I added Roo to the sobriquet to symbolise his Australian roots. I cannot recall anyone calling him these names to his face, yet by the same rule there was always that air of self-confidence. When he was being asked about how he performed at any of the sports in which he had participated in, he said that he was a winner and he made sure that he maintained his standard. It was something that I admired about him, and as he discussed the exploits of Don Bradman, Lindsay Hassett, Neil Harvey and Richie Benaud, and I about George Headley, Ramadhin and Valentine, Weekes, Worrell, Walcott and Constantine, my youthful intuition convinced me that he had a bee in his bonnet about the 1932/3 tour by England to Australia when Harold Larwood and Bill Voce, both Nottinghamshire fast bowlers bowling to a packed leg side, curtained the Australian batsmen from scoring runs freely, hence the bodyline concept. We finished our cricket discourse with him promising to come to see me play; it was then that he told me that he was a right handed fast bowler and left handed batsman, and that he also played football. It was quite an interesting revelation in that as a cricketer I bowled right handed and batted left handed. The following morning after breakfast, Mrs Fraser requested that I come to her office and she told me that her husband was quite impressed with my understanding of cricket and that it was largely due to sports as to why he finished up working in tourism. From what she told me his ambition was to be a vet but from what she told me of a failed business venture of his father it resulted in him leaving Australia for California, where he did a number of jobs as film extra, waiting on tables, caddying, and life-guarding. I could make sense from what she told me about his early predicament, at least I guessed that he had an understanding of the struggles of people like himself who had to make things happen for the betterment of themselves.

True to his word he did come to see me play against a team from Clarks Town that had players like Gowie, Strachan, and Batts, who played nethersole cricket for Trelawney and in the Crum Ewing Competition for Long Pond Sugar Estates. On the day I bowled seven overs, two maidens, one wicket for thirty four runs and I also took a catch at second slips. At work the following morning Malcolm told me that he was impressed at the way by which I moved the ball. He said that the catch I took at second slip was as good as Neil Harvey. I was pleased with the compliment, which helped to bolster my confidence that there was a place in cricket for me.

The job at the hotel came to an end in the April of 1951; there was no Summer Season then but in order to keep staff on their books they operated a scheme whereby if members chose they entered a pool which meant they worked one week in every month to keep the establishment in good condition. It also gave one the opportunity to learn other skills such as cooking, bartending and gardening. For me it was part of the learning curve and I have never regretted that I availed myself of at least knowing what to do in these areas.

I worked for three months, considering that the basic wage was low I was able to put into context the extent by which tips compensated for that. My first priority was to join a 'partner'. A partner is one of the oldest Jamaican forms of saving whereby a group of people come together and pledge to save an allotted sum of money over a given period and where each member gets the total amount saved on a rotating basis. The sum total of a partner is that it is built on trust, mutual respect and the encouraging of self-esteem and self help through thriftiness; to this day I have never failed in being a member of a partner.

I had taken the job at the hotel as a short-term measure with the intention that I could still work and prepare for the third Jamaican Local Examination, which, if successful, would see me going on to Mico Teacher Training college. The truth of the matter is that although I spent as much spare time in following the curriculum, and with the able support of Lloyd Chin who was later to become a stalwart in the National Workers' Union and Staunch People's National Party Activist in North Western Saint Ann, and Livingston Brown who became a high-ranking Civil Servant, cricket overshadowed everything else to the point that at one stage I decided that I would work toward building up a business for myself by investing in a car or a boat that I would rent to visitors during the tourist season. All these proposals were possible, especially in the light that when I worked at the hotel I always encouraged guests to use the Kanawa, our fishing boat, to go out to explore the reef. Selvin Lamont and Jacob Leslie were always on call and we all benefited financially.

I saved enough money to afford the rare privilege of buying my own cricket bat, flannels and boots made by Noonan Riley from Keith; for me it was rewarding in that I no longer had to depend on any of my relatives to give me money, which in a number of cases they could hardly afford, to pay for my subs and for travelling to play away matches. I will always continue to be grateful for their help when it was most needed and as such I see the importance of stretching out a helping hand whenever it is needed. My parents have always stressed that giving is the act of receiving and that a closed hand will never let anything in.

The break from the hotel was an opportunity to indulge in spear fishing, which as a result of tourism was just beginning to take off on the Island. Selvin Lamont, Vannie Alexander, Noel Seivewright and I were the pioneers in Discovery bay for this brand of sport, between us we shared two goggles and two snorkels. We had no flippers and our guns were home-made, nevertheless they were quite effective, or put the other way, our skills at shooting underwater were excellent.

I enjoyed the discipline of getting up at four in the morning and rowing out to sea as far as Salem, where the Hedonism Hotel now stands, and spearing all the way down the coast to Discovery Bay. Next day it would be rowing down westward spearing from the Marine Laboratory off the Queen's Highway, down to the Grand Lido at Braco. As I have said we were pioneers and as such were constantly being warned by the older fishermen who constantly regaled us about the dangers that lurk under the sea, such as sea cats, the Jamaican name for an octopus, that were so big that they could suck us into their nostrils or wrap us around with their tentacles and drag us into the deep. It is fair to say that I have had the experience of fighting off sharks and barracudas, the most determined of the two from snatching the prize fish at the end of a spear gun, or using a stick to ward off seagulls who would swoop into the boat to take fishes. I have also been stung by jellyfish, pierced in the fingers and sole of the feet by sea urchins, and lost spear guns to fishes that proved too strong to be captured. It was all part and parcel of an adventure tied in with the necessity to make a livelihood and to put into some kind of perspective, not only about the concept of the survival of the fittest but man as a predator and hunter.

I also came away from that experience that some of the most beautiful scenery on Jamaica's north coast lies under the sea and now that I am in the autumn of my life when the season of renewal arrives I would sincerely hope that my wishes for cremation becomes the order of the day and the ashes be taken to Discovery Bay and sprinkled outside of the Channel where as a young child and later in the processes of growing up I watched from my veranda overlooking the harbour the waves coming in and from which swimming, rowing, diving and fishing all added to creating fun, for obtaining food and a livelihood.

The best laid plans will continue to be aborted by circumstances beyond one's control. The hurricane of 1951 was a reminder of that fact, and although it was not as severe as the hurricane of 1944, it did damage part of the roof of our house, destroyed fish pots and pimento trees, from which the berries were just about ready to be reared. Fortunately my savings and the money from the selling of Sam Bull was enough to buy materials, which meant that my mother did not have to take out another loan from the bank or us waiting on the Government for assistance, which as far as I can remember always meant waiting forever and a day and as I have always said, 'promised are comfort for fools'. Being born and raised in a country where hurricanes have a pattern of damaging the roof of houses, even with that reality I cannot remember a hurricane being called Rufus, be that as it may, the fact that I had savings to put towards the repairing of our house was a confirmation that saving for a rainy day in as far as I was concerned meant that not only could I buy an umbrella but also that I would have to go back to work in the hotel whether I wanted to or not.

As anticipated I was called to come back to the hotel when the 1952 season started in December. A fortnight into the season I noticed that nothing had changed in terms of my workload and I was still on the same wages, so as I was a year older, with this in mind, I wrote a letter to Mr Fraser asking for a meeting to discuss my wages. I detected that there was a change of attitude towards me both by Mr and Mrs Fraser and I assumed that they were upset by my letter asking for a rise. It was about ten days after I had sent the letter that I received an acknowledgement informing me that changes were about to take place which would benefit every member of staff. Other members received a similar letter and like in any working environment there were a number of speculations as to what the changes would be, with a full house and as always a thriving passing trade and tips coming in like barges, morale amongst the staff was quite high and as such staff awaited the supposed changes with an open mind. At least I did until Don McLaren, a Glaswegian who was the accountant, told me in confidence that the new changes would see every member of staff getting a rise. My rise would be an extra ten shillings, but the sting in the tail was that instead of staff accepting tips directly from guests they would be placed into a pool which meant that those staff who had no direct contact with guests would also benefit in the fortnightly payout. To me it sounded a very fine arrangement until McLaren said to me, 'You know what that Australian bastard is going to do, he will use some of that money to help with the rise in pay, and the rest will go towards paying off his gambling debts'. I had no reason to disbelieve the fact that Fraser was a gambler as quite a few times I had witnessed him with his friends who were not guests at the hotel ordering bottles of champagne from the bar, spraying it about or using it to wash their faces. These acts of behaviour would always get Gordon, one of the bar waiters, saying, 'Bwoy de Jaguar win big today'.

I was later to understand that he gambled at everything, poker, golf, horse racing, that being said I wondered why McLaren should have imparted such information to me and what he wanted me to do with it. I was not to know until later that both men worked for the same company who had the contract for running the hotel, and there was bad blood between them, resulting from a game of golf where they both accused each other of cheating. For my part, being from the old school where 'see and blind, hear and deaf and dumb also' has always been prominent in the general order of things, in my life experience I decided that whatever misunderstandings Fraser and McLaren may have had it was for them to find their own solutions to sorting it out as it was for me to find my own when the occasion would eventually arise.

Driving with Rose Pare to see one of the cooks, who was admitted to the St Ann's Bay Hospital for an operation to his appendix, it was good to share with her some of the experiences that I had and the places of interest that I walked past when I was in that same hospital four years previous when I was struck by lightning. Passing through Priory I pointed out to her the house where it is accepted that Marcus Garvey, one of Jamaica's national heroes, was born; she had never heard of Garvey, nevertheless she was interested to know more about him, how from such humble surroundings he had done so much for the uplifting of black people, not only in Jamaica, but worldwide. I was a bit surprised that throughout the journey both ways she made no mention of my letter to Malcolm Fraser or any of the changes that were supposed to be taking place.

Prior warning was given about the meeting to take place regarding the changes and it was planned for immediately after breakfast and even staff who would be on a day off were encouraged to attend. To the letter as it was related to me by McLaren was what was conveyed to us on the morning by Malcolm Fraser. As I have said I believed in the principle, some people did not agree with it and suggested that those members of staff who had no contact with guests should be paid at a much higher rate than those who had contact. This did not go down too well with some people. My question to Malcolm was that in the light that I have always been requested to write songs and recipes in my best handwriting should the rewards be placed in the tip pool. His response was 'definitely Stennett'. The for and against the idea was discussed long after the meeting and within two days there was a box placed near the newspaper stand for gratuities. In every environment where people gathered there will always be that element who get a buzz out of taking what has often been said, then times embellishing them to some source from above. Realizing that Lambert was one such person, I said that 'I would not ask guests for money but if I do a service which pleases them and they tip me I would not place it in the tip box'. The following morning I was in the room that adjoins the kitchen, cleaning some silver and eating a banana, when Malcolm Fraser came in and shouted, 'Stennett, come into my office'. I suppose that my slow response was not to his approval as Rose Pare rushed in saying, 'Widdy, Mr Fraser wants to see you now; he is spitting feather'. He was more than spitting feathers when I entered his office; he was more like Goliath and Appolon all rolled into one ready to devour me, his face was red and his eyes piercing through, he was certainly in the mood for war as he pushed away his leather chair from his desk and was well into my face. 'Stennett, don't you know that you are not supposed to eat on the premises and furthermore what about the rumours that you are spreading about the new tip system; do you know that I can fire you immediately?' All through his tirade I was as cool in Jamaican lingo as 'Miss Martha's donkey', still staring into his face with a half-clench right hand ready for him because he was known to throw punches when he was in a rage. As far as I was concerned that morning he would have had to kill me and I was ready to die in defending myself. He may have noticed that I was ready for a showdown and in the process of moving back to his chair I said, 'Mr Fraser, can I answer your questions? 'Of course you can,' he replied. Firstly I said, 'I see so much food being wasted in this hotel, having a banana should not cause you to be so upset, and as for tips I know exactly who told you what I said only I know that he did not tell you that the system can be exploited'. That being said he went into another range and said, 'Stennett, you bring that bastard here and I will personally deal with him'. My response was, 'Mr Fraser, those people are now back in New Jersey and Massachusetts'. 'Those communist bastards, supporters of Adlai Stevenson,' he said as he thumped the desk.

Finally, 'Mr Fraser, I said, you threaten to fire me as you can see I am not wearing the hotel jacket, every piece of clothing that I am standing in is mine so I am willing to go, but once I leave here I am going to St Ann's Bay and will be lodging my case with the National Workers' Union and although we have no Union here I know that there are members of staff who will follow me out because we are members of the PNP. From a domineering and forceful figure he was now more like a pussycat and said, 'Stennett, you don't have to be that drastic, let's sit down like two men and find a way out which is quite simple. You keep all the tips that you get, making sure that nobody sees you, and in addition whenever you want to go and play cricket just let me know and I will deal with it, but Stennett this discussion must stay in this office'. At this point we shook hands and on turning to leave I said to him, 'One more thing Mr Fraser, my cricket team need some gears and I am wondering if you would like to donate some gears to them'. 'I will certainly see to that', he said and with that I departed from his office to find some curious members of staff wanting to know the reason and outcome of why I had been called into the office, with Lambert around it was convenient to convey a story about Malcolm Fraser's interest in lending support to the village cricket team. My bit of spin was that there was the possibility of me being picked shortly to represent the parish, which would mean that I would be given time off to practice. There was a feeling of good will expressed in my favour and I felt quite reassured that I had come out of what could have been a very nasty situation with not only mine but Malcolm Fraser's confidence and credibility intact; I would live to fight another day.

Within two days of the peace treaty between Malcolm Fraser and myself I was forced to defend him in circumstances that could easily be interpreted as part of the plot of a thriller movie. As Deputy Manager at the hotel one of the roles of Malcolm's wife was to arrange the weekly floor shows. These shows had various themes and the cast was made up of staff who received a little extra money in their pay packets. The theme on this particular night was 'Pirates of D'Bay', which depicted a boatload of pirates landing ashore with muskets and bayonets with the intention of taking pots of gold from the natives but the natives outsmarted them by allowing the women to entice them into drinking too much rum and dancing, and in their drunken state they started fighting amongst themselves. My role was as a native helping to pour rum for the pirates, but it was real rum and these shows attracted patrons who were not guests at the hotel. As the majority of people partaking in the act were dressed in period costume I noticed that Malcolm Fraser was struggling with three men, which at first I assumed were part of the act. However, when I passed I heard him say, 'Stennett I need help, get the boys'. By this time one man had a stranglehold on him as if they were intent on dragging him away. In the process of getting help I took hold of 'barkwood', the two foot long Lignum Vitae Staff that Corporal Coward, the Security Man, carried with him and started to beat the daylights out of the man who had the neck hold on Malcolm. Other members of staff also got involved and in the heat of the battle I heard the stentorian voice of Corporal Coward shouting, 'Masterman, give me my staff so that I can lawfully execute my duty'. By then the men had let go of Malcolm and Corporal Coward escorted them off the premises as they shouted, 'Malcolm you have been rescued by your black dogs, we will be back'; with that they jumped into their Morris Minor convertible and disappeared into the dark. It was obvious that Malcolm was hurt and badly shaken up as he retired to his cottage, but as they say the show must go on and it certainly did until the wee hours of the morning.

It was business as usual the following day and some guests talked at how much they enjoyed the evening but felt that things had gotten out of hand a little, making reference to the fracas. There was a lot of speculation as to whether what happened was play acting or was it for real. When Malcolm did emerge, which was in the late afternoon, he had bruising to his hands and a black eye which suggested that there was more to the incident from the previous evening. If he was embarrassed he did not show it and my guess was that he carried his injuries as a badge of honour, and in his explanation to us of what had led up to the incident was according to him that the men had not only made nasty comments about his wife but also about us, as members of staff. Then there was a consensus amongst us that our actions in defending him were justified, especially in the light that when the men were leaving, and I must say they left fully realising that they were in flight telling Malcolm that he was rescued by his Black Dogs, I personally had no grumble about that and I felt good knowing that I was fighting for the underdog, In any language or circumstance three against one was not on, not as far as I was concerned.

It is rather interesting or uncanny that in 1983, almost thirty one years after that incident I was faced with a similar event at the Manchester Regiment Pub on Chester Road, Manchester. It was four days before Christmas and my friend, George Blissett, and I were having a drink in the lunch hour. One could say that it was our local, the Landlord at the time was Jack Thomas, a Yorkshire man in every sense of the word, who made it quite clear that like its cricketers Yorkshire people are the best in the world. His wife, Trudi, was from Austria, two of his sons, Robert and Nigel, also worked in the pub and whereas they would sing the praises of Len Hutton, Fred Trueman, Geoff Boycott, Brian Close, George Hirst, Raymond Illingworth, Dickie Bird, Chris Old and many more, George and I would regale them with the exploits of George Headley, Learie Constantine, Gary Sobers, Roy Gilchrist, Wes Hall, Michael Holding, Clive Lloyd, Viv Richards, Gordon Greenidge and Desmond Hayes. The pub was an ideal location where other sports were being discussed in an atmosphere of conviviality with its diverse clientele. On the day in question the place was quite busy over and above what is normal, it being the festive season. Trudi, in the process of collecting glasses and calling 'time gentlemen' went across to a table where four men were drinking and at the point of collecting the glasses one said to her, 'Fuck off and get those black b******* out first'. Jack, who was also assisting her, heard what he had said and went over and said to him, 'You have not only sworn at my wife but you have used a term relating to my customers, will you please leave?' Suddenly they all jumped up and started raining blows on Jack, one had hold of his tie as if he wanted to strangle him and the next thing I noticed was that Jack was completely bald and still struggling with them when his toupee fell to the ground. Without further ado Blissett and I intervened and with utter disregard to the Marquis of Queensbury's rules I got in close with some heavy body shots to the rib cage of the one that held on to Jack's tie. In the meantime, Blissett was working away at one, the other two ran off and by this time most of the customers had made quick exits as if it had nothing to do with them. Maybe it didn't, but by the same rule I felt that at least some of the people who had seen and heard what had happened could have intervened before it came to that stage. By the time the police arrived everything was over, but as I understand all four men were outside waiting for Blissett and myself to come out so that according to them they could 'give us a good hiding'. Obviously they ran when they saw the police.

Christmas came and went and nothing had been said to our families until the New Year when over drinks we mentioned the incident and someone asked the question if there was any reason for us to defend a white man against another white man. My answer was in the context that it was not a matter of taking sides with a white man against another white man, it was a situation of standing up for someone who over a period of time I was able to form a meaningful and genuine relationship forged through sports. Like my Jamaican experience it was to find resonance in what Edmund Burke said: 'All that is necessary for the triumph of evil is that good men do nothing'.

P.B.H. Coward, a private in the West Indian Regiment and later a member of the Jamaican Constabulary Force where he attained the rank of Corporal and even after retirement he was referred to as Corporal Coward, was one of the people who did so much in helping me understand the vagaries of human behaviour within a working environment. He had a son and a daughter and said that I was the grandson he never had. Some people saw him as an odd ball, him being a member of the Jehovah's Witnesses, although he preferred to be called a Millennial Dawnist. As far as I can remember he was the first person to embrace that religion in Discovery Bay.

He was the only member of staff who was on first name terms with Malcolm Fraser and I was rather pleased when two days after the incident Corporal told of Malcolm's measure of respect for me based on the way in which I stand up for myself and my community without making a noise and also my depth of loyalty to friends. According to Corporal, Malcolm could well see me playing a role in the political and social life of the Jamaican people.

It was quite interesting hearing Corporal relating to his early days in the army and police force, and how an over-indulgence of alcohol, women and gambling almost destroyed him and how his prowess at cricket and music, which were the contributory factors to his near demise, were the same factors that helped in his escape and rehabilitation from what was a near fall from grace. He said, 'the bone dice and the card pack can turn millionaires into paupers overnight'. On the Malcolm Fraser incident he said that the very theme of the evening\s floor show, 'Pirates of D'Bay', was a throwback to the old days when several European countries in their quest for expansion and colonial dominance travelled to the Caribbean and fought each other and in the midst of their squabbles the blacks, who did the menial jobs, found themselves sometimes fighting for their masters against other blacks. He smiled and said, 'Masterman (the name he dubbed me), history will continue to repeat itself; there is nothing new under the sun'. And for that reason, like the search for gold and the cultivation of sugar, citrus, coffee, coconut, and bananas by the Europeans, who in the main were empire builders, castaways, bondsmen, religious zealots, political refugees and escaped criminals, tourism will to some extent bring across similar kinds of people to Jamaica seeking to create wealth, fun, relaxation, and a tan. How right he was as during my time working in the hospitality industry I came across or met an interesting cross-section of people who, if truth be known, and in some cases it did happen, their antecedents were to say the least chequered. By the same rule I had the

91

good fortune of meeting people such as George Shearing, the blind English-born pianist and composer of 'Lullaby of Birdland'. He was the first person to have given me a fifty dollar tip; who said the English are not big tippers? I have also met Larry Adler, the world famous harmonica virtuoso and composer Noel Coward, who wrote 'Pygmalion', Ian Fleming the creator of James Bond; both Fleming and Noel Coward lived in the north coast parish of St Mary in Jamaica. Other people that I have met are Thomas Dewey, a Governor of New York and Republican Presidential nominee in the forties, Christopher Soames, son-in-law of Sarah, daughter of Sir Winston Churchill, Mr and Mrs Walter Robbins, who had connections with Warwickshire County Cricket Club and were regular visitors. They were noted for having their famous Lea and Perrins sauce. I always looked forward to Macy's Group, the big American chain store, coming; they left no stone unturned in enjoying the Jamaican hospitality.

The Mento Band of Leebert on Banjo, Glen on lead guitar, Natty on Rumba Box, George, lead singer with Maracas, serenaded them with songs such as 'Mommy by belly hurting', 'The Big Bamboo' and 'Hold him Joe'; one of their favourites which was almost like a welcome song which went like this:

When you come from America to this land called Jamaica, you have the
sunshine all the while as you drive and smile mile for mile.
Cool an gay so long ago, so long ago,
The first Jamaican rum you drink it move your head and you start to think
Cool an gay so long ago, so long ago.

My first visit to American was in 1969 and the first store in which I made a purchase was Macy's near Central Park in New York. Amongst the goods that I bought was my favourite aftershave, Mennen. I started using that brand of aftershave in April 1952, a gift from my brother Noel after our cricket team amassed a total of one hundred and ninety two against Rio Buenos. In their first innings they got thirty three and in their second innings they made twenty seven; I had match figures of four for nine in the first innings and six for fourteen in the second innings. It was at that match that I came across Jack Mercer, formerly of Sussex, Northampton and Glamorgan, who was then Chief Cricket Coach in Jamaica. He suggested that for my height, I was only five feet six inches tall, I was taking too much out of myself to bowl fast and I would be more effective as leg break or spin bowler. More about Jack Mercer will be revealed in a later chapter of this work but as I have said it is over fifty three years since I first used Mennen and I am still young at heart and an application of it to my persona still attracts almost the same comments, 'What's the aftershave Whit, it is lovely' from very fastidious ladies.

Another person that I met as a result of playing in that match was Bunny. He was two years older than I, born under the same star sign, Aquarius; both of his parents were dead and he was being looked after by an Aunt. He was from Upper Trelawney and was a cunning left arm googly bowler and whereas Martin Bell, with the same action, would throw his arms in the air and shout 'Jesus wept' when he beat a batsman, Bunny would stand akimbo and say 'you ole fu fu fucker'. Irrespective of your trade, profession, or calling, cricket was the leveller, at least on the field of play. He was looking for work and I reckoned that if I talked to Mrs Fraser, although there were no vacancies at the hotel, I might be able to persuade her to take him, which would mean that he could play for my team.

Mrs Fraser was quite amenable to my suggestion to start him as a general hand, shining shoes, washing dishes, working in the garden and any other chores that became necessary. With the tip system being in place and working Bunny's wages were one pound five shillings per week, not a lot for a nineteen year old, but a job is a job and at any rate he expressed a desire to be a 'Coco Cook' and his nice laid back attitude made Mammy Beck, the Pastry Cook, take to him like a duck to water.

Not so Simmons the Chef,who for whatever reason always tried to belittle him; whenever he did this in my presence I would challenge him and he would always say, 'This have nothing to do with you Mr Cricketer'. Things got to a head one morning when Bunny was asked to make an omelette. The consensus amongst the kitchen staff was that it was properly made but Simmons would have none of it and he was ranting and raging and even threatened to throw Bunny out of the kitchen. In some way his behaviour was consistent on the grounds that I have seen him almost bring cooks to tears and once he was satisfied that his wishes were carried out he would seem to come back down to earth. Whenever he flew off the handle Mammy Beck would stand in the middle of the kitchen and would sing, 'All hail the power of Jesus name name let Angel's prostate fall'; she claimed that it had a hypnotic effect on Simmons.

I was also planning on how I could do something to him that would take him down a peg or two; adjoining the kitchen and pantry was the cold storage and every so often it was his duty to have a stock-taking. The rule was that whosoever entered the storage they would have to put on a suit similar to that worn by skiers. They would also have to enter their names in a book as to the time that they entered and they took the lock and key with them. On the day in question I watched him as he entered the cold storage whereupon I took a demitasse spoon and wedged the door and wandered down onto the garden and from there to under the Naseberry Tree where we, as staff and sometimes visitors, would join in to help put the world to right. We discussed everything worth discussing and I often wondered what time the leaves had to wave to the breeze as I am sure some of our tales had no foundation. Nevertheless it was worthwhile shooting the breeze; it helped to stave off depression. It was like Bedlam or even worse when Simmons emerged from the cold storage; he was ashen, white and stiff like a board, so much so that he was put in the sun to thaw out and was given several glasses of brandy to drink in the process. Whilst Mammy Beck was praying, other members of staff started to investigate as to who could have done what in Jamaican saying, 'Joke to you, death to me'.

Simmons was swearing like a drunken sailor, hinting at what he was going to do with the person who did it. I had my alibi that was being backed up by Royland, one of the gardeners, and certainly it couldn't be Bunny because it was his day off. There were even suggestions that what occurred was as a result of somebody resorting to supernatural forces, and in a Jamaica where, like in Haiti, voodoo and in the Dominican Republic Santeria are vestiges of West African animistic religion, the Obeah man or woman is sometimes being consulted for either bringing good or bad luck. I don't believe that Simmons entertained any such thoughts; he knew that somebody did it - the question was who? The next morning, when Bunny came into work and heard about the incident, with his customary akimbo stance, he said to me, 'Sten, a beh,beh,bet that is you fu-fu-fuck him up'. If he was expecting a response from me all he got from me, like the excellent cricket umpire that I turned out to be, was a head slightly moving from the side followed by 'not me'. Having said that, whenever there were disagreements in the kitchen over the preparation of a meal and Simmons lost his cool, Mammy Beck burst into 'All hail the power of Jesus name'. When it came to bring forth the royal diadem I would chip in, quietly of course, with bring forth the silver 'essatimed', demitasse spelt backward. Within days the incident was hardly mentioned; it died its natural death and the various Celebrity Cooks programmes on television are in reality what take place in some of the best eating establishment's worldwide, which reinforces the argument that chefs have very large egos.

Prior to Malcolm Fraser making his public announcement to the staff that he was leaving the hotel, he called me into his office and in the presence of his wife and Rose Pare, thanked me for my loyalty to him. He also said that he knew about the valuable land owned by my family and that he could get investors to help us develop a portion of it for tourism, or failing that he could make arrangements for me to go up to Canada and do a course in tourism. All very good propositions, and although I cherished the idea of working for myself, I was still conscious that there were monies outstanding on the land and the priority was to have it paid off. I knew that fortune favours the brave but at the same time neither my mother, my brothers or myself were ready to think outside the box and in more ways than one we were supporting the adage that 'where there is no vision the people perish'. Be that as it may, I did not come across another Australian until I played in a Civil Service Cricket Competition match, Manchester Inland Revenue versus Manchester General Post Office at Radcliffe in 1961 when, after the match, I went into the bar of the club and during the conversation this man came over to congratulate me on my accuracy in terms of line and length. He finished up saying, ''The opposition didn't have a clue in dealing with the fucking Yorkers'. I was to learn that he was none other than the great Australian all-rounder Cec Pepper. Like Malcolm Fraser he said it as it was and did not give a damn.

CHAPTER SIX

Lose me and let me go

I WAS totally convinced that the story about the three parrot fishes, 'wise before time', 'wise in time' and 'wise after time', that the Reverend Woolley, who pastored the Discovery Bay Congregational Church from the fifties into the sixties used to espouse in his sermon, was intended for me. As the story went the three fishes were brought inshore by a heavy wave and found themselves in a crater. Wise before Time took every opportunity to escape back into the ocean and the first wave that came along. He told his other two friends that he was going and off he went. Wise in Time waited for a stronger wave and told Wise after Time that he was going and off he went. As it happened no other wave of any consequence came and a fisherman came along and thrust his harpoon into Wise after Time.

Although I accepted that the story had some relevance to me, I was at a loss to put into context with what Parson Woolley had in store for me. Common sense dictated that I kept my counsel and continue to do what I knew was good for me and if and when something presented itself that was the making of Parson I would deal with it in my own way. Things started to become clearer on the following Sunday; after Church Reverend Woolley said to me that he was happy to continue being Chairman of the Village Cricket Team and that he intended proposing me as First Team Captain and would I be willing to accept? I replied in the affirmative and at the meeting I was elected unopposed. In my acceptance speech I asked that members give me their support and that I would be making every effort to continue to uphold the tradition of the Club.

My first match was travelling to Stony Hill to play against the Stony Hill Approved School Team; the School provided training in woodwork, printing, baking, carpentry, farming and music for boys from the age of fifteen to early twenties who were either orphaned or had brushes with the law. Sports such as cricket, football and athletics were very central to the maintaining of discipline and pastoral care within the institution. The cricket team consisted of members of staff and students who played in The Senior Cup Competition at the time. One of the senior members of staff was R.E.K Phillips, who was later to become a member of Jamaica's Diplomatic Corp when the country gained independence in 1962. He served as a Consular Officer at the Jamaican High Commissioner's Office in London in the late sixties.

Lose me and let me go

The match almost proved to be my undoing in more ways than one in as far as cricket was concerned we were outplayed in every department of the game; for a start they won the toss and elected to bat, our bowlers, I used six on the day, made little or no impression on the opening batsmen, Noel Gay and Nestor Ogilvie, who carted us all over the park. To make matters worse Ogilvie was dropped behind the stumps by Jacob Leslie off the second ball of Lloyd 'Bugsie' Daay's first over. The barracking and sledging from the Stony Hill spectators was out of this world. The score was one hundred and twenty for one when Gay got out; caught at short mid on by 'Marshie' Marshall off the bowling of Crampy Williams for sixty five; at that moment they declared and we went in to bat. Our openers, Lloyd Daay and Dick Campbell, got us off to a good start but once they went, other than Marshie who put up a brave fight, we were bowled out for sixty two; for me it was quite a steep learning curve and I believe that we all consoled ourselves with the musical rendition of the School Band during tea. I was quite fascinated by their brass section playing 'Run Mongoose', 'Linstead Market' and the calypso 'Please Mister Don't You Touch My Tomato'.

More was to come to add to my woes as Captain of the team before we left Discovery Bay. The arrangements were that those of our supporters who had relatives in Kingston and did not want to watch the game at Stony Hill should contact their relatives who would meet them at Parade in Kingston and they could spend the day with them providing that they can take them back to Parade at 11 o'clock at night when our transport would be leaving for home. The same applied to those supporters who had travelled to watch. After the game we all boarded the transport back in to Kingston. I was in charge of the team both on and off the field; it was quite a daunting responsibility, especially in the light that some members of the team were twice my age, and like the Police Officers and three other members of the team who had first hand knowledge of the night spots in the city, I was more like the sheep following the goats. Country bumpkins some of us were, and some of us could not tell a waltz from a mambo but that did not matter, we had money in our pockets, we were cricketers intending to have a good night out and the Kingston girls were quite prepared to make it a night to remember.

There is an old saying that 'good company keep late hours' and at ten thirty when I reminded the group that we had to be at Parade at 11 o'clock the response was, 'relax skipper, the night is still young, we only live once'. That night not even Superman could pull them away from the Silver Slipper Club in Cross Roads. Up until then I did not drink any type of alcohol and neither did I smoke, I never have anyway, but I could dance and that night I was forever on the floor.

It was well past 2 o'clock in the morning when the club closed and we had to walk down to Parade to face the wrath of Reverend Woolley and Mr Brammie, a Deacon of the Church who umpired the match. Some of our supporters felt cheated that they missed out on spending more time with their families. Floor, the driver of the truck, was not bothered in the least and in any event he had enough sleep and was quite refreshed to drive us home.

There was no doubt that I was seen as the villain of the piece and on the Monday when my brother, Egbert, came to see me he was not pleased about what he had heard and expressed his concern that I was falling by the wayside and that the sooner I found myself a full time job, as opposed to working during the hotel season for six months, and the next six months, according to him, fooling around, playing cricket, and swimming the better off I would be. It was during this discussion that I found out that the interest that Reverend Woolley had shown by getting me to captain the team was part of a strategy that my two brothers, my mother, Teacher Sudlow and the Reverend Woolley had devised to get me to leave the Country and to take up a job in Kingston and the opportunity to continue with my studies. It was their second attempt and there were others that followed.

At the cricket meeting following the Kingston episode, Reverend Woolley left no stone unturned to point out the error of my ways and in apology I asked if it was the wish of the members that I resign. There was a resounding 'no' whereupon Reverend Woolley asked if my apology was accepted and the consensus was 'yes'. After the meeting Emeriah Johnson, the most senior member of the team, took me to one side and said, "Skipper, it is one of the best nights that I have ever had, you made all the old men feeling young again". Mr Brammie said, with that old twinkle in his eyes and youthful smile, "From what I heard you boys had a ball; it is a pity that I was not there". The remark above all remarks relating to the incident came from Racketeer Leach, who said, "The time is fast approaching when they will have to lose you and let you go".

In my quiet moments I analysed all the remarks that were being echoed both openly and privately during and after the meeting and came to the conclusion that there was far more depth in them and that they had relevance to the three fishes, Wise Before Time, Wise In Time, and Wise After Time. In actual fact, during the meeting I was not slow to observe that the body language of some of the benefactors of the club, who in the main had connections with the church, was not conducive to what they were saying. My observations were confirmed on the evening when the club met to choose the team to play against James Hill in Clarendon, where Reverend Woolley originated from. Amongst James Hill's claims to fame is that the well known

Jamaican writer and poet, Claude McKay, was born there. McKay migrated to the United States in the nineteen twenties, settled in New York and with other writers such as Langston Hughes, Eugene O'Neil, and performers such as Paul Robeson, Bessie Smith, and Louis Armstrong, in conjunction with political activists such as Marcus Garvey and W.E.B. Dubois, helped to put the community of Harlem on the map. Their creative and accumulated talent gave birth to the Harlem Renaissance. Like Mckay, Reverend Woolley was a very proud Clarendonian.

Outside of cricket the club encouraged open dialogue and debates that involved wide-ranging subjects such as music, politics, religion, farming, and fishing. These debates always took place after the teams were selected and the theme of the debate following selection for the James Hill versus Discovery bay match was, 'Does things always seem to be the way they are?'. For the debate was Reverend Woolley, against the debate Lloyd 'Bugsie' Daay. Three years my senior he was one of the long line of Daay/Fairweather family from Helicon who excelled in the fields of academics, business, sports and music; in this regard he was more than a worthy debater and on the night he did himself proud at the way in which he presented his case. In his conclusion he said that with a good command of the English language sometimes things that are not the way they are can be seen to be that way, citing sermons by some preachers, including Reverend Woolley, who sometimes used examples to make their points and if some of the examples are properly examined they would fall short of reality.

Reverend Woolley did not take too kindly to the remarks and requested that Lloyd withdraw his statement and if he did not do so he would be asking that his membership from the club be taken away immediately. Failure to do so would result in him resigning as Chairman for the club and all arrangements for future matches cancelled forthwith. Lloyd decided to dig his heels in and would not budge; the impasse of both men immediately created two factions within the club with their own agendas. It was now getting quite late into the night and as first team captain I asked that the meeting be concluded provided that we would come back the following evening to see to what extent we could resolve the situation. Teacher Sudlow requested that my suggestion be a motion which was accepted by a majority; as always our meetings ended in prayer. That evening it was the longest prayer that I have ever heard from Mister Brammie. I am now convinced that God heard it because what is now being envisaged to be a heated meeting on the following evening took more than half an hour to resolve in an amicable fashion after Teacher Sudlow, in his capacity as Chairman, located the incident of the previous evening in Shakespeare's 'Love's Labours Lost' where commonsense is as important as education.

One could hear a pin drop in the basement of the Discovery Bay Congregational Church when Teacher in his summing up of the proceedings opened the book that he placed on the table and read the words from Biron, one of the Lords who attended to King Ferdinand of Navarre: 'To seek the light of truth while truth the while doth falsely blind the eyesight of his look light seeking light doth light beguile'. Hardly had he finished reading when the Reverend stood up and went over to Lloyd with outstretched hand and asked that the whole incident be forgotten, reminding the packed room that the art is about agreeing to disagree and like cricket it is what is interpreted by the player or the various spectators as a good batting stroke or a bowler bowling rubbish. Lloyd shook his hands amidst thunderous applause from those who attended the meeting. It was as far as I was concerned, 'All's well that ends well'. The reality was that in the next couple of days I would be leading the team out on home ground and I was determined to get the team to rise to the occasion and not to have a repeat of The Stony Hill game.

In terms of fast bowling Emeriah Johnson and Percy Bell were my role models, both left arm quickies; they could move the ball both ways. Emeriah had the knack of getting his bouncers rising at the best of batsmen, who in most cases, in the process of taking evasive action, would glove the ball into slips. At Stony Hill I bowled him number five, recognising that he was peaking and in any event it would be good to seem him playing out his remaining matches at home. Things could not have fared worse for him, or for that matter for myself; when I opened the bowling with him and Roy Walford, a St Ann Parish player playing for James Hill, got thirty four off him in the first over, comprising of three sixes, three fours and tow twos. It was good from a spectator's point of view and I could feel and observe the body language from the team, especially my two other fast bowlers, John Gallimore and Lloyd Daay, contempt and resentment that was building against Walford for taking their idol to the cleaners. My instruction to Lloyd, bowling from the seaside end, was 'let it rip at Walford'. I had enough cricket savvy to understand that he would be doing just that but a Captain must be seen to be communicating with his bowlers. First from him to the other batsmen was a gentle medium pacer to which he played and got off the mark with a single, leaving Walford to face the music. Lloyd took one of the longest runs that I have ever seen only to see his well pitched up ball being dispatched to the mid on boundary for four. The crowd went wild and amidst the din there were voices egging Lloyd to 'shake him up with the pace' and to Walford, 'Hit the pace man hard and high'. The next ball from Lloyd was a beamer to which I had to go up to him and ask him to apologise to both batsman and umpire. Walford played out the remaining over showing a modicum of caution and respect. I continued with Emmie until he got three wickets for over a hundred runs; in a way it was rather sad to know that it was his last game for his club that he served with undivided loyalty playing to the best of his ability and at the same time passing on advice to younger players in true cricket tradition. He led the team off to tumultuous applause. It was a case irrespective how good one is Anna Domini will always prevail. After his playing days were over it was always a pleasure to seek his advice and whenever I go back to Discovery bay I would have a drink or two with him; As I understand his grandsons are continuing to carry on from where he left off!

In this match my ability as a captain to make decisions on the field was to my mind being tested during the duel between Lloyd and Walford when Lloyd bowled a short pitched ball that smacked right into Walford's jaw. Well, you must remember that in those days helmets were unheard of, as usual or what was expected. Lloyd went to apologise, to which Walford waived him impolitely. Next was a note delivered to me by John Gallimore, who was fielding at deep backward square; it was from Reverend Woolley and it read, 'Stennett take Daay off immediately'. Between overs Gallimore said to me, 'Wha appen Parson send you love letter?" My reply was that it was just a reminder that I was down to read in Church the following day. Well as sure as night follows day, I had no intention of taking off the man who I knew deep down was keeping the opposition in check. Given that Walford was still at the crease fighting for dear life and in the process keeping the scoreboard ticking over, at one stage when I looked in the crowd I could see Reverend Woolley holding court and as far as I was concerned I was in charge and was not prepared to be pressured by any spectator, be they chairman or Preacher. As I got older I was able to understand some of the vagaries of Jamaican or, for that matter, Caribbean cricket in terms of how as a sport it became embedded in the body politic of a society that experienced oppression by a minority over a majority, and as a result both groups had different points of view which were perpetuated by an autocratic minority which in turn created a harshness in those from the enlightened majority that the way forward for self expression, self-esteem and self-determination is a basic human right, and if cricket or sport provides the vehicle for attaining them why not use the opportunity.

The two hundred and eighty runs that James Hill posted on the board gradually paled into insignificance through the determination of Lloyd Daay, Sibert Hall, Marshie Marshall and Glen Thomas. Victory was made all the more sweeter when Walford congratulated me for the way in which I captained the game. I took the compliment as a vindication against any suggestion that I should take my best bowler out of the attack; once again common sense dictated that there was no point in attempting to bring to the notice of players things that could create any kind of misunderstanding. As I have said before I was the youngest player ever to lead the team and with some players who were much older, it became important for me to revise some of the strategies that I used when captain of my School Eleven. Central to the strategies was the combining of my cautious and defensive attitude, some people have refereed to it as being laid-back, and the ability to take calculated risks located in a state of mind wherein there is a justification for taking the responsibility for my actions.

I was rather flattered when in the process of passing compliments regarding my captaincy, Aston Pickersgill, who was the Overseer for the Public Works Department in Discovery Bay, mentioned that there would be a vacancy for a Store Room Assistant at the construction site of the Coast Road between Discovery Bay and Rio Bueno, The Queens Highway. Aston Pickersgill was the father of Bobby Pickersgill, a People's National Party Member of Parliament in Jamaica and the Minister for Transport and Works.

The job in the stores was a far cry from that in the hotel in that it was heavy and dirty. That I did not mind because I was accustomed to it and always kept myself fit. The fact is that the environment was quite hostile in terms of language and behaviour, it was the first time that such a large scale construction project had taken place in the village, hence it attracted a wide cross-section of personnel, from one day casual labourers right up to very skilled engineers and artisans of all descriptions. Some of the machinery that was being used, such as twenty tons Euclid Dump Trucks, Graders and Barber Green Machines were first introduced and used on that site. The vast majority of the tractors were from Massey Ferguson, so one can imagine the excitement or the interest that I had when I arrived in Manchester in 1959 and realised that not only was Massey Ferguson only a few miles from Moss Side where I lived, but there were men from the various Caribbean islands working there. I even applied for a job there, but was unsuccessful; nevertheless, they had a cricket team and a very good one as well that played in The South Lancashire Cricket League and I had the great pleasure of playing against them for many years representing The National Dock Labour Board and Post Office Engineers.

The wages as a Stores Assistant were five pounds seven shillings and six pence per week and was paid fortnightly, but with overtime - and there was a lot of it - I was sometimes taking home twenty five pounds per fortnight. This was good but by the same rule overtime was beginning to encroach on my cricket practice. As I have said, people from different parishes came looking for work; on reflection it reminded me of the gold rush days in the United States and this is why I use the word people because it embraced women who would appear from nowhere, especially on pay day. Some came to make sure that when their menfolk got paid they took the money from them so that they could neither buy or pay for the tomato that they credited from women who captivated them with their smiles and their wiles. I have seen many men who have had the wind taken out of their sales publicly, both by legitimate partners and 'sweetie pie' sidekicks. They became sharp learning curves for me and underlined what the good book said, 'That behold your sins shall find you out".

Within six weeks of my employment I was given the job of helping to employ the causal labourers, in some cases it could be for two days, a week or a fortnight; it all depended on the needs of contractors and sub-contractors. This again was a very interesting learning curve for as I was in a position to know a majority of the men within five miles of my village, either through family connections, cricket, the church or politics, those from farther afield posed problems, especially those who used sobriquets. So for instance, a man from Clarendon would give his name as Clarendon, if he was from Old Harbour you knew him as Old Harbour, but these same men would be known to the woman who sold food on the site by different names and by a different name by the shopkeeper where he credits his rum until pay day. Some of these guys were what is known in Jamaican lingo as 'Fly by Nights'. In 1979, when I took the job as Youth Leader-in-Charge of the Green Hill Youth Centre in Oldham I had the experience of coming across names such as M. Ilk, K. Elloggs, S. Ugar, B. Read on the register; it was all part and parcel of youthful behaviour intended to outfox an adult in authority In essence I had seen it many years before at the construction site at Discovery Bay, the only difference being it was being done then by grown men, which underlines the fact that there is nothing new under the sun.

Walking to work one morning a man stopped me enquiring if there was any way that I could put a word in for him so as to get a job, I had never seen him before and as we walked along to the site and in talking it transpired that he was from Borrobridge in the Dry Harbour Mountains. Amongst other things that he told me was that he was good at cricket and as it happened there was a need for extra hands that day and he was taken on for two days. On the evening of the first day he asked if I knew of a place to stay, I told him that adjoining our kitchen was a store room which we used for storing wood for cooking, the padding for the donkey and clothes just in case it rained. It was not three stars but by the same rule it was dry and airy and above all it was near to the kitchen. He liked it and within days he made himself a nice wooden bed and a mattress from the dried leaves of the banana tree. He also turned out to be a good worker on the site and was getting regular work. I was also benefiting with him living at my house in that we would rise early in the mornings, tend to the goats, pigs, hens, the vegetable and flower garden, have a practice at cricket under the mango trees and be at work for nine o'clock. Life could not have been better either for Sam Lord or myself; at work he referred to me as Mr Stennett, out of work he called me Mass Whit; he insisted that respect be due.

After receiving my fourth pay packet from work I enquired of my mother how much money was outstanding on the house and when she told me I decided that with my savings from the hotel job and the hands of partners that I was throwing plus the monies earned from selling pigs, goats and eggs we would be better off paying off the loan. My mother was not happy with my suggestion, citing that she did not want to see me without money to live on or to further my studies. My determination won and on the day when I took time off from work and went with her to pay off the loan at Browns Town Benefit Building Society at Musgrave Square it was one of the happiest days in my life. I was to have the same feeling of accomplishment and freedom from paying off for the roof over my head in the year 2000 when I paid off my mortgage for my house. They were definite acts of losing me and letting me go.

There is an old saying, "That when things are going well plan for crises". This was to manifest itself when Sam, whilst he was at work, was involved in a fight which resulted in him being arrested and consequently losing his job. So far I was the only person that knew him well enough to stand bail for him, the problem was I was too young and the general consensus amongst relatives and friends was that the very way in which he turned up almost from nowhere, though he did say that he was Sam Lord from Borrobridge, there was no evidence or indication that on being bailed he would stay around to go to court. I believed that although it was only a short time that I had known him I was willing to take a chance, so I asked my Uncle-In-Law Elkanah Williams to stand surety on the understanding that if anything went wrong I would pay him the fifty pounds. I also contacted Lawyer Barrett, who was my father's solicitor, to represent him in court. On the day in court the complainant failed to appear and it transpired that he was on bail pending trial for wounding in St Mary. The same applied to his witness, who, according to him, saw Sam head-butting his friend. Sam's lawyer requested that the case be thrown out on the grounds that it was a case of self-defence; the Magistrate ruled in his favour and he was discharged.

Whilst we were having something to eat a woman came into the shop and recognised Sam. When she greeted him she referred to him as Daniel, immediately he took her away and it was about ten minutes before he returned. Sam introduced me to her as Mr Stennett, his boss. Her name was Peggy; at least that is what he told me but then I started feeling uneasy and could understand what relatives and friends were saying that this man could be telling lies about who he really was and about his whereabouts. At least I consoled myself with the fact that I did not have to pay any kind of surety, and with him not having a job to go back to I would employ him to tend the goats, pigs, chickens and the vegetable and flower gardens.

After finishing lunch he took Peggy shopping and from my observations it was clear that they had things in common and he was trying as hard as he could to be nice to her. Looking back on his actions that day was a reminder of the Jamaican story which gained currency throughout the generations of the man who on being released from prison decided to be an itinerant preacher and during one of his sermons in a village he saw a man in the crowd who was also in jail with him, and in trying to get the man to refrain from letting people know who he is was he shouted out, "Man from afar who sees me and knows me say nothing for I will see you later".

It was evident that Sam was upset because he kept rather quiet after he left Peggy. It was only when we arrived home that he told me the true story about himself. Between tears he talked of an early life without a mother or father and the extent to which people took advantage of his good nature; in reality he was not from Borrobridge but from Upper Manchester and his name was not Sam. The reason why he came down to Discovery Bay was really to drown himself as a result of the pressures of two women who were always putting him in court for maintenance of his children. Peggy, who he met by accident on the day of his trial, was the one of three women who never pressured him and he was twenty five years old. I reassured him that I would not divulge anything that he had said to me; it was the opportune moment for me to offer him the job of working for me at thirty shillings per week, in addition he could also use the wood on the land to burn or to make white lime for house-building on a fifty fifty basis. Included in the proposal was that he had to repay the ten guineas that I had paid the lawyer. He agreed to all the proposals.

In as far as is also known as mitigations, reasons for either granting or refusing bail and sureties, clients should be given opportunities to mend their ways, either through a variety of community sentences or custodials where there are no other options available. The fifteen years in which I served as a Lay Magistrate within Manchester City Magistrates' Court in England was to remind me of my early experiences with Sam in Jamaica. To appreciate that though as human beings we may fall by the wayside for the same things, we are all unique, no two individuals are the same and when one is called upon to make judgement there are so many factors that have to be taken into consideration and by the same rule not allowing our own biases and prejudices to stand in the way. Hardly had things settled down than Sam found himself in more controversy; this time an over-zealous member of the New Testament Church of God at Old Folly reported to Elder Higgins that my mother had somebody living on her premises in sin. Apparently Peggy was now living with Sam and the Church wanted him to leave. I intervened and argued that I was the one who employed him and was paying his wages and part of the arrangement is that he lived on the premises and as far as I was concerned Peggy was causing no trouble. I was to tell them that the eggs, vegetables and flowers the elders received from my Mother, and the tithes that she paid to the church, were all due to the efforts of Sam. Elder Higgins was a reasonable man and exhorted his members to pray that Sam be born again, which would mean that he had to marry Peggy, which I guess was music to her ears when she heard that if Sam would learn to save. He was always borrowing; he would get paid on Friday and in most cases by Wednesday it would be the customary, 'Boss man, what about a raise until Friday?" which meant that he was always owing me, but as my father always said, "lend is lend, give is give" and as such I was not prepared to be taken for a ride; hence whenever I paid him it was always minus what he borrowed.

Most Saturday evenings we would go down to the Bay to listen to the village band playing, which he joined playing the harmonica. Sometimes he would disappear and would be away until the shop closed and everybody went their separate ways. I was convinced that his disappearances were to see another woman, and I have never seen him smoke and if he did smoke Ganja I would have smelt it or seen the tell-tale signs in his eyes. Whenever he went out on other evenings Peggy would always shout at him, "You go on you going to Fenneh".

He had so many excuses as to why he was going out, sometimes it was the band practising for a dance, or it was to do with making arrangements to cut trees for making coal. In a way we, that is my sisters and I, when we had relatives staying with us, liked it when he went out on his missions as it gave us the opportunity for Peggy to regale us with annancy and ghost stories. Sam's homecoming was always heralded with the music from his harmonica breaking the stillness of the night. On entering the yard it would change to religious music and I am sure it did something to his girlfriend, who would always greet him with, "you come back already". It was as if she knew what he was up to and his singing off tune was always, "Now the day is over".

One Sunday night I had a dream that a white man came into my yard, kicked the door open where Sam stayed, tied him to the tamarind tree in the yard and started to beat him with a whip; at every stroke of the whip the man was saying "give it up" and he continued hitting him until he passed out, leaving him lying naked on the floor.

On my way back from work on the Monday I told my Uncle Mate Wallace of the dream to which he tried to ascertain if I had read any books or an article in a newspaper where somebody had been flogged. I cold not recall any such incidents, whereupon he reminded me of Belshazar's dream in the book of Daniel where he failed to interpret his dream regarding the writing on the wall which read 'Mene Mene Tekel U', to which Daniel interpreted as "thou art found in the balance and found wanting". He concluded that dreams have their own way of revealing themselves and my dream could be related to any one. I went home and did not tell my mother or anyone else about the dream, yet what was strange is that Mate made references to the biblical Daniel, the very name that Peggy called Sam on the day that I attended court with him in Brown Town. Come Tuesday up until Wednesday he did not tap me for a raise and from my observations he was as normal as usual. On the Thursday morning we did some cricket practice under the Mango trees and like me was excited about the match coming up, a Boys Town Eleven from Kingston led by Clinton Bell, one of our Discovery Bay boys who had gone to live in Kingston. Boys Town was the club that the well known West Indies test player Collie Smith played for.

It was about two thirty on the Friday morning when there was a loud banging on the back door of our house; it was Peggy almost hysterical, shouting, "mother, mother, Mass Whit come quick, come quick". I hastily got out of bed and on entering Sam's room he was just in his underpants and awash with perspiration and repeating over and over, "I am redeemed, I have given all to the Man on Calvary". The first thing that came to my mind is that he was getting off his head, at least that is what I told my mother and sisters who by then were all awake with the commotion. When my mother came into Sam's room, he was reasonably relaxed as he asked my mother to read a Psalm for him, to which she read Psalm Thirty Two, "Blessed is he whose transgression is forgiven whose sin is covered". Following the reading we all knelt as mother said prayers, Sam interjecting occasionally with "I am redeemed". Prayers over he was at ease with himself as he started to tell us of his dream of being chased into the yard by a white man and a dog and before he could enter his house the dog got hold of him, which allowed the man to hold him, bind him to the Tamarind tree in the yard and then start to beat him mercilessly with a whip until he was stark naked, at every stroke of the whip the man was shouting, "Give it up or else fire for you". In between relaying his experience he started crying and, although not uncontrollable, it was difficult for me to erase from my mind the feeling that he was not having some kind of mental breakdown, especially when I remembered that he contemplated drowning himself at one time. Adding to my misgivings relating to his state of mind was the fact that there were similarities with our dreams and other than relaying my dream to Mate and no one else I knew the difficulty that would arise in me trying to convince my Mother or my sisters about my dream.

On my way to work the following morning I stopped by and informed Mate of what had transpired the previous night; he was rather philosophical about the similarities of both dreams, starting from the premise that the dog in

Sam's dream was an indication that there was a dark side in his life that he needed to give up so as to enjoy inner peace. Like myself he erred on the side of caution that Sam could well be experiencing a mental breakdown, adding that "no madman is going to stay on my father's premises. I will be going up there today to see what is happening". These remarks left me wondering if what I have often heard in the village that Mate was the son of my grandfather Samuel Stennett was true. I can remember asking a senior female relative of mine if there was any truth in what I was hearing, her response was, "Boy, what is hidden from the wise and prudent is revealed to babes and sucklings". I was then fifteen years old, certainly not a babe or a suckling, but wise enough to seek information that was relevant to me.

On my way home from work I met Mate coming from my house, according to him there was nothing to indicate that Sam was smoking Ganja which would affect his state of mind and as such, he was prepared to accept that in his dream he had some kind of spiritual awakening that would help him to come to terms with his addiction to gambling and that I would have to help him, and it is for that reason why our dreams were so close. On parting he said, "Boy, this is what God sent you to do to help people". I was eighteen years and five months old and although I was fully aware of what responsibility entailed from the passing of my father when I was eleven years old, I did not feel comfortable at the thought of giving support to a man who had an addiction to gambling.

When I arrived home Elder Higgins, Bro-Joe Ward, Sister Currie, Sister U.U. and Sister White were sitting on the veranda. I greeted them and after having finished my dinner Mother asked that I join them in bible reading and prayer for Sam, who was in the back yard making a fire, the smoke intending to chase away the mosquitoes. There was something special about the making of this fire when Sam called us and showed us his gambling board for playing Crown and Anchor and a number of dices which he placed on the fire. It was only then that it dawned on me that all the time when he was making various excuses why he was going out and would disappear from band practice leaving me to assume that he had another woman, he was gambling in the bushes using a bottle lamp to provide light. To top it all he was hiding his gambling equipment under an old upturned oil drum under the Tamarind tree. It was obvious that there were discussions regarding his new experience with Elder and the other church members, who decided that he would be placed on penitent ground for three months to make sure that he mended his ways and then he would be accepted into the church. His girlfriend would also have to find a place to live separately from him and if they were still in love with each other they could marry then; that very evening Peggy left to stay with one of the church sisters.

The following morning Sam was up at his usual time, playing on his Harmonica, "Old things are past away and everything made new". For me, if anything was made new is when he told me that he could neither read nor write and he would like me to help him; I can't say that I was surprised in that I grew up with people who were in similar positions and unless they tell you it was difficult to find out in a majority of cases; they were always good at calculating money and if the occasion should arise when they feel that they would more than likely to declare that, "nobody is going to give me a six for a nine". Helping him to read and write gave me tremendous satisfaction, but one day, when I asked him to bowl at me during cricket practice, he told me that he was a new person and that old things have passed way. I knew then that he was following instructions from the church members, including my mother, and felt somewhat disappointed that I was helping him to acquire a much needed skill and he was not in a position to help me with my sport, all because he was born again. I was even more disappointed when I realised that h e would no longer be at matches leading the chorus of "Boss man give me some skin", an indication for me to bowl short-pitched deliveries to batsmen shaking them up. This action was later to prove my demise and ultimate loss of my job with the Public Works Department when in a friendly or curry goat match I hit one of the top brass with a bouncer, and even though I apologised, which I always do when I hit a batsman, he did not accept my apology and Jamaica being how it was at the time, in terms of who held the handle and who held the blade, a case for my dismissal was wrapped up in the guise of promotion to a part of the island that I had no desire to go. In Jamaican parlance it was a case of "giving me a basket to carry water". But such is life and I have always used negatives to achieve positives. I was not unduly bothered, firmly believing that perseverance will always conquer.

As I mentioned earlier in my experiences as a Lay Magistrate in England where some clients get a number of chances to mend their ways and failed in the process, others who have had one chance made serious efforts and have never been in court again. Sam was an example of the latter, proving as he once said that all he had ever wanted was the opportunity to prove himself. In time he was admitted into the church, married his girlfriend Peggy and eventually made contact with his children and started to support them.

I was completely thrown off balance one evening when I came in from work to face a man who I accepted as being changed for the better in a mood of defiance; there was no point asking if he was angry, the question had to be what had given rise to his anger. The answer was that a relative of ours, on my mother's side, whom C.L.R. James in his book "The Future in the Past", and especially at the period in time in Jamaican said that, "There are the Browns intermediates who cannot by any stretch of imagination pass as white but who will not go one inch towards mixing with people darker than themselves". She lived in Kingston and worked as a stenographer in a Lawyer's office. As it happened she had come to spend a few days with us and during her stay she referred to Sam as 'Yard Boy', whereas I am sure that my mother would not allow her to get away with that kind of behaviour. I would have to say my piece, after all I was the man of the house and a man had to do what a man had to do so I told her that Sam was a grown man and should be treated as such, and had it not been for him the struggle to make ends meet would be much more difficult, whilst she did not make an open apology to him her attitude towards him did change, and I am sure that many years after, when she experienced a series of misfortunes starting with the death of her husband and the loss of their business which saw her migrate to the United States to start a new life. Whether it was by coincidence or fate, of the two jobs that she shared, the one looking after an elderly lady at nights was obtained as a result of a friend knowing a friend, one of those friends was one of Sam's granddaughters, both of them were complete strangers. Yet in some way, through our family there were things that happened in the past that as far as I can gather when they got to know each other better in a society where so many isms help, to dictate one's way of life they both yearned to go back home. On one of my many visits to the United States I did meet my cousin and during our conversation it was interesting to hear her talk about the days in Jamaica when people knew their places and how since Independence every Tom, Dick or Harry can address people irrespective of who they were in any old way, for all the wishy washy liberalism that she expounded about America giving one the opportunity to succeed. I came away convinced that deep down she prayed for a return to the days in Jamaica when Yard Boys were ten a penny and opportunities for progression were limited to the chosen few and not the many.

The match against Boys Town, like all the matches against Clubs from Kingston or the planter elite ones from the Sugar estates, attracted its more than extraordinary large amount of spectators. An added feature of interest to this game what that the wicket on which the match was being played was the one that was dug up and a new one laid. I was part of that vociferous minority who expressed the view that it was a backward step and would not be in keeping with providing of good cricket for players and spectators alike; our argument was based on the material that was being used to make the wicket. As Captain for the team I was hauled up before the Committee for leading a breakaway group. I defended the stance that we took, reminding the Committee that events would either prove us wrong or right, and if wrong we would have to agree that our pre-judgement was wrong. I was not prepared to take another hiding like we had from the game at Stony Hill; our team was prepared as we have always done to fight to the bitter end, in other words playing to the best of our abilities.

I won the toss and as usual batted, I have never done otherwise from the first ball that Lascelles Davis, who at the time played senior Cup Cricket for the Railways in Kingston, bowled at Jack Murphy who opened the batting with Sibert Hall. It was evident that our misgivings about the state of the wicket would be justified. In my over sixty five years of playing and watching cricket I had never seen anything to compare with that day. The ball did everything out of the ordinary; players suffered bruises to all parts of their bodies. It is a miracle that somebody did not get killed or seriously hurt considering that at the time head gear and body guards were unheard of. The one hundred and thirty seven runs that we made was through sweat, blood, tears and good fortune, which always favours the brave and by the end of our innings the feeling amongst our team was that the opposition would be asking that we call the match off or play on the practice wicket.

No such request came from them other than sweeping the wicket; they had come to play cricket and the crowd wanted to see a good game. I opened the bowling with James Marshall, the Grand Uncle of Xavier Marshall who plays for the West Indies, from one end and Lloyd Daay from the other end. The Boys Town batsmen were experiencing similar traumas to ours and I decided to sacrifice speed for spin and brought in Rupert Williams, a slow left arm bowler, who had one of the most impressive lengths and the ability to bowl making the batsman in cricket jargon play at "the wrong un", bowling from one end, and from the other end Martin Bell, a left arm back-of-the-hand spinner. He was very difficult to read and he was the one who when he beat the batsman would throw his hand in the air shouting, "Jesus wept". Rupert on the other hand would ask the batsman, "Did you read that one?" Except for Clinton "Charlie" Headlam and Bunny Shaw, and given that Boys Town did not field their strongest team against us which certainly was not our fault, they had no answer to Rupert and Martin, who had match figures of four for sixty five and five for fifty respectively. To see us winning by two runs it was a wonderful victory, added to that was the open-mindedness on the part of the majority of Committee members who sanctioned that the wicket should be dug and a new one put in place to acknowledge that their decision was wrong. Without being big-headed we told them, so in life we all can be right at the same time, and we can be wrong at the same time, it is all about give and take.

Two people that were to have a positive effect on my life as a result of this particular match were Doctor Lenworth Jacobs and Clinton "Charlie" Headlam. The then Medical Officer of Health for the Parish of Saint Ann, Doctor Jacobs was a near white upper class Jamaican who, with his wife Mrs Beth Jacobs, from a similar background, made and left an indelible mark in terms of their invaluable contributions to the upliftment of the Parish in medicine, education, sports and every civic endeavour, central to these contributions were the emphasis that they placed on motivating the masses to a level of understanding of their own awareness that they must be a part of nation-building. The Beth Jacobs Family Planning and Early Childhood Education Project in Saint Ann's Bay is a legacy of Mrs Jacobs' philanthropy, dedication and commitment to the Parish.

Dr Jacobs was arguably the Doyen of St Ann cricket, he more than any one else encouraged and created opportunities where cricket as popular culture embraced those who had a passion for the sport, irrespective of their colour, class or status, to show off their talent in an organised way that reflected the game in its finest tradition that embraced good on and off the field. He stressed the importance of cricketers being good ambassadors for themselves, their club, their parish and their country. I was over the moon when he himself invited me to come to Saint Ann's Bay to play in a friendly game against a team from Trelawney; a similar invitation was extended to James Marshall. On the day of the match a car was sent to pick us up at The Discovery Bay Square at nine o'clock. We were there from eight o'clock; it was an opportunity not to be missed, in fact I hardly slept on the night before the match.

There was a feeling of excitement, anxiety, anticipation and accomplishment all rolled into one as I walked through the gates of the club, which is now where The Marcus Garvey Secondary School stands. We were early and as time progressed other players and spectators started to arrive. It was the second time in my cricketing life that I was to change in a proper dressing room; the first was at Stony Hill. Playing for the Trelawney side was Roy Gilchrist, who three years later made his debut on the 1957 West Indies tour to England as a fast bowler and was acknowledged as one of the fastest and most hostile bowlers the West Indies has ever produced. Providence decreed that Trelawney won the toss and batted; it also decreed that rain prevented the game finishing before I had to go in to face Gilchrist batting at number seven. Who says that God does not answer prayers immediately? As far as I am concerned he did answer mine that day because Gilly was firing and as James Marshall and myself watched him we both concluded that he must be the fastest bowler that God had ever blown breath in his nostrils. Not only that, it appeared to us that he had no respect for batsmen. Be that as it may, it was exciting watching him running up to the wicket and jumping up as if to increase his height and delivering the ball at a tremendous speed. I was rather amazed that a man who bowled with so much hostility and venom would be so quiet, almost shy to a point. My opening gambit to him was "Paceman do you touch the iron", meaning did he do weight training; it was

112

interesting when he responded that he was about to ask the same question of me. He did use weights, but when I told him about my experience of being struck by lightning some six year previous, in addition to expressing at how lucky I was to be alive, he felt that I had the ability to make myself into a useful medium pacer with a deadly Yorker. It was quite flattering.

Over the years, I was to develop a wonderful relationship with Gilly; it all started with Doctor Jacobs inviting me to play in that friendly game against Trelawney. As I have said he was always stressing the importance of self-actualisation and when I told him that I was leaving for England to seek work, to play cricket, and study to be a teacher in physical education, he was quite pleased that I chose to live in Manchester, not only citing the hospitality and generosity of people in the North of England as to why my decision was a good one, but also that there was a long tradition of West Indian cricketers playing for various clubs in the Lancashire, Central Lancashire and Cheshire leagues, and that Manchester United Football Club and Lancashire County Cricket Club were part and parcel of the sporting life of Manchester. Without a doubt Dr Jacobs was mindful of the path that could be taken at the time by someone like myself who appreciated that cricket had value systems that had to be adhered to so as to achieve any kind of social or financial rewards. It was not unbecoming of him that on leaving his office on the day to say my farewell he said, "Stennett, keep you eye on the ball, bat straight and above all be a good ambassador".

Charlie Headlam was little above five feet tall but remembers getting the Gleaner in the fifties and turning to the sports page for the cricket scores of the Senior Cup Matches played in Kingston, or the results of the Nethersole Cup Competition played in the rural parishes, or The Crum Ewing matches played on the Sugar Estates. Week after week Clinton Headlam, playing for Wembley, would always feature making runs and taking catches. His impression of me after the Boys Town Match was in the context of how I captained the side, pointing out that from his observations the majority of the players were older than I was. In total I bowled five overs during the match as a result of changing the bowlers; but that was sufficient for him to recognise my ability to bowl both inswing and outswing and, above all, the deadly Yorker. I took two catches in the slips and he was equally praiseworthy. On realising that I had a brother who was living in Kingston he encouraged me to go there where I would have a better opportunity to play better cricket. I know that both my mother and two brothers would most definitely support his line of argument, but as far as I was concerned I was happy to stay in the country away from the bright lights and the hustle and bustle of city life. That being said I kept abreast of his achievements and the general consensus island-wide was that his performances warranted a

113

place on the West Indies team, but in the Caribbean at that time in a number of cases it was the situation of the man in favour as opposed to the man in form.

Charlie eventually migrated to England, settling in Manchester and played professional and semi-professional cricket in the Huddersfield League, The Central Lancashire League, The Lancashire and Cheshire League, The Saddleworth League and the South Lancashire League. I remembered him playing for Holmfirth in the Huddersfield League in the 1970's when I worked for The General Post Office in Manchester and Charlie informed me that they were looking for a bowler and he had recommended me to them. He said, "Sten, with your ability to move the ball and your Yorker you can pick up a load of wickets in that league". I felt honoured that he thought so highly of me but could not take up the offer because I was in the planning stages of moving from the Post Office to start my course at Manchester Polytechnic, now Manchester Metropolitan University.

Charlie continued playing cricket until he was almost seventy and it was rather ironic that when he suddenly fell ill and was admitted into Trafford General Hospital and I went to visit that in the presence of his daughter, Colette, although it was evident that he was suffering we chose to turn the clock back and revisited the old days playing cricket in Jamaica. One of the many stories that gained mileage throughout Jamaica was the time when Wes Hall, one of the greatest fast bowlers in the world, played for Barbados in an Inter-Colonial Game against Jamaica at Sabina Park. The first over that the six feet two inches Hall bowled to the diminutive Headlam, he drove the first two balls passed Hall for four runs. Rattled, his third was a bouncer which had Charlie sitting down on his backside only to look up to hear Hall saying to him in his strong Bajan accent, "Boy you thing I come here to make sport, this is war". When I relayed the story to Charlie, he eased himself up from his pillow and ,with that radiant smile that was his trademark, said, "Sten, how did you remember that it is true". He continued by saying, "Sten, in those days helmets were unheard of"

Throughout the long years that I knew him I have never heard or witnessed any kind of bad behaviour coming from him; he was indeed a great ambassador for cricket. No wonder Alan Rae, who opened the batting for the West Indies and who figured largely in the 1950 Test Match against England at Lord's when he scored 106 and as the win by 326 runs resulted in the famous Calypso "Cricket lovely cricket", called Charlie 'the little gentleman'. As we reminisced in the hospital it was refreshing that his daughter was there to hear some of the stories about her father, who earned the right to be a cricket legend, a role model and a mentor. As I was about to leave I recalled him saying, "Sten, we have talked for a long time. I completely forgot to ask how you are doing with your course". He was making reference to the course that I started in September 1997 at Manchester Metropolitan University for a Masters Degree relating to sports people as role models and mentors. Looking back his question was an interesting one in that in 1974, when he recommended me to play at Holmfirth in the Huddersfield League for expenses, I was making preparation to go to the same institution to study for the Certificate Course in Youth and Community Studies. He died four days after I visited him in hospital and, as if to add insult to injury, on the morning when I was getting ready to attend his funeral at which I was to pay a tribute in the celebration of his life, I received a telephone call from Jamaica that my eldest and only surviving brother, Egbert, had passed away. Two days after Charlie's funeral I was on my way to Jamaica, which during the long flight afforded me with the opportunity to reflect on the impact that both men had on my life. From their own perspectives I came to the conclusion that both in a sporting and non-sporting context and in their own individual styles they had as fathers, husbands, brothers, friends and in keeping with what positive role models and mentors should be, fought good fights, ran good races, finished many courses, and with their passing it was important that I continue to emulate them.

My next match as Captain was away to Hope Bay near the beautiful Somerset Falls in the Parish of Portland where its lush vegetation and thick undergrowth provided a safe haven for the maroon freedom fighters in the earlier part of Jamaica's history. Descendants of the Maroon are still living in the Parish. Surrounded then by banana, coffee and other provisions, with a small river running beside, the ground could only be reached by a kind of Bailey bridge. It was one of the most picturesque that I have ever played cricket on. Added to this was that the team consisted of players with the surnames Jump, Dunbar and Afflick; even one of the umpires was a Jump. It was a case of either being caught, bowled or run out by any of those three names. Be that as the case, our team was not daunted by names, we played all comers to the best of our abilities, as they were to find out when they won and elected to bat and in the process their openers Jump and Dunbar got them off with a solid start. Dunbar especially was a very good batsman with an array of shots; when he went caught in the slips for 37 the score stood at 57 for 1. Next in was another Jump, who with his namesake took the score to 67 for 3; the other batsmen found life difficult playing Rupert Williams with his slow left armers from one end and my right arm fast medium inswingers and outswingers from the other end. Match figures read Gallimore 6 overs 2 maidens 2 wickets for 32, Barrett 6 overs 1 maiden 1 wicket for 29, Williams 11 overs 3 maidens, 4 wickets for 40, Stennett 12 overs 3 maidens, 3 wickets for 45. With extras Hope Bay totalled 158 runs.

With a batting strength of Murphy, Marshall, Alexander, Campbell and Barrett, followed by a lower middle order of which I was one and a lower order which could get runs if required, 158 seemed a mere formality, but as they say in cricket, it is a funny old game, it is never won until the last ball has been bowled. What a truism, as I was to find myself going in at number six when we still needed 50 runs to win. Dunbar made inroads into our batsman by bowling just short of a length, inducing batsmen to come to him. Watching him bowling I decided that I would be taking my usual leg stump guard and bat at least a foot from the popping crease, thus making his short of a length ball much easier to play, being left handed he had to bowl around the wicket to me. His first ball I hit him clear out of the ground into the river, the spectators went wild and Dunbar was not amused. The next balls were successive fours, in Jamaican cricket jargon I was seeing the ball like a bread fruit and as such I was willing to make hay whilst the sun was shining.

I remember Jacob Leslie, who had the speech impediment and who was batting with me saying, "Whitty Boy, look like 'Tita' Maud pray for you lath night". At least it looked that way as we stayed together to win the match; I was 38 not out. It was altogether a great game and the spectators were not in any way inhibited to show their appreciation for the duel between Dunbar and myself, who were both members of the fast bowling fraternity; his comment to me as we walked off the field was, "today is your day until we meet next time". My response was, "I will open the batting". It was all in good fun and the after-match nourishment of bussue soup, jerk port and roast bread fruit was well in keeping with the tradition regarding the hospitality of Portlanders. There were even suggestions amongst some of the members of our team that we were served Injun Coney; an animal which resembles a rabbit and is only found in the Parish of Portland. Like the bussue, which is some kind of shell fish and is noted for its aphrodisiacal propensities and the thousands of visitors both local and international who travel to Boston in the eastern end of the Parish for the Annual Jerk Port Festival, it has acquired its own popularity and validity as to its effectiveness. It was certainly not something that I could ascribe to for the very fact that when I played in that match I did not drink the soup, and events to which I had no control decreed that I never had the opportunity to play cricket in the Parish of Portland again.

CHAPTER SEVEN

Expanding the Vision and Raising the bar

THE ALL-Island Celebrations of 1955 commemorating 300 years of British rule in Jamaica was of great importance to me. Throughout the Island villages came together and through collective worship, sporting, artistic and other events, which culminated in a grand finale at the Parish Capitals, provided a showcase and an opportunity and appreciation of the richness and diversity of the country's people in an integrated society. Over that period in radically diverse groups of Africans, Europeans, Asians, Chinese and Jews, all with differing agendas as to why they settled in Jamaica and how they faced and dealt with the various challenges for survival, would ultimately lead to the creation of nation-building with one common objective. Interestingly, that seven years after the 300 celebrations in 1962 when Jamaica achieved independence the motto was 'Out of many one people'.

One of the many village events that I was involved in prior to going to Saint Ann's Bay for the Parish Finale was a cricket match played between the over-forties and the under-twenty fives; and, as I was to learn during the match and many years later, that the ripe old age of an eagle is better than the youthful age of a sparrow. The fact that we lost the match was testimony that brains will always have an advantage over brawn and on reflection put into context an experience I had when I visited Jamaica in 2001 and was asked to play in the past students' eleven against a present student eleven. I was no spring chicken, yet by the same rule I knew that my level of fitness could take me through the 20 overs a side match. I could be a grandfather to any member of the present student eleven and as such I expected that respect would be due; not so in as far as a young fast bowler who I overheard telling his team-mates that he was going to let the Englishman smell the red cherry. The Englishman he was referring to was me. I believed that his anger stemmed from the fact that on the previous day there was a discussion at the beach regarding the positive performance of England against the West Indies in England. At the time, in as far as he was concerned, living in England made me an English man and for that reason he was going to let me pay dearly. Well, I was seventeen like him; full of youthful vigour and eager to prove myself but he has never been twenty, never mind being over sixty. I was due to bat at number three and immediately the first wicket fell I gave Pushu Ward, one of my contemporaries, some money to get a round in, my preferred choice was a double J Wray and Nephew over-proof white rum followed by a single. I knew that it would take much more than that, even under the fierce July sun, to cause me to start singing, 'What do you do with a drunken cricketer'. That being said it was sufficient for me to take the pads off and excuse myself from the fiery and hostile onslaught of a young tearaway fast bowler by the name of Williams. Truth of the matter I did not travel over five thousand miles away to be terrorized and maybe put in hospital, besides in three days I had to give the keynote address at our past students' dinner.

There were a number of similarities with the game of 1955 and the one of 2001. There was youthful bravado, there was cautiousness born out of experience, and above all a meeting of minds made possible through a sporting event where it created an environment where the past could be revisited, the present consolidated and preparations made for the future. In the 1955 match I recalled Bunny, who stuttered bowling his googlies to Mr Sterling, a veteran of the second world war and an employee of the Public Works Department, an extremely good batsman who could cut and drove with great skill and dexterity. He had a cork leg and always had to use a runner, as usual when Bunny beat any batsman he would say "Yu yu fu fu fucker". On his third time of beating Mr Sterling he said to Bunny, "Son you can use that word all day but if ever you use the word Mother I will stop the game and get the Police to arrest you. Now do you understand?". A sheepish and repentant Bunny replied, "Yes, Mother Sterling".

At the end of the match Mr Sterling told us about the accident he received travelling from RAF Sealand in Chester to RAF Filey in Yorkshire resulting in his having been fitted with a cork leg. His story of life in the air force and the opportunity that it afforded him to play cricket was quite interesting to me. Central to the theme of his discourse was that if one cannot make a living playing cricket it can provide one with the opportunity to find a way to make a living.

A week after Jamaica 300 Grand Finale, along with Vin "Uncle Money" Cover and Llewlyn "Bugs" Faulcher, I was back at Saint's Bay to join the over three hundred men who answered the advert in the Jamaica Gleaner for recruits for the Jamaica Battalion. All three of us saw the army as a stepping stone towards what we wanted to do with our future lives. Vin wanted to be with the Royal Electrical and Mechanical Engineers, "Bugs" wanted to be a motorcycle dispatch rider and I wanted to work in the Stores, which, hopefully, would give me the opportunity to play cricket.

With over 300 men applying for twenty vacancies it was simply on the one hand more dogs than bones, on the other it was a reassurance that I had the ability and confidence to motivate Vin and "Bugs" that rather to run the risk of waiting for the bus which could be full before it reached Discovery Bay we would be better off rising early and walking the fourteen miles, after all we were looking at careers in the Army where fitness was crucial. The suggestion and action was justified as we were to discover later in the day that the bus broke down after leaving Runaway Bay; at least we were on time to start the test, and the consolation was that a month after we all received letters from the Army informing us that we had passed, but the fact that they had reached their target figure our names would be placed on file and as more vacancies arise we would be considered. I have always said that promises are comforts for fools, and all that letter and several other promises that I was to receive regarding my progression added to my resolve in expanding the vision and raising the bar. From the trio that went to enlist for the Army Vin was the first to move. He was starting work as an Engine Room Attendant on one of the Liners that transported the bauxite Ore mined by Reynolds, Jamaica mines from Ocho Rios to the Gulf States of America. He rose through the ranks to attain the position of Chief Engineer. Bugs was next when he joined the Jamaica Constabulary Force and after his initial training he was assigned to the Motorcycle Division.

As I have said, in Society at the time, and it is still the case where opportunities are limited, especially if one is from the group of have nots, nothing can be taken for granted; it means that preparation, prayer and perseverance must at all times be central to aspirations, visions and dreams. Hence when I was told that there would be a vacancy for someone to work in the Stationery Sores at Tower Isle Hotel I immediately sent off a letter applying for the position and within three days I had received an answer for me to attend an interview, taking along with me two letters of recommendation; one was from my last headmaster, A Spencer Sudlow, the other was from Donald Redwood, Accountant at The Columbus Inn Hotel where I worked.

Nine people turned up for the interview, which was in three parts starting with each candidate giving an oral presentation lasting for five minutes before a panel of three people which included Frank Abbott, Director of Personnel, Mr Rouse, Controller of Stores and Maintenance, and Godfrey Brash, whose promotion to the Accountancy Department created the vacancy for which we had applied. Following the open presentation we were requested to do an hour-long written test, which consisted of writing an essay on 'The Importance of Tourism to Jamaica' and a general knowledge and arithmetic test. At the end of the test we had a forty five minute break for lunch. On going back to the interview room six names were called out and they left the room with Godfrey Brash. I was one of the three that was left to be interviewed individually. As I have always said I believe in myself and this day proved my point, whilst not downplaying the importance and the skills that were necessary to perform the job effectively and to which I did have some experience. I came asking myself if they really wanted someone to work in the stationery store, be in charge of the incoming and out-going mail and file all the dining room, bar and miscellaneous checks used by resident guests in the hotel or they wanted a General Manager. This was an indication of the depth of the interview to which I knew that I had given my best shot and found solace in the adage that 'when men on earth have done their best angel in heaven cannot do better'.

Four days after the interview I received a letter offering me the job with the view of starting within a week and that a response was needed by telegram whether I would take or refuse the offer. The starting salary was six pounds seventeen shillings and six pence per week, paid fortnightly, including meals, accommodation and uniform; it was eight to four thirty Monday to Friday and on Saturdays eight to twelve. Extra hours worked were compensated at time off in lieu or 'TOIL'. A member of the kitchen staff from Retreat near Content in St Mary noted for his sense of humour was credited with the following: "If you cannot retreat you must content and though all prospect seems good, only Tower Isle is TOIL". Prospect is the plantation near Ocho Rios where visitors can tour the plantation either on horse back or train to view fields of sugar cane, banana, citrus, and a variety of trees both native to Jamaica and from other parts of the world.

Developed by the late Sir Harold Mitchell, an English aristocrat landowner and philanthropist who took young men from underprivileged backgrounds and trained them as cadets and with a variety of skills that they acquired found employment on the estate. It was whilst playing cricket in a Tower Isle Eleven against a Saint Mary Eleven at Prospect that I once again came across Jack Mercer, who two years previously when he saw me playing at Rio Bueno suggested that I should resort to bowling leg breaks instead of pace; so impressed was he with my performance at this game that he told me that his contract as Chief Coach for Jamaica was coming to an end and then he would be joining Northampton and if ever I migrate to England I should contact him and he would arrange that I have a trial for the county. I was rather flattered that a man of his experience saw so much in me, but although more than once I contemplated travelling to England I was not prepared to take Jack Mercer seriously, besides I was determined not to leave Jamaica before I reached my twenty first birthday. Playing for Saint Mary was Lester King, the Jamaican fast bowler who played for the West Indies against India in 1961 and against England in 1963.

Approximately twenty five miles from Discovery Bay, Tower Isle, later named Couples, was owned by Abe Issa, recognized as the man who from the early 1950's placed tourism on a new high in Jamaica and was like another world to me. It was the first time that I had left home to live and work. However, whatever apprehensions I had regarding coming to terms with a new environment dissipated within days as Brash did everything in helping me with aspects of the job. He was an excellent instructor and the fact that I had some experience in that area of work made communication much easier. That being said, on the morning before I left home to start the job, as was customary before prayer to read from the bible my mother requested that I read Psalms 12, "I will lift mine eyes unto the hills from whence cometh my help". As one of the three people who were part of the interview panel I asked Brash to tell me about my performance on the interview; a very studious man who listed his interests as reading and playing chess, his answer to my question was as calculated as it was revealing and there was no doubt in my mind that there was a consensus with the panel that I was the best applicant for the job. Even though I did not talk more about myself, on this note I gathered that Mr Rouse said that, "Any young man who walked fourteen miles to join the army and was the first to arrive for the interview was good enough for him". That was an indication of my commitment and over the years I have proved that "I can talk the talk and walk the walk". By the same rule the panel found my experience of being struck by lightning an interesting one; in time this was to become my calling card both to staff and visitors alike at the hotel and for that matter throughout my life.

With over one hundred and fifty members of staff that not only reflected the 'out of many, one people' reality, there was also an amalgamation of occupations, political, religious, cultural and sporting interest groups. The story going round at the time which gained currency and validity was that the House of Issa concept was to create employment and training opportunities whereby employees could work themselves up through the ranks. Other considerations for staff welfare was the emphasis that was placed on providing leisure time facilities for employees. It was there that I was to develop my skills as a footballer and also add table tennis to my list of sporting activities. The hotel prided itself in the fact that the same amount of care that was placed on preparing meals for the guests the same applied to that of the staff. An interesting aside is that I have never liked soup but on one occasion when Mulligatawny soup was on the menu I tasted it, found it appetizing and from that began to appreciate soup as an integral part to any meal. Over time I was to become adept at making soup, but more about that in a later chapter.

Six months into the job I was summoned to see Mr Willard Samms, Chief Accountant; except for exchanging courtesies I had never had the opportunity to speak with him on a one to one basis. Always smartly attired, studious, with eyes as if looking into the deep recesses of one's mind from behind thick lens horned-rimmed spectacles conveyed the impression that he was assured and confident of himself and his position in the organisation. He wasted no time in stating his reason for wanting to speak with me. Firstly, from his own observations and also from other employees he was pleased with my performance, not only as it related to my work but also to the cricket and football teams in which I was involved. He said that having read the essay that I wrote when I came for the interview for the job there is no reason why I should not make the effort to study towards achieving a career and suggested that I should do a correspondence course in Bookkeeping from Bennett College in Sheffield, England, and from that I could combine theory with practice. At the end of our conversation he informed me that in my next pay envelope I would be awarded a rise of an extra one pound ten shillings, making my salary seven pounds seventeen shillings and six pence per week.

Although I have never envisaged being a bookkeeper or to be stuck in an office as a career I consoled myself with the fact that to be successful and happy it was important that I made the most of the present which would enhance my future. I was aware that I was at the right place where I could dream dreams and have visions. My level of expectancy had been raised and when I came across a copy of Ebony Magazine, created and published by John H Johnson, an African American who challenged negative stereotypes of black people. He described the magazine as a medium that made an effort to seek out the good things, even in the face of adversity, people who have made it against all odds. In essence I believed that he was speaking to me and from the day that I acquired the magazine in April 1955 I have always bought it. The same applies to my two daughters, Patricia and Angela. Ebony celebrated its 60th anniversary in 2005 and on the 8th August 2005, two days after some of the members of the Jamaica Society, Manchester, of which I have been a member since its inception in 1962 when Jamaica achieved its independence, met to discuss the events of the 43rd Anniversary Celebration in the process of telling them that on that very day it was 57 years when I got struck by lightning, the news came on the television that John Johnson had passed away; he was 87 years old. Earl Graves, publisher of Black Enterprise Magazine said, "We have lost a legend, a pioneer, a visionary, as an American he was ahead of his time. Ebony is part of Americana now and the black world". It was Jet, the sister magazine to Ebony that highlighted the viscous and racist murder of the Alabama teenager Emmett Till by the KKK.

It was interesting that once I started the course from Bennet College how many people I discovered that were taking courses by correspondence from overseas institutions in a number of subjects ranging from engineering, accountancy, religion, history and sociology, and over time we became a nucleus of dreamers inspiring each other to reach new heights. The enthusiasm became contagious and on numerous occasions when we wanted to break from the rigours of work and study we would meet at the back entrance to the hotel, which like Hyde Park in London always had a soap box from where one could put the world to right. From the mere fact that employees were drawn from a number of backgrounds and experiences these discussions embodying every subject under the sun were very illuminating. It was not uncommon to sometimes have guests joining in these discussions or debates, which were well organised with a chairman and recorder who would have his exercise book to jot down points of interest. My favourite chairman was Stu McIntosh, The Head Chef, an authentic Louis "Satchmo" Armstrong look-a-like even down to his graveled voice. A very articulate man who grounded himself in the pursuit of philosophy, and a penchant for travelling, a book that he carried with the stamps of the various countries that he visited working on cruise and cargo liners in their catering department validates the fact that he had been around the world more than once. He was head-hunted from the Waldorf Astoria Hotel in New York and it was from him that I further developed my interest in boxing as a spectator. He was a walking encyclopaedia on the sport and was never out of The Ring magazine, published by Nat Fleischer. On the subject of making efforts to achieve he said that, "You cannot soar to the heights with the eagles if you are hanging around with the chickens". On women he said that, "they should be angels abroad and devils in bed". Throughout the three years that I knew him I have never heard him swear, yet by the same token one knew that whenever he started walking or rather rocking from side that things were not running to his expectations, his disapproval peppered with the words 'absolutely baloney', 'kaput', 'poppycock' and 'I run a god damn tight ship and I expect every man to know his job'.

Of the many things that I admired about Stu is that he did not bear grudges; I recalled the time when someone slipped into my room whilst I was in the bathroom and stole my money, a brand new pair of Three Castles shoes, and a suit length imported from George Odom from Bradford, England by an employee of the hotel who had just started in that line of business. In trying to help me come to terms with my loss Stu started from the premise that I had not followed the golden rule of man, mind thyself and the extent to which I had made it easy for the theft to be committed. In keeping with Shakespeare he reminded me that the person who stole my possessions and not my good name and it was important that I put it down to experience and move along. Within weeks of the incident the person I suspected of relieving me of my possessions was caught red handed and given a thorough working over before he was handed over to the police, that was the then Jamaican thing. I doubt if the status quo has changed.

123

George Oddom and Lennard's were two of the traditional English Mail Order Companies that Jamaicans dealt with just after the ending of the second world war and there is the story that with the advent of migration to Britain many Jamaicans who settled in cities or towns where they had connections either through correspondence courses or importing goods were always keen to make contacts with these institutions. As it happened two Jamaicans arriving in Bradford went to seek out George Oddom. Instead of a large factory it turned out the business was being run from a small shop, however they were made to feel welcome and after being shown around they had the opportunity to view a range of materials whilst looking at an eye-catching bit of material. Mr Oddom said to them this is going at twenty five shillings per yard; the most loquacious of the two Jamaicans, astonished at the price of the material, said to his friend, "Rass Clot". On hearing this Mr Oddom replied, "No sir, it is the best mohair on the market".

If my interest in sartorial appreciation was heightened at Tower Isle it could in no way match with that of my political and religious awareness. There were people who were Anglicans, Baptists, Roman Catholics, Methodists, Presbyterians, Adventists, Humanists, Christian Scientists, Jehovah Witnesses, Revivalists, Rastafarians, Buddhists and Bahai. Over time I was able to read, or at least browse, through some of their literature which was freely available at the same time and I had the confidence and the willpower not to have been taken in by everything that I read. There were also a significant number of people who were members of fraternal organisations such as Masons, Buffalos, Mechanics, Forresters, Rosicrucians, Elks, and in a number of cases adherents of the organisations and some members of leading churches kept quiet about their membership, suffice it to say in times of crisis they showed a high level of commitment in the supporting of good causes. Like the Churches and fraternal groups members of staff were supporters of the two major political parties, the Jamaica Labour Party and the People's National Party. Their party allegiances were reflected in membership of the Bustamante Industrial Trade Union (BITU) of the Labour Party or National Workers' Union (NWU) of the People's National Party. There were also those people who espoused their belief in communism, Garveyism, Marxism and Leninism; again I had the opportunity to read literature on these subjects and at a time when Jamaica, in line with other British Caribbean Islands, was moving towards the formation of a West Indian Federation and ultimate independence political debates were at the back gate.

With my earlier awareness instilled by my father and members of his generation on the impact of Marcus Garvey on the Jamaican Society, I found great pleasure in not only listening but contributing to the debates that were in keeping with the creating of a system that would enhance the future for all

Jamaicans. It was during one of these discussions that Francis, one of the cooks, lent me a copy of The Blackman, one of Garvey's publications. Dog-eared and crumpled with age, it was obvious that it had seen better days, notwithstanding that it carried a list of the policies that Garvey intended to implement if he was elected to the Jamaican Legislative Council in 1925. I was drawn to many aspects of his manifesto, in particular to those that stressed the importance of providing schools in all the main towns in Jamaica where students would be able to study at night in the pursuit of furthering their education and also employers having insurance policies to take care of their workers during sickness. As a young man just beginning to make my way in life I felt that Marxism did not have an appeal to me for the very fact that I could not identify or have a wider world view of an industrialised society such as Britain. In time, as knowledge increased I was to become more aware of the vagaries of European societies and the correlation between Capitalism, Socialism, and Nationalism and the strategies that I would need to devise for my own survival, whether at home or abroad.

Despite Francis, the cook, showing enough interest as to lend me the copy of The Blackman, I have never told him that I was doing a correspondence course in Bookkeeping. At least he knew that I was very keen on sports, hence when he suggested that I join the National Workers' Union and work myself up to be a Union Rep. I was rather taken aback in that other than through sharing in discussions and our interest in Garveyism, we knew nothing of each others background yet he saw it necessary to encourage me to pursue a career in which I would be able to influence changes for the betterment of people; in essence he was helping me to enlarge my vision and I was glad that he reminded me that in order to fulfill my potential I would have to stretch my faith to the limit.

Two days after joining The National Workers' Union I walked into the staff dining room, which was a cauldron of agitation and planned revolution. I had never witnessed anything like that before; there was no doubt that things were reaching confrontation level. All I could hear were, "This is Jamaica and not the deep south of America", "Every man is a man" and "One out all out". As it happened Jenkins and Johnson, two bar waiters, whilst on their day off in Kingston met two guests at the Hotel, man and wife, who were sightseeing and asked them to join them for lunch at the Myrtle bank Hotel, also owned by the House of Issa. Whether it was an over zealous member of the Tower Isle executive staff or a jealous member of the Myrtle Bank staff who saw them, it was never made clear. Like the Jamaican Calypso that was quite popular at the time, "I nearly lose my life in Spanish Town because of a talking parrot that was around", Jenkins and Johnson were reported for fraternizing with guests from the hotel and without even making any attempts to ascertain the facts the management made a decision to fire them. The decision was leaked and even before they had seen the management, which again reinforced what I learnt even before I went to school that dogs who take a bone to you will also take a bone from you; hence the importance of seeing and be blind, hearing and be deaf, and to be dumb likewise.

It soon became evident that whatever discussions that were being held between the local union representative and management things were moving towards a go-slow and a possible walk-out by dinner which usually started at seven o'clock. I have never been involved in a strike before but after hearing the reasons why these two workers were to be fired I made it quite clear that I was prepared to join those who would be walking out; as it happened the whole matter was resolved without any further action and likened to 'a storm in a tea cup'. Even so R A Brown, the local union rep, attested to his skills as an effective negotiator in the same diplomatic mould as John Foster Dulles, the American Secretary of State who used atomic weapons as the vehicle to stave off the threat of communism in the fifties.

In their effects to nullify the strength of the union amongst the rank and file members, management devised a strategy by re-classifying the structure and status of staff so whereas originally the decision process was centred around a few people; more became involved, which helped boost morale amongst the staff. These experiences helped in shaping my decision that one day I would go into representational politics; in this respect I was rather fortunate to have met Sydney James from Ocho Rios, Political Activist, owner of limousines that ferried tourist throughout the island and proprietor of the Cotton Tree Club situated on the main road leading out of Ocho Rios to Tower Isle. It was noted for its excellent preparation of Jamaican dishes, and first class entertainment provided by aspiring local musicians to showcase their skills, which led to a majority of them being recruited from the Cotton Tree to work in the prestigious hotels in Jamaica, other Caribbean Islands and on the cruise liners. Comrade James, as he was popularly called, was fearless in articulating the needs of those who were less fortunate, central to that was the emphasis that he placed on people making efforts to improve themselves. One of his abiding messages was that 'Manna stop fall from heaven, God help those who help themselves'. These words struck resonant chords within me and the more I observed his way of working with people the more that I was able to appreciate that the person who does not have the capacity to conceive a dream is the person more difficult to motivate.

It was not uncommon to go in the club, or whilst you were there, to see Comrade James holding court with leading sportspersons, politicians, union officials, or for that matter people from a wide cross of interest, especially those who had their allegiance with the People's National Party. It was during one of these sessions that I met Thossy Kelly of The National Workers' Union, who mentioned that Ruskin College at Oxford, England, offered correspondence courses for members of Trades Unions worldwide. I was already pursuing my bookkeeping course from Sheffield and did not want to 'change horses mid-stream'.

In this world there are always those people who will stop at nothing to upset the apple-cart, some will even go to the extent to create conflict and controversy in an empty house. This was to reflect itself one morning on my way to work when Comrade James drove up and stopped his car and angrily accused me of wooing one of his members of staff, who in Jamaican lingo 'was one of his squeeze'; according to him from information that he received we were seen shopping in Kingston. Nothing could have been further from the truth because on the day he mentioned when we were seen together I was at work, reason being that I chose to work that day other than taking my time off in lieu which would make it possible for me to travel to Grange Hill in Westmoreland in two weeks time to play cricket.

This particular girl, Sadie, was a cashier in the Club and the first time that I went there she told me that I reminded her of Frankie Lymon, who led the group that sang "Why do fools fall in love". From that day onwards whenever I entered the club she would give a waitress money to put in the juke box starting with none other than Frankie Lymon, followed by "Roses are Red" Bobby Vinton, "Fever" Peggy Lee, "Love me tender" Elvis Presley, and "It's only a paper moon" Nat King Cole. She must have spent a fortune on the jukebox and as far as I can recall, other than us sharing an interest in star signs under which we were born, I was Aquarius, she Sagittarius, which according to us we were compatible, it was a relationship that was as pure as the driven snow, or let me put it the other way round, I had enough street savvy to read the signs emblazoned on Comrade James' white shirts proclaiming "Sadie is mine!" and being from the old school where lessons are constantly being imparted that there is no honour in fooling around with your friend's or boss's woman, or for that matter other men's women period. There is no way that I would want our relationship to be otherwise. I had a feeling that Comrade James realised that there was an element of malicious gossip intended to destroy his relationship with Sadie and one day, when I went into the club, she told me that she had been accepted by a hospital in Leamington Spa to study nursing. It became all the more clearer that my assumptions were right and that the decision that I made to declare myself persona non grata from the club would not have been healthy; that being said I had never heard anything about Sadie and in time Sydney was to become a local Councillor and in perpetuating his memory for his contributions to the upliftment of Ocho Rios and its people, James Street has been named after him. I learnt so much from a man who had a great sense of humility in his service to others.

Notwithstanding our platonic relationship, when Sadie left for England in December 1955 I realised that there was a strong message in what she implied as her going away to better herself, her leaving was also a reminder that "parting is so much sweet sorrow", yet for all that I was determined that I would never leave Jamaica until after I attained the age of twenty one, besides at the time I had a job that I enjoyed, I was enjoying my cricket, in a nutshell life could not have been better.

It was important that in keeping with my mother's Pentecostal tradition of no alcohol, no smoking and no secular music under the roof that I had a quiet family get together at home and one where everything within reason was permissible to mark my twenty first birthday. I chose the Alterry Beach Club at Priory near Saint Ann's Bay for the latter, everything according to prevailing jargon at the time when things are running in order was "just copasetic"; it had to be for the sole reason that I started saving towards it when I started the job at Tower Isle. The strategy that I used for saving towards this event was one that I had learnt from my father when he worked in Cuba and shared accommodation with other people. He obtained an old oil tin which he filled with disused oil and molasses. For eighteen months he secretly placed all his loose coins. I dare say that when I told Fitzhenly, who shared accommodation with me and Adassa, the cleaner, that it was my intention to make honey they poo pooed the idea and dismissed me as an oddball. I am sure that if I had told them that I intended to put money into it they may have thought differently of me, but there again who would want to place their hands into sticky goo to fish money out but as the old saying goes, "Where there is a will there is a way". That being said there was no smell to the stuff, I made sure of that by putting the occasional tip of Bay Rum and my Mennen aftershave into it, a way of keeping everybody sweet and that was the way that those who came to my part looking pretty and very sweet after much eating, drinking, swimming and dancing under a cloudless moonlit night to pulsating music provided by the Serenaders Calypso Band to songs such as "Night Food", "Penny Reel", "O Miss Ida don't you lift up any wider" and many more that left little to the imagination, but, of course, that is what Calypso is all about and the object of my party was to make it a celebration that was real and to reflect the words that were written in one of the many cards that was read by Joe Daay, one of my school friends with whom I played cricket and who was the Master of Ceremonies on the evening, about passing through this world but once, and the onus was on people to do good things in the present life because they may never have the opportunity to pass the same way again.

I was 13 years old and This photo was taken a week before I was struck by lightning on the 8th August 1948. It was defining moment in my life and came literally as 'a bolt out of the blue'.

My Grand Aunt Edith Hyman, who imparted many words of wisdom to me. She died when she was over 100 years old. I communicated with her up until her death in 1978 at the age of one hundred and two; I have always stressed that longevity is on my mothers side of the family and it could be as a result of their diets. It was from Granny Edith that I learnt the skills of making cakes for any occasion, making guava jelly, orange marmalade, tamarind balls and curing meats and fish. Her motto was, "Eat some today, and preserve some for another day."

Above: In my gymnasium in the back yard at Discovery Bay - check out the pecs.

Right: This photo was taken on the day of my 21st birthday.

The handsome young fellow above was mistaken for the jazz musician Miles Davis, the singer Sam Cooke and the boxer Ezzard Charles. One thing for certain is that it IS Whitty Stennett.

My mother and my youngest sister Lyn enjoy the sun outside our house in 1957.

My Cuban girlfriend Gloria Alvarez - she survived the harrowing journey by boat from Cuba with her family, escaping the regime of Batista. She eventually moved to Miami and despite corresponding we eventually lost touch with each other.

Above The New Testament Church of God at Old Folly, where my mother was secretary for 40 years and below, the plaque that was laid there in her memory when she died in 1999.

DEDICATED TO THE MEMORY
OF A FAITHFUL SERVANT
MAUD STENNETT
WHO SERVED IN THIS CHURCH
1948—1988

HER WORK ON EARTH IS DONE
AND HEAVEN'S CROWN WON

R. I. P.

Two views of Bro Eggie House, which my Grandfather, Samuel
Stennett, built in 1893. The original roof was thatched.

**My brother Noel when he worked at the General Post Office
in Kingston, Jamaica.**

I laid two memorial stones to my parents when I visited Jamaica in 2002. Above left, the one commemorating my father, Joseph, and right, to my mother Maud.

My mother during her visit to Connecticut in January 1974.

Above: The first Hurricane that I experienced was in August 19944. It destroyed a large part of our house. The indomitable spirit of the Stennets resulted in almost a completely new structure, which was severely damaged in August 1951 by Hurricane Charlie, rated then as the worst of the 20th Century. Our resolve was severely tested and a better structure was erected which stood firm against all the other storms until September 1988 when Hurricane Gilbert, the master of all hurricanes, struck and left our beloved Harbour View Cottage a total wreck. My brother-in-law, Locksley Clarke, surveys the ruins below.

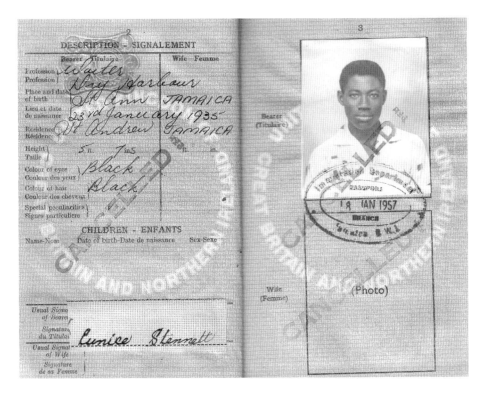

DESCRIPTION - SIGNALEMENT

	Bearer - Titulaire	Wife - Femme
Profession Profession	Waiter	
Place and date of birth Lieu et date de naissance	Dry Harbour St Ann JAMAICA 23rd January 1935	
Residence Résidence	St Andrew JAMAICA	
Height Taille	5 ft. 7 ins	ft. in.
Colour of eyes Couleur des yeux	Black	
Colour of hair Couleur des cheveux	Black	
Special peculiarities Signes particuliers		

CHILDREN - ENFANTS

Name-Nom	Date of birth-Date de naissance	Sex-Sexe

Usual Signa of Bearer
Signature du Titulaire

Eunice Stennett

Usual Signa of Wife
Signature de sa Femme

Bearer (Titulaire)

Wife (Femme)

(Photo)

18 JAN 1957

Have passport will travel. In 1959 Jamaica had yet to become an independent country so passports were issued by British Foreign and Commonwealth Office. I travelled to the motherland on 12th August, 1959. I can recall in the process of packing my case, Granny Edith and my mother were not happy that I was taking my cricket bat and cricket boots with me; they said that from what they heard it was always raining in Manchester.

Here I am on my wedding day with Gwen on 14th January, 1961 at the Claremont Road Congregational Church in Moss Side. The officiating minister was The Reverend Dorothy Havergal-Shaw MA.

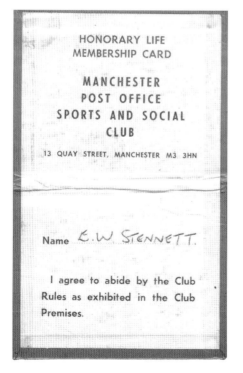

HONORARY LIFE
MEMBERSHIP CARD

MANCHESTER
POST OFFICE
SPORTS AND SOCIAL
CLUB

13 QUAY STREET, MANCHESTER M3 3HN

Name E.W. STENNETT.

I agree to abide by the Club Rules as exhibited in the Club Premises.

My Post Office Sports and Social Club Life Membership card.

With my soul mate
Rennie Henry when
we were members of
the Manchester
Regiment of the
Territorial Army
based in Ardwick in
1961.

In army fatigues at
Millom camp in
Cumbria
in July 1963.

Above: The GPO team of 1963 that played in the Manchester & District Wednesday League. Front row (l to r): Tony Clough, Roy Tomlinson, Frank Johnson, Derek Hill, Euton Christian, Tommy Conroy. Back row: Tommy Horniman (Manager in suit), Terry Lawton, Frank Coglan, Me, Carl Garner, Mick Mannion, Ken Knight and Tony Mills.

Below: The National Dock Labour Board team in Salford. Front row (l to r): Ken Hamilton, Carl Marriott, Stan Boyd, John Stephens, Gerald Essue. Back row: Guy Hall, John Rourke, Alvin Stephens, Myron Hull, Me, Philip Burton, Hermon Bogle, Brian Nolan, Phil Morris and Newton Currie.

This picture appeared in the Manchester Evening News in 1963 when I was 28 years old. I was blowing up a hot water bottle, showing the power and capacity of my lungs. All those years in the open air in Discovery Bay had not been without their benefits.

Above: 1976 and that great West Indies team are in town. Michael Holding, the fast bowler, takes centre stage at Old Trafford as he passes on some of his skills to St John's Youth cricket team. From left to right: Dennis Pitterson, Junior Powell, Cedric Powell, Junior Binns, Glen Pitterson, Dave Thomas, Holding, Cedric Edwards, Earl Stephens, Ricky Coleman and Carl Duncan.

Below: St John's Youth team again with myself as coach on the left standing. Next to me is Rev. Tony Durrans (Chairman), then Trevor Barclay, Cleveland Blissett, Junior Powell, Ricky Coleman and George Blissett (Treasurer). Kneeling (from l to r) are Jarvis Brown, Earl Stephens, Dave Thomas and Cedric Edwards.

In the 1970s I appeared on the Tom O'Connor hosted game show Zodiac.

Officials of St John's Cricket Club with representatives of Bass North West Brewery, who handed over cricket gear to the club in May 1980. From left to right: Myself (Secretary), Rev. Chris Ford (Chairman), Mr Anthony Price (Area Manager - Bass), Victor Lovelock (Captain), Mr Stewart Livingston (Director Outside Operations - Bass) and Mr Charles Kelly (Landlord - Shrewsbury Hotel).

The day following the revelry, my brothers, Egbert and Noel, and myself went to see Mate Wallace and, although he was not in bed, he complained of not feeling well, which was the reason for his absence from the family get together at my house to mark my twenty first birthday. This was much more than a meeting of minds, it was the acknowledgement of my attainment of manhood and the responsibilities that it carried. There was the sense of elation on my part that so far I had faced the challenges that life offered and with self-determination I was willing to continue. I was aware that they felt the same way too and in between preparing a meal of tripe and beans, which is one of my favourite dishes, I used the opportunity to field a number of questions that would have to be answered in adult fashion, and by the same rule putting gossip into some kind of context. I was keen to establish if Mate was our true Uncle and the story relating to how he came to acquire that name was a fictitious one, no doubt my eldest brothers knowing the answers to most of the questions that I wanted answering but feeling that we were in the presence of the most senior of the male relatives so respect was due. In as far as Mate being an illegitimate son of my grandfather, making him our biological uncle, there was no doubt about that by the same rule he expressed his own sadness that his mother chose to have given him her name, Wallace. His acceptance of the fact was grounded in the knowledge that he knew who was his father and his father had never neglected him. In fact the plot on which he lived was given to his mother by his father, Samuel Stennett.

His account of how he got the name Mate was completely different from the one that I heard growing up, that on one of his trips on the Banana Boat from Jamaica to Boston in the United States, he took the mate's uniform to be laundered and when he collected it he wore it to a speakeasy joint to impress the women that he was the Mate on the boat. Unfortunately for him the entertainment got too much for him and he was escorted on board the ship, both the Officer's uniform and himself the worse for wear. On arrival in Jamaica he was paid up and never sailed again. With the exception of having on the Officer's uniform when he boarded ship, all the other information relating to the incident was false and I could sense the amusement in his voice as he relayed what really happened. It started on his second trip when he met Sarah, a woman from North Carolina who was living in Boston. They became friendly and on his third trip she invited him to her apartment and after a meal they went to bed. She had never mentioned to him that there was someone else in her life so it was rather frightening when he heard a loud banging on the door demanding admittance and threatening to shoot whoever was inside with her. According to Mate he hastily started to dress and with presence of mind ripped open the bag with the Officer's Uniform, believing that the irate suitor would have some respect for him. He hid behind the door as she nervously slipped the night latch and true to his word the man did have a gun in his hand to which Mate hit with all the strength that he could muster. The gun fell to the ground and he kicked it under a table and made good his escape through the streets of Boston to his ship where he had to seek out the officer to explain his plight, which was accepted.

The ship had another day in port before sailing and for his protection he was locked away in a room; hence the rumour that he was arrested for passing off as the Mate in charge of the ship; according to him his action was to preserve his manhood, the honour of the Stennetts' name and the pride of being Jamaican. His revelation was well received and I was a bit surprised that my brothers had never mentioned it to me; their explanation was that it is always best to find out things for myself within reason. My eldest brother, Egbert, during the conversation reminded Mate that for all the years that he has been living with his woman, Miss Maggie, to the point of having grown up children, it was important that he gave her the legal status of a married woman. I suggested that by the way in which he responded that it was a long and on-going debate, then as I left the last thing that Mate said to me was, "Whitty I know that sooner or later you will be travelling abroad but when that time comes if you are twenty five years old always tell white folks that you are thirty or thirty five because even when you are eighty some of them will still call you a boy". How right he was as I was to experience quite a number of times.

When I went back to work Noel Harrison from Parry Town, who worked as a waiter and was also doing a correspondence course in electrical engineering, came to see me in the Store Room informing me of his intention to travel to England. His decision was based on the encouragement from his brother in law, Yankee Campbell, who had come back after two years and was planning to go back. Yankee, in his Ford Zephyr Six bedecked with lights, was a real man about town in Ocho Rios, hardly had Noel left the stores when Seymour Williams, another waiter, came in to tell me that he was also planning to leave for England. I could hear the travel bells ringing but the travel bug was far off in terms of stinging.

Within a fortnight of my meeting with Mate and my two brothers I received a telegram that he had died, almost two hours after he took the marriage vows on his bed in the presence of Reverend Wooley, my brother Egbert, his daughter Gwen and Sister Samuels. His sweetheart, Maggie, and himself lived together for over thirty years before he finally married her and I was later to understand that his argument relating to marriage was that true love was stronger than a piece of paper or a silver or golden ring and living happily ever after was a work of art. His passing was a great loss, not only that he was a source of good advice, but he was my only surviving uncle on my father's side.

On the morning of his funeral a small boat with four people on board was towed into the bay by Larky Williams, a local fisherman. The occupants, runaways from the oppressive regime of General Batista of Cuba, had nothing except for the clothes on their backs, which were in an appalling condition. They were not the first, neither were they the last to have landed in the Bay; what was unique is that before their boat touched the shore it sank; an indication of its seaworthiness and the Herculean task that the four members of the Alvarez family performed in using their bare hands to bail the water from the boat. No wonder that they were so weak even to wade ashore had not it been for the assistance of the people on the beach. The possibilities were that occupants on the boat could easily have lost their lives as a result of the deteriorating physical conditions, but despite the meagre resources that we as members of the community had at the time within hours of landing ashore, and in keeping with the way that we were brought up to believe that in the act of being kind to strangers we could unknowingly be entertaining angels, they were provided with food and clothing to await being taken to Saint Ann's Bay Police Station where they were interrogated. In the case of the Alvarez they were to remain at Discovery Bay for four days. On the evening of the second day they came to watch us practice for a match against Oracabessa Cricket Club and it was after practice we took them to the Alcazar Club, not far from the Cricket Ground. Through Claude Scarlett, the local interpreter, I was made to understand that Gloria Alvarez had a likeness for me, according to him I reminded her of Sam Cooke, the African-American singer/songwriter. Her Uncle Pedro tended to differ, saying that I looked like Miles Davis, the African-American trumpet player. Her grandmother Maria saw me in a different light, likening me to a young Ezzard Charles, the African-American world heavyweight boxing champion from 1949-1951. Whilst I was not completely swept away by the tide of adulation in terms of my look-a-like to their African-American cult heroes, it was quite refreshing that nine year old Carlos recognised me in my own right as a cricketer who had the skills to adapt to baseball and do well at it. A further logic to thinking at the time some fifty years ago could well support the argument that the demise of Caribbean cricket is to some extent due to more youngsters in the region being attracted to basketball and baseball.

Gloria was a year younger than I was and of the four, her English was much better than the others and in our conversation during dinner, a mouth-watering delight prepared by Riley the cook at the Alcazar, which started with Pumpkin soup, the main course of rice and peas, fried plantains and coleslaw, for dessert Banana Delight, followed by coffee, she explained to the group of us who sat with them the harsh conditions that existed under Batista in Cuba and the extent to which those people who opposed him were being persecuted.

As representative of the New Revolutionary Movement that stressed the importance of a Cuba for all Cubans irrespective of class, creed, status or colour, it was obvious that the Alvarez were supporters of Fidel Castro and like other members of their family, who a year previously had fled from Cuba, finally settling in Miami, they bemoaned the fact there were many who were not as fortunate as they were to survive the rigours of the high seas, and as such they were looking forward to a future where their lives would be better and they would have the opportunity to serve the cause of the revolution outside of their country than being in it. This philosophy has stayed with me from the very day I arrived in England.

Typical of all light hearted moments in my life when discussions take on board and in no particular order music, sports, gardening, a book that I have read, golf, or cooking. That evening started with the uniqueness and high standard of Jamaican cuisine that started with the first inhabitants, the Arawaks, who left us with some valuable recipes made from sweet potato, cassava and corn. Then the Spaniards, who introduced the banana, plantain and citrus except the grapefruit, and animals such as pigs, goats, and cattle; other Europeans followed and then Africans, Asians, and Chinese, all adding to the vast array of Jamaican dishes. On this point there was an agreed consensus, even to the extent of our Cuban host extending 'Gracias' to the chef, but when it came to the subject of rum, there was no denying that there was a gulf as wide as the 90 miles between Jamaica and Cuba in terms of whether Bacardi was as good as Jamaica's J Wray and Nephew White Rum. What was rather interesting was that whilst Pedro was singing the praises of Bacardi he was enjoying his fair share of Jamaican Rum Punch, calling it Mojito, colloquially speaking he was giving credence to 'when the rum is in the wit is out'.

Be that as it may and on reflection none of us who were involved in the discussion that night would have envisaged that in time Castro would nationalise the Bacardi Rum Distilleries in Cuba and the result of his action would see Bacardi as a multi-national organisation using its political and economic strength to successfully stem the flow of better rums from other Caribbean countries. As I said, we did not have the vision to foresee the political or economic impact of Rum in the Caribbean, but on the night Hopeton James, who was a member of the group, had enough street savvy to avert a situation that could have easily got out of hand when he went on stage and in true Billy Eckstine-like fashion started singing "All the Way", followed by "The Lady is a Tramp" and finishing with "Passing Strangers". The ovation was tremendous as he made his way back on stage, not to be outdone Pedro went on stage, borrowed the guitarist's instrument and after a brief discussion with the other members of the band he started playing Mambo

Number five, giving each member enough time to fall in with their own chord patterns. By the time they had come together the dance floor was packed. Giants at improvisation, Benjie Fairclough on tenor saxophone, Charlie Ward on drums, Kenneth Edwards on trumpet, Joe Hickling on clarinet, Pedro on guitar and Glen Thomas on banjo, they played from Bach to Boogie that evening and at the end of their session there was the feeling that we were all caught up in the rapture.

But, as they say, the night was still young and in the process of patrons southing for more I was literally pushed on stage according to my friends "to do a number", and although Gloria Alvarez felt that I looked like Sam Cooke, and her Uncle Pedro said that I reminded him of Miles Davis, to which I felt was a more appropriate comparison, I was a great admirer of Nat King Cole and because the Church was the bedrock on which we built the foundation to perform I was not daunted by my opening number, "You are my funny valentine", followed by "Answer me oh my love" and finishing with Sam Cooke's "Darling, you send me", to which I struggled but was rescued by Hopeton James, who at the end called Gloria on stage and a trio finished with "When somebody loves you". Kenneth Edwards doing the trumpet solo could only be described as heavenly, or in other words a night made for the opportunity to understand that from the beginning of time, music and food served as an instrument that records our collective emotional sojourns in this world where sufferings, pains, sadness, happiness, and celebrations are all central to the journey of life.

Sadly, these ironies were to present themselves that very evening in the person of none other than the diminutive Dick Francis, who, despite his stature, would go to any lengths to disrupt an event. To describe him as "a nasty little piece of work" was generosity in its extreme. For a start he was much younger than any member of the group involved with the party for the Alvarez, the custom in those days was that age groups interact with age groups, and except in the case where a younger person had a particular skill in academics, sports, music, agriculture, where he or she would be admitted to a senior group the lines of demarcation were clearly drawn and adhered to and custom dictated that it created no controversy or conflict. Dick was always determined to buck the system and on the evening in the height of the celebration he appeared from nowhere with both hands in the air imitating that they were guns and shouting at the top of his voice, "Viva Batista, away with Fidel Castro".

Dick's exit from the club was like a bullet from a gun, hotly pursued by Pedro, who obviously was swearing in Spanish. He was followed by Claude "Leatherneck" Scarlett, and Constable Cunningham from The Discovery Bay Police Station, whose duty it was to see that the Alvarez did not abscond; fortunately Maria and Carlos had left for the station immediately after dinner and did not witness the event which in part was as serious as it was funny. Some of the patrons did leave the club but I stayed with Gloria and in the process of dancing to the band playing "The breeze and I", I reassured her with the words, "Have no fear Prince Stennett is here," to which she replied, "You a prince, I will be princess you promise". Well, as I have always said that promises are comforts to fools, at that particular moment I felt that I could easily be the fool rushing in where angels fear to tread but consoled myself with the fact that the following day I had an important cricket match to which I had invited her family to watch, safe in the knowledge that from what I had gathered they would not be leaving for St Ann's Bay until the following Monday, which meant that we would be able to continue where we left off after the match.

As the band started playing their signature theme "My Mother's Eyes", Pedro, Claude and Cunningham came back into the club. Through Claude Pedro conveyed his depth of anger and frustration that he experienced as a result of Dick's actions, but was also grateful for the kindness that he and the rest of his family received from the majority of the community.

On my way back from the beach on the following morning Claude Scarlett informed me that plans for the Alvarez staying until Sunday had changed and the vehicle was on its way to transport them to Saint Ann's Bay and they would like to see some of the people who had shown so much kindness to them prior to their departure. Seven people came and it was clear that as interpreter, Claude found it hard going translating the out-pourings of gratitude from the Alvarez's and the best wishes in keeping with goodbyes from the local folks. For my part there was a bit of disappointment that they would not be around to see me playing cricket at competitive level, but as the old saying goes 'circumstances alter cases' and as such there was nothing that I could do to stop a Government process from taking its course. The best I did was to write my name and address on the back of a used Four Aces cigarette pack and passed it to Gloria to which she politely accepted, adding that she would write to me when she settled down in Miami. As the police van drove away I wondered to myself what life had in store for them, would we ever meet again and if Castro did gain control of Cuba and things started to go wrong in Jamaica would he entertain Jamaicans in Cuba. I did not have a crystal ball to gaze into the future, besides I was conscious of giving priority to the cricket match that was to be played that very day.

Based on the fact that I was some twenty five miles away from home and was not able to practice with the team as often as I would have liked and just able to come on match days as Captain was not something that I relished. There were also younger players coming through, besides as Captain for nearly three years with a record of leading the side for twenty seven times, playing in all fourteen parishes of the Island, losing eight, drawing four and winning fifteen, at one stage we won six matches on the trot which I felt was quite good, but as they say all good things must come to an end and it was my final match and I was determined to finish with a win.

What with all the wining and dancing until the wee hours of the morning on the day of the match, not to be in tip top condition would be a disaster. Truth of the matter is that from an early age I had disciplined myself to rise early and in the process of maturity discovered that I could boogie before a game and the lost energy in boogieing could be replaced with my own concoction of honey, cerasee, and egg white, on the other hand being a student of the old school had taught the lesson that boogieing before a match not only saps the energy but it also blunts the sharp edge for aggressive competition. To break that rule in my time would almost be like suffering the same fate of being banished into the wilderness of aching heart by women if they found out that a man is a 'kissing and teller'. Oh how times have changed with both electronic and news media portraying people who are willing to discuss every aspect of their private lives and several encounters, whatever the circumstances I will continue to be a student of the old school when it comes to my private life.

Highgate, the team that we were playing, won the toss and as was expected elected to bat. I had just about finished setting the field with the intention of opening the bowling with John Gallimore when the two opening batsmen walked in, one was Campbell who I knew was one of the key people who caused me to lose my job with The Public Works Department. Rather than keeping his mouth shut he turned to me and said, "Eh boy, you still around, I'll see you off today". I was quite upset but I kept my cool, fully realizing that to do otherwise would be an advantage to him. He would be taking first knock whereupon I decided that John would bowl from the other end. My first ball to Campbell he drove me through the covers for four. This was the prelude for Dick Francis, who was chased by Pedro Alvarez on the previous evening from the club, to start barracking me with the words such as, "too much night life", "drunk man can't bowl" and "Fool, fool, captain". Next ball got the same treatment like the first and other spectators joined in the barracking, which is part and parcel of the Caribbean cricket scene where spectators take no quarter, or give no quarter in showing approval or disapproval. My next ball was the Yorker straight into the blockhole which he managed to deal with, but the next ball saw him sitting on his back side. It was sweet music to my ears when Dick and his cohorts barracking, egging the umpire that I was overstepping, was drowned out by spectators with the words "Come on Stennett shake him up, he is not your daddy" and "Bruise him, give us some skin". As if to respond to my followers my next ball was about the most perfect bouncer that I have ever bowled and in the process of taking evasive action he took his eye off the ball, which smacked him flush on the jaw resulting in him being taken off the field quite dazed. Other than being bruised there were no breakages, but he did not take any further part in the match. Although I was quite upset at his behaviour towards me, which I felt was quite disrespectful especially in the light that when I had him sitting on his backside and had gone down with other players to enquire of his well-being, his response was "F...k off Stennett". I honestly had no intention to hurt him, although there were people who felt otherwise, so in my after-match speech, which was customary, in the process of using the opportunity to announce that it was my last game as Captain I openly apologized to Campbell for my actions, which was not intended; as a true cricketer he informed the audience that the war of attrition was entirely of his own making and that he was looking forward to a return match in which he would personally show me that batsmen not bowlers are the Kings of cricket. By the same rule it was quite refreshing when to a tumultuous applause from the audience he intoned that any fast bowler who lacks the ability to intimidate batsmen within the rules of the game should be arrested without bail for impersonation, as the Gods might have decreed we had never met again either on or off field to continue where we had left off.

A further logic of not only the teams achievement but my own ability as a fast bowler was further reinforced after the match when Ronald Seivewright gave me a letter; on opening it I discovered that it was from Alan Shaw 'Pharaoh' Campbell, owner of the Innswood Sugar Estate in Saint Catherine, who had watched the earlier part of the match, went away and had come back for the end. The sum total of the letter was based on my performance on the day and from what he had been hearing about me as a player the offer of a job working as a Scale Clerk at Innswood. Obviously I was pleased by the offer in that by working for the company it would give me more opportunity to play cricket at a much higher level and the possible entry into the national arena and beyond. Although this was my ultimate ambition I have never ever entertained the idea to work in a sugar or rum-producing environment neither for love nor for money. This prejudice was largely due to the oral tradition that brought into context the harsh realities of plantation life in Jamaica and the extent to which earlier generations of Stennetts, at the risk of life and limb, made tremendous sacrifices to escape armed with this sense of awareness. I wrote a letter back to Mr Campbell, who incidentally was not related to the Public Work Campbell, thanking him for recognizing my ability as a good cricketer and the offer of a job, which I would not take up, for the sole reason that I was in employment that I liked.

Expanding the Vision and Raising the bar

Over a drink on the evening after the match, Claude Scarlett told me that prior to leaving for Saint Ann's Bay on the morning Maria Alvarez, who was not present when Dick Francis did his 'Viva Batista Salute', had read the tea cups and it showed that in time Dick would be shot dead. I had by then become so accustomed to the future manifestations of soothsayers, clairvoyants and the like I have always kept an open mind. Maria's was treated in similar fashion as the discussion widened to other subjects, mainly about cricket and the person who would be most likely to take over from me as Captain. One of the many interesting aspects of the discussion was that when I took over as Captain the club was struggling financially, but as they say success breeds success which reflected itself in people contributing generously to the club both in cash and in kind. One of the most expensive elements of expenditure was transportation and it was not uncommon that when travelling to away matches transporter operators like Lanny Lynch would charge us three quarters of the cost and the remainder would be placed in the Club's kitty. I recall Cecil Robinson, one of our local butchers, donating a match ball on the day of the match he turned up with members of his family and friends to watch. At one stage of the game one of the opposition batsmen was hitting the ball all over the ground and Cecil was upset and sent a message via Rook Barrett, who was fielding at long on, that I should change the bowler. I took no notice of him and continued with the bowler. The batsman hit the ball into the crowd near where Cecil was standing, he got hold of the ball declaring "This is my ball" ,which he placed in his pocket, mounted his bicycle and rode out of the ground with some of the players and spectators chasing after him to retrieve the ball. Gully Mouth, a constable at the police station was riding his bicycle on the way to the match and was concerned that the people chasing Cecil were about to do him harm, no doubt they would have done gentle persuasion resulting in him giving back the ball and the game continuing. We did win the match and Cecil, like other benefactors, continued to make their valuable contributions to a cause that was integral to the building of a sustainable community, leadership development and the creating of opportunities where visions could be expanded and bars lifted.

137

CHAPTER EIGHT

Planning for the Exit Strategy

ONE OF the many vagaries that I have learnt throughout my working life is the extent to which large employers and I have reasons to support my argument that sometimes those people who are elected to serve and protect the interest of the workers collude with each other in making decisions that are out of step with the wishes of employers.

Call it downsizing, modernising, voluntary redundancy or whatever, the end result is always the same; the worker being disenfranchised. That being said it was not surprising when it became common knowledge that Arthur Collard, the General Manager at Tower Isle, was paid up and moved on to greener pastures. Hardly had he departed when a shaft of new measures were introduced that saw departments being amalgamated, resulting in staff cuts and an increase in the workload with less staff. Overnight, from an organisation that was running quite smoothly with staff morale at a high standard, cracks started to appear in the structure bringing into focus the effectiveness of the union in terms of how they presented the case of the workers for proper settlement of severance pay. It was evident that not enough time was spent at looking how these issues should be dealt with. Hence there were expressed feelings of frustration amongst members of staff, both from those who wanted to stay and those who wanted to go.

I was one of those who wanted to go, I was twenty two years old and knew that the seven years that I had spent in the hospitality industry had provided me with the necessary hands on skills, starting from gardening through to book-keeping to managing my own small ten bedroomed guest house, which I anticipated building on my own land; that is if I was willing to use the title to raise the loan to complete that project. Over-cautiousness put paid to that dream and over time I had to concur and reluctantly admit that where there is no vision people do perish.

Common sense and practicality dictated that for me to move forward, not only in terms of playing cricket at a higher standard than that which I was used to playing in the country, but also to further my education, I would need to give in to the long-standing and stubborn resistance that I mounted to leave the country to live and work in Kingston. There was no getting away from the fact that the decision to leave the North Coast, with its beautiful beaches, turquoise blue and clear water which I got to from my house in ten minutes, fresh fruits and vegetables directly from the trees, wide open spaces where I was able to wander and get away for solace and a number of other things connected with country life, was not an easy one, but as the saying goes, I had to take the will for the deed. At the time and in no particular order both options were important for my progression.

Adjusting to life in Kingston was much more than I had expected. For a start, I was hampered by not having the Third Jamaica Local Examination Certificate, which made entry much easier into jobs with the Prison Service, The Fire Service, The Post Office and Mental Health Service at Belle Vue, the only Health Service Agency at the time that employed male nurses and took people on for casual work on a daily basis. In my case I was taken on in that capacity with the General Post Office on King Street, starting at one pound two shillings and six pence per day or six pounds thirteen shillings and six pence per week, much less than what I was earning in my last job where food and accommodation was provided and I did not have to pay to travel to work. In addition to all that it was the worst environment that I was to work in; it was every man for himself, a dog eat dog world. Central to that was the constant Kingston person versus country person, similar to the North/South divide in England. An interesting aside was that even the person who had come to Kingston a day previous to another automatically became a part of the group that saw the newcomer as a country bumpkin, one to whom it was easy to sell the clock at parade, or get to buy round upon round of drinks. I was not Slick Whit, neither was I Dumb Whit, and especially that on my first visit to the city some years previous when my wallet was stolen I was more than prepared to deal with some of the distractions. I lived near to Constant Spring at the time, which meant travelling by bus to and from work every day, and for that matter anywhere that I wanted to go in the City. This situation was resolved by buying my first bicycle, a Raleigh, for fifteen guineas. The very day I bought the bike I opened an account with The Victoria Mutual Building Society at their Duke Street Office in Kingston. Having dealt with my mode of travel, which meant a bit of saving and also developing the skills to 'bump and bore', which is riding behind other bike riders and motor cars and when the opportunity arose you overtake them; more than once I have had narrow escapes from serious accidents and in time, after witnessing a fatality, I desisted from the practice. It was as a result of this experience that I went back to reading the bible and to pray, a practice that I gave up a year previously. I felt that I was too busy even to give thanks to God for so many mercies and blessings that were coming my way.

Paying out for food which I could prepare myself was certainly not good economy, and mindful that there was merit in the philosophy that one should have their breakfast, share their lunch with their friends and leave their dinner for their enemies, getting up early in the mornings to prepare my meals was more fun than a chore, at least I was sure what I was eating. As far back as I can remember and throughout my life I carried a prejudice regarding eating outside of my own home.

For all the distractions Kingston was still the place to be at the time, especially in the light that the country was in another phase of change that was leading up to independence. My job as a casual worker involved delivering telegrams sometimes, loading or unloading incoming or outgoing foreign mails, working in the circulation or the parcel department, and after about six weeks as an auxiliary worker, for three months I was attached to the Telegraph Department. It was a cushy number that carried a fair amount of perks, such as getting tips or tickets to go to cricket, boxing, or the cinema from offices, or shirts, socks and sometimes shoes from some of the large department stores.

At the end of the three months probationary period I was taken on permanently; in the meantime a new Postmaster General was sent out from England in the person of Colonel Joe Green, a retired Army Officer. According to the oral grapevine he was sent out by The Colonial Office to keep that vociferous element within the rank and file of the Post Office who saw independence as the only way for Jamaica in check. There was even talk that there were members of the Communist party in that group. Contrary to rumours that Colonel Green had come to root out Communists, or to keep agitators quiet, he was from the outset a man who wanted to promote the well being of the worker. Rather than sitting in his office he was prepared to meet and talk with staff irrespective of their position. This did not go down very well with some members of staff in supervisory positions, particularly when he suggested that the Post Office be a closed department that would make it possible that a person could enter, say as a cleaner or watchman, and through internal examinations work themselves up to at least middle management positions. The hostility against the proposal from some of the group who were in management positions, especially those who got those positions not by merit but by grace and favour, was quite vicious.

I was neither surprised or envious of the hostility that was being voiced. I was fully aware that such was the nature of things in a society where some people were still willing to deny or ignore the harsh realities of the majority of people in their community, so when I overheard two people expressing their disgust for a man who as a result of their position in the organisation would dearly love to be in his company, but the only thing that was making that impossible was the fact that in their own words, he was encouraging every Tom, Dick or Harry in Kingston and those little country boys to take exams to be like them. One went as far to say that he was making plans to go to Britain. Listening to such comments strengthened my resolve to succeed and so on the following day I went to Saint George's Extension College and enrolled to prepare myself for the internal examination . If and when it did happen I was also mindful of what one of the two people had said about planning to travel to Britain, maybe like myself, but for different reasons. I was also making plans for an exit strategy.

Maybe had I not refused taking some clothes to the laundry for a clerk who worked in the Telegraph Department, I could well have spent a longer time there and played cricket for the Post Office much earlier but I could not grant a favour to someone who had the cheek to say in my presence that these stupid country boys should be bundled up and sent back to whence they came. Ordinarily I would have ignored the comment, but that day must have been a bad day for me and I retorted that it takes a stupid person to know a stupid person. Late in the afternoon I got a letter from Squire Gordon, one of the workers who had the responsibility for sorting out the telegrams for us to be dispatched. When I opened the letter it had no name or address to indicate who it was from, it simply stated, "Stennett you will be reported for insubordination with dire consequences". My response was as follows:

> *To whom it may concern and I know that the person who has written to me threatening that I will be reported for insubordination with dire consequences is either a ghost or a nincompoop for the very fact that he or she does not have the guts either to put their name or address or to sign their silly threat to which I am using this medium to say go to hell where you will be burnt to cinders.*
> *I am*
> *E W W Stennett*

I gave my reply to Squire Gordon requesting that he gave it to the person who had given him the letter to give to me the previous day. I was in no doubt that it was delivered and whilst the Bible is a reminder that one should not judge so that judgement would not be meted out, having said that I was convinced of who had sent the intimidating letter. I decided that there was no good reason to let anyone else know of what had taken place, to do otherwise in an environment where gossip and innuendo could well be described as the order of the day would be committing social and surely economic suicide.

My suspicion was confirmed as to who had wrote the letter to me when a bulletin was placed on the noticeboard requesting players to take part in practice matches with a view to selection to represent The Telegraph

Department versus Parcel Post in The Inter-Departmental Competitions. It is from these matches that players were eventually selected to represent The Post Office in The Carib Cup Competition. Eighteen names were placed on the board, which by design was the beginning of my elimination process from the team whereby on the evenings that we had to practice, either I was the chosen one to do overtime, which I had to do unless I could get a swap which never happened, or I was given a batch of telegrams to deliver in opposite directions of the city. It might sound trite to believe it but because I firmly believe that no one has the right to deny another person of their experience, I will state my case of which I am certain that when a boy has lost a father at an early age and has been able to come to terms with it and move on positively, no person other than God can or should phase them ,so when those little tin pot clerks and supervisors were hatching their plots it was of no concern to me whatsoever.

In actual fact it was more than a blessing in that it gave me the opportunity to see some of the most appalling conditions under which people were living, especially in Western Kingston. I could never understand why a majority of those people who were from the rural areas of Jamaica chose to leave an environment where for all its shortcomings at least the ability to grow one's own food was a better option than living in squalid conditions in areas of the city where no provisions were being made either for essential services or housing.

Up until that time, save for a one year lapse in which I did not read the Bible, from time to time when it became necessary I would revisit John Bunyan's Pilgrim's Progress. I read Dale Carnegie's How to Win Friends and Influence People and The Power of Positive Thinking by Norman Vincent Peale. I was a regular subscriber to The Reader's Digest and Ebony and bought The Daily Gleaner every day. I was never short of something to read and as such when I bought a copy of "I am No Slave" from the Author and Publisher Stennett Kerr-Coombs and started reading it I immediately knew that over the years and up until the present time my understanding of self and all that it involved in terms of identity, determination, and preservation remained intact, which placed me above and beyond any considerations and illusions that any one should see or treat me as a victim.

Almost before I could get to the middle of the book, although I had enrolled at The St George's Extension College to do a course, which would start in September, I went to Chetolah Park School, which had the distinction of having one of the most powerful female Jamaican teachers as its head, Mrs Edith Dalton-James, and paid the fee and sat for the Third Jamaica Local Examination in July 1958. When the results were published in late August I had passed with a distinction in English and, of course, my pet subject

142

History. I was then twenty three years old and at the crossroads whether I should stay in The Post Office, join The Police Force or travel to England.

My first cricket match was in May of 1958. By then I had been transferred from Telegraphs to the Circulation Department, with much heavier work involving opening the mail bags from every part of the country, placing the contents onto wheelbarrows or in large skips where they were emptied into large piles and from there to large tables until they were finally sorted for delivery. Given that it was hard work there was a better feeling of camaraderie, due mainly to the fact that a majority of us were from the country. One of the jokes which gained some currency is that 'we were hewers of wood and drawers of water'. Be that as it may we could give a good day's work for a good day's pay as opposed to some of our city fancy dans, but that was the way that the cookie crumbled.

I was to learn two days previously before my first game that had it not been for Miss Tomlinson, popularly known as Miss T and who came from a near white upper class family, I would not have been selected. Apparently some relatives of hers had seen me playing next door to a pitch at Constant Springs Post Office for a team which consisted of gardeners, carpenters, masons, and other occupations and upon enquiry regarding my performance found out that I worked down town for The Post Office; the tongue of good report was in motion and nobody but nobody could deny Miss T. I was in and I knew that I had to give a good account of myself and above all to validate the tongue of good report.

The match, an inter-departmental one, Circulation versus Telegraph A, played at Tinson Pen Oval, being near to the sea it was ideal for any medium pacer who had the ability to bowl the inswinger, or outswinger on a good length. Telegraph won the toss and opened with Rowbotham and Williams, who got off to a very good start. Other than a few balls that I bowled before the start of the game, Anderson, our Captain, had never seen me bowl before, so it was only fair that he introduced me as the number four bowler. By then the two openers were still there having a field day. My first two balls Rowbotham dispatched to the boundary for successive fours. That was as far as he got as the next few balls were played quite circumspectly. The last ball of the over was the outswinger, which he played at resulting in first slip taking the catch; it was my first wicket playing on a ground in Kingston and I will never ever forget the feeling or the moment Circulation won the match. I finished up with six overs, 1 maiden, 47 runs, 3 wickets and I also took a catch fielding at second slips. I went back to work the following day with a sense of achievement, especially when Miss T, who was not at the match, said to me, "Stennett, I heard that you had a good game yesterday, keep it up". But of course not everyone was as complimentary, some of my detractors referred to me as 'a muscle-bound country boy using strength to bowl', others said that I was lucky and that my run up to the wicket was too fast. Some of the criticisms were quite ridiculous, but I ignored them being a scholar from the old cricket school where the taught lesson is that some people who cheer do not know why they cheer and some people who jeer do not know why they jeer.

It was a lesson that I learnt well and I was to play other matches for the Post Office, not without their controversies which ultimately broke the proverbial cmel's back in terms of my exit strategy - more will be revealed in the later part of this book.

If Joe Green, who incidentally was the last Postmaster General from England to head the Post Office in Jamaica, did not get his way in making the organisation a closed department, there was no way that the intermediaries, who were the buffer between him and the lower grade staff, could stand in his way in the reorganising of the whole structure that saw staff who never lived or worked in the country being transferred and staff from the country coming to the city.

It was a very chastening experience for some people who suddenly saw the importance of seeking allies from the very group whom they had objected to, being part of meritocracy to challenge Joe Green hardly was that possible. We had our own battles to fight in that reorganisation was also affecting us with the introduction of a rotating system where, for example, one week I would be in the Circulation Department, the other week I would be in the Bulk Letter or Parcels Division. The intention was to give all-round hands on experience of the workings of each Department. Every Department had their unique characters; in The Circulation Department there was Mr Newman, whose sobriquet was the Phantom. He knew the operations of the Department inside out and he did not suffer fools gladly, he was straight and direct both with his praise and criticism. I recall when I swam from Gun Boat Beach, off The Palisados Road, to Bournemouth Beach in the then annual Pepsi Cola Cross The Harbour Race, the following day when my work colleagues were making much of me, Phantom broke up the back-slapping interlude by announcing, "Mr Stennett, you are getting too popular, next move I will be sending you to Parcel Post to rotten". On the other hand, there was a spate of pilfering where it was alleged that persons within the department were in collusion with outsiders to sign for registered items, which resulted in handwriting experts from the Police Department being called in to test handwriting. When it was my turn Phantom said to The Chief Superintendent of the Department, "Mr Fox, leave that sportsman Stennett. He does his work and like the Chinaman, he sees no evil, do no evil and speaks no evil". Another occasion there was Smallpiece the Watchman, who would often fall asleep in the canteen. As it happened Joe Green and Phantom were having a walk around inspecting the building. On hearing the heavy snoring, Phantom went and stood over Smallpiece saying, "Sleep on Mr Smallpiece, sleep on, because as long as you are asleep you have a job, but when you awake you will be out of a job, so sleep on". The quality of mercy prevailed and Smallpiece was suspended for two days and on return to work got a job loading and unloading mail van,s where he had no time to even scratch his head, never mind slipping across the road to the bar for a Q.

In the process of reorganisation Joe Green was to find himself coming into conflict with the Postmen who did deliveries in and around the city. These rounds were valuable to these man and any change was seen as the destroying of a way of life for men who joined the service very young. Some had joined the Army and volunteered to serve overseas and on return went back to their jobs as Postmen. Loyal Servants to the British Crown Overseas, at home they were determined that their militancy would win out.

Phantom was to find himself more on the side of management as opposed to that of the workers and when he suddenly fell ill and was off work for a long time a card was placed on the noticeboard intended for him. The quote was from Ecclesiastes Chapter II Verse 13, which read, "If the clouds be full of rain they empty themselves upon the earth, and if the tree fall towards the South or toward the North in the place where the tree falleth there it shall be". The card was taken down and the general consensus was by one of his cronies. In the meantime there was some kind of truce where both sides were like dogs barking but not biting.

Phantom got better and on his return to work he personally placed on the noticeboard a card in his own handwriting quoting from Micah Chapter 7 Verse 8, which read, "Rejoice not against me O mine enemy when I fall I shall rise again, when I sit in darkness the Lord shall be a light unto me". Almost immediately a meeting was called requesting management fire the Phantom on the grounds that according to one worker, "He had come back to mow us down". There was very little that management could have done to accede to the demands of the workers. Phantom was to have the last word when he stood up and faced his detractors, telling them, "You can beat me but you cannot beat my word"; such was the measure of the man who for all his faults I did admire for telling things as he saw them.

Whether by accident or by design, Phantom's return to work saw me being transferred to the Bulk Mail Department and not Parcel Post "to rotten" as he said he would. The Bulk Mail Department dealt with items that could not be classified as letters because of their size, neither could they be classified as Parcels because of the contents within them. They were mostly newspapers, catalogues and books. The man in charge of the Branch was none other than

145

Mr Blake, otherwise known as Colonel, an Ex-serviceman of the Second World Ward who saw active service with the British Army in Belgium. He was a disciplinarian in every sense of the word. The first morning that I started he said to me, "Mr Stennett, there are some things that I need to let you know. Firstly, at all times I will address you as Mr Stennett and I will expect you to address me as Mr Blake. Secondly, you are provided with a uniform and I am expecting that not only you wear it but it must be clean at all times and your shoes like your cap badge must be properly polished. Thirdly, I expect that you work with your colleagues to make this place spick and span at all times, team work must be the ideal. Fourthly, as young men I know that from time you will be involved in discussing a number of topics but try never to reach a point where you want to settle your argument with a fight. At times we have to agree to disagree. Finally, Mr Stennett, I will never ask you to do something that I cannot do myself. These are the rules and providing you try and stick with them I don't see why we should not get along".

Colonel Blake did run the branch like a crack army unit and I take it that Joe Green got a visit, which was always unannounced and resonated a sense of pride in him; every aspect of the job had some link with life in the Military, which I found quite fascinating and when I arrived in England and joined the Territorial Army getting used to the way of life was quite easy. During one of Joe Green's visits to the Branch I was in the midst of telling my colleagues what it was like swimming across the Harbour. So as not to give the impression that we were simply wasting time, Colonel told him what the discussion was all about; rather interestingly he stood listening and at the end asked what was the highlight of the experience. I told him that it was being able to look up at the mountains and to appreciate how beautiful Jamaica is. It was rather refreshing when he concurred that it was the very same impression that both his wife and himself had when they sailed into Kingston Harbour. As he was about to leave Colonel said to him, "By the way Sir, Mr Stennett was once struck by lightening", to which he replied, "Provided you had heard the blast you are alive". When he left Colonel said, "Lads, I have made sure that Mr Stennett's name will be mentioned in Dispatches". I guess that must have been music in his ears as we all started clapping and shouting "Good one Colonel".

Compared to the Circulation Department there was a much better bonding amongst those who worked in the branch, young men we were with our strengths and our weaknesses and also our vices and our virtues. My vice was playing the Chinese Numbers Game, Peaka-Pow and Droppan. It all started when Dick Francis, of the Alvarez fame, who I got an apprenticeship as a motor mechanic with John Crook, one of the leading importers of motor cars in Jamaica at the time, came to see me one lunchtime telling me that he had a dream in which my Uncle Mate told him to tell me that I should use the number three bus. Dick insisted that I lend him some money to buy number three which in Drop Pan signifies Dead Man. I gave Dick five shillings, telling him to use one shilling for his lunch and the remainder for buying number three. As he made his way in the busy lunchtime crown up Mark Lane where the Peaka-Pow Shop was situated, I said to myself, ' bye bye Dick, bye bye my five shillings'. I returned to work thinking that I had been taken for a ride, this was definitely not the case when just as I was about to take my bicycle from the rack to ride home Dick appeared with one of the widest grins that I have ever seen. Excitedly he informed me that number three played and my share of the pot was five pounds twelve shillings, with the five shillings that I had given him for his lunch he bought the same and got one pound eight shillings. On my way home I stopped at Miss Kirlew's, who operated a bar at Mary's Brown Corner and who also ran a partner, to find out if I could join. As it happened she ran two partners, one for thirty shillings per week which had twenty people, which meant that in the year each person would receive two pay outs. The other was one pound per hand for ten people which meant four payouts in each year. I took both hands based on what I was taking home even without overtime, which was quite infrequent when working the Bulk Mail branch.

Whether it was the gambler's lucky streak that kicked in or it was the fun derived from working out which numbers are most likely to be played on certain days, thanks to Dick this venture was beginning to prove profitable, and I dare say very profitable that it is if I was willing to up my stakes. Caution dictated that winning with small stakes meant big smiles, losing with big stakes meant bigger cries; in essence I was winning enough not only to pay my partner but to save so as to satisfy my fetish buying shoes. The downside to playing the numbers was that one ran the risk of being arrested if caught buying on the premises or losing out on substantial amounts of money if during the time of the premises being raided the raiding officers confiscated the cash. There was one theory that in a number of cases when these raids did take place it was a collaboration between the owners and the raiding officers, who split the spoils amongst themselves. In all my time buying numbers it was only once when a raid took place. I had gone in to find out what numbers played so when the Officer asked my name with the view of prosecuting me for purchasing numbers I challenged him on the basis that I had no numbers on me to prove that I did make a purchase. The Chinaman agreed and as a result I walked off the premises and I could tell that the police officer was annoyed. At least that was what Joe Daay, my friend who was a serving officer at Central Police Station, told me. It wasn't long after that incident that the said Officer was suspended from the Force for taking bribes. Over the years changes saw Drop Pan and other forms of gambling being legalised and whenever I go to Jamaica I always make sure to buy my favourite number three Dead Man, number thirty two, Gold …..number 35 Vagina or Goat. More often than not I would win at least enough to buy what I want.

As I have always said, I started hearing about the birds and the bees as an eleven year old youngster fielding in the slips with the senior members of my village cricket team. Just how they were able to talk in parables about the female spectators sitting beyond the boundary and at the same time holding on to some fantastic catches sill remains a mystery to me. Learning about what the birds and the bees do was to follow much later, almost in tandem with my progression as a cricketer, so when Kenny Rowe, one of my colleagues from St Elizabeth's, who was one of the three postmen assigned to take Bulk Mail on cycles to various addresses, promised to take me around to show me some of the clip joints on his round, I can't say that I was over-enthusiastic. By the same rule I introduced him to playing the numbers so courtesy demanded that I acceded to his request. Some of these places were dimly-lit Rum Shops with a jukebox and in the majority of cases barmaids with smiles and curves to match, sufficient to induce the combination of a miser and a teetotaller that from time and within reason at the expense of thriftiness and abstinence the name of Baccchus is worthy to be praised.

These shops were also venues where dominoes were being played and every topic under the sun discussed, sometimes in over-animated fashion. Others were much bigger establishments offering the same fair ,and in some cases were favoured by more adherents of political parties. The large establishments on Kenny Rowe's round were ones that were synonymous with a song that was being pumped out on Radio Jamaica at the time. The words were, "Money is King, it can get you almost anything, when of the lady you are not sure money can open the bedroom door". These establishments and the clients who used them often attracted the rebukes and ire from the fire and brimstone preachers who would always conclude that if daylight should suddenly take place after nine o'clock at night in Kingston it would be of great surprise to see some of the people who patronised such establishments. Whether the preachers were speaking from experience or hearsay was made much more clearer when Kenny Rowe mentioned to me the second time when I went out with him that it was not so much as the people who used the establishments but it was the people who owned them; some were leading members of the community. He was further to inform me that outside of making deliveries in the areas his other interest was strictly business, in that as a result of a relative who was a serving member of the Jamaica Constabulary who knew of his bookkeeping skills through working with the West Indies Sugar Company, who recommended him to one of the proprietors to do his stocktaking, word got around regarding his skill and within a short time he had four shops he was doing the books for and would have taken two more, that is if I wanted to help him. This was based on the fact that he heard that I was doing a correspondence course in bookkeeping from Bennett College in Sheffield, where he himself had done a similar course. His ambition was to travel to Canada where he had an Uncle and as far as doing stocktaking and keeping books was according to him something that I was not keen to do. Having said that the few times that I did go around with Rowe was to prove a sharp learning curve in my understanding of another aspect of my City life. For instance, I was to learn that people who hire barmaids would rather the maid wear slippers as opposed to close up shoes whilst on the job, preventing them slipping money into their shoes. Other tricks were male friends drinking all night and not paying. The most common of the tricks was barmaids filling bottles with water and placing them in cases of the genuine stuff; this practice was mostly applied to white spirits such as Gin, Vodka and Rum.

Kenny Rowe knew all the tricks and one of his golden rules was never to drink where he did his part time job, one of his favourite watering holes was Doris Bar on Johns Lane, popular with newspaper hacks, sailors, seamen, soldiers, policemen, in fact people from all walks of life. I recalled when I became a Local Councillor in 1993 representing the Clifford Ward in The Metropolitan Borough of Trafford. Peter Garde, one of the Mayor's Attendants, on learning that I was Jamaican, told me of his experience as a cadet working on a ship that went to Jamaica and going into Doris Bar when he met, according to him, this beautiful Jamaican lass. Hardly had he sat down she was on his knees whispering sweep nothings in his ear to the point where the money in his wallet sent him a telegram informing him that it needed spending, saving that it was about to explode to which he immediately responded by opening his wallet and gave the young lady a pound note to buy the drinks. Two rounds came to seven shillings and sixpence, almost at the point of finishing the second round and she got up and politely told him that she would be returning with twelve shillings and six pence change. That was the last he saw of her, the year was 1958. Thirty five years later he was still waiting for his change, reflecting rather philosophically that it was all part of growing up, which rang a chord with me when Kenny Rowe said to me, "Sten, you need to have eyes in the back of your head and your brains working overtime because some of these women will take milk out of coffee". Contrary to popular belief that Kenny was burning the candle at both ends and that he was god's gift to womanhood, he was a sober and intelligent man who knew how to live with all types of people without causing offence.

One of his philosophies was based on the creating of situations where it was possible to avoid conflict with others. In my time I had witnessed women engaged in fights with other women for the menfolk, but the one that was to astound me was when I saw two women raising blows on each other for a man who in the process of dynamiting fish had his entire wrist blown off. When it was explained to me the reason why they were so attracted to him the knowledge was one that passeth all understanding. That being said it was even more hilarious that when a man to whom Kenny had lent some money, instead of repaying him he took two of his friends to beat Kenny, who was little over five feet four inches tall. Undaunted by their threats, Kenny went and got two women to defend him. Like the biblical Goliath, one of the two ruffians was disrespectful to the women but one was far from being phased as she held him by the collar of his shirt, pulled him in close and head-butted him saying, "That's from my little Kenny". Rather than retaliating the man mounted his bicycle with his two accomplices chasing behind shouting obscenities at the two women. A smiling Kenny said to me, "Sten, always have women to protect you, they will never let you down, especially if you treat them good". Over the years I was to prove him right, giving credence to the adage that, "The hand that rocks the cradle rules the world".

CHAPTER NINE

Messages in the Winds

THE HURRICANE of 1958, though not as severe as that of 1944 when I was nine years old and the one in 1951 when I was sixteen years old, did leave its share of damage and the social and economic hardships and sufferings allied to such damages.

Whether it was through providence or destiny why I had chosen to take my first seven days leave from the Post Office during the week that the hurricane struck I will never know. It was my first time of going back after six months in Kingston and I recall on the second day on my way from the beach, two of my friends, Pole Reid and Pat Wilmott, invited me to come along with them later that evening to shoot birds in the Old Fort bushes where The Kaiser Bauxite Company built an airstrip during their operations in the area during the early sixties, and it is still being used.

The gun, a single barrelled twelve bore was owned by Mrs Mahala Kennedy, one of the local land Baronesses who was the licensed keeper. She loaned the gun to Pat Wilmott, whose father was a Member of Parliament for North Western St Ann. Knowing Pat, I am convinced that he would have persuaded her that his dad's licence covered him. To be fair Pat had a reputation as a good shot following in the footsteps of his father and I felt confident as he explained the precautions that we needed to take, for instance not going over a fence or a gate with a loaded gun. As far as I was concerned the experience of firing a gun at a bird in flight would be another notch to my sporting portfolio. That was never to be because as we took up our positions the plan was that Pat would fire first, Pole would follow and I would be last. As we looked up there was a flock of White Belly flying towards us when I said "Mark over Pat", to which he aimed and fired but the shot did not exit. Pole took the gun and peered down the barrel, in a split second I raised my hand hitting the barrel of the gun only to hear it going off. The secretion of flight took over and the perspiration flowed freely as I headed for home, passing a number of people who I knew were concerned as to why I was running so fast; in my younger days they would not need to ask why I was running, the answer would have been I was running from an irate man whom I had called a nickname, who, if he managed to catch me would more than likely give me a good hiding. I was noted for calling people names that stuck, but none of them have ever laid hands on me; I was too fast on my legs. That was the prerequisite if you were in the habit of calling people names!

I was no youngster at the time, I was twenty three years old, or in other words I had put away childish things so naturally when I got home that evening, panting like a horse, wet with perspiration, my mother was quite concerned, even more so when I refused to have dinner, my favourite stew peas and rice followed by carrot juice. Mother knew that it would be pointless exerting any pressure to ascertain my predicament, as for me I expected the prelude to the worse would be bawling signalling that there is a tragedy. My own calculation in terms of the time that it took running from the Fort bushes to my house and the time that Mrs Kennedy would have waited for Pat to return the gun before raising an alarm was moving much further away from panic stations, but even then my mind was far from being at ease. It was around twilight when Pat and Pole turned up at my house, apparently Pole fainted when the gun went off, fortunately for him, Pat as a serving member of the Army and Air Cadet Force applied his skills in first aid. In the process of trying to relive the experience it was beginning to get more clear that of the three of us, Pat was the only one who had a sense of what had really happened. Pole had no recollection of hearing the explosion and to my surprise Pat said that when I ran off it was in the opposite direction that I went and I did turn back whilst Pole was sitting on the ground. I had no recall of what he was saying other than feeling relieved that we were all still alive.

As I have alluded my Mother was a fountain of wisdom and generosity, in all the time that I knew her I cannot remember any one coming to our house and not having something to eat. As all three of us sat around the table she remarked of smelling sulphur to which Pat, a man blessed with the gift of the gab, told her that we went shooting birds and the one that he shot when I went to retrieve it, a mongoose, got to it first and I gave chase after the mongoose. He continued with his spin telling her how good I was with a gun, to which she replied that with the exception of playing a musical instrument I was like her Uncle Fred who was good at cricket, very good at swimming, and good at shooting both with a catapult and a gun. As far as using a catapult I could hold my own amongst the best of my contemporaries and my mother knew this, hence she did not buy Pat's line of argument at how good I was at using a gun. Female intuition on her part dictated that there was no good reason to contradict my friend, suffice to say that when my friends left that evening whilst I did not give an exact account of what had happened she was nevertheless quite upset to know that I had used a gun or was in the company of somebody whom I did not ask if they had a licence to use one.

Listening to her was enough to make me realise that if there was a situation where the police had to be called we would be in trouble, which ultimately would make it rather difficult for me to realise my dreams. Fortunately, nothing happened, but on the other hand if it had it would more than likely be Pole who would have suffered the most, given the fact that according to him he did not hear the explosion. His explanation was that when he was on the ground he "was playing mongoose", in other words pretending. Well, I have always known and the whole village recognised that he was the best dancer for miles around, no doubt he wanted another string to his bow and maybe to see himself as the fictitious mongoose that Pat referred to did something to his ego, which helped to reinforce my belief that even in the time of conflict and discomfort one can find humour. That being said my Mother's quiet but riveting words of rebuke were enough to see me keeping away from guns until when I travelled to England and joined the Territorial Army; as it turned out I was a pretty good shot but more about that later.

Recognising that my feeling of well being had been somewhat deflated my mother, for the evening's family devotion before retiring to bed, chose that I read from Ephesians Chapter Six, which starts, "Children obey your parents in the Lord for this is right". She insisted that I read Chapter Twelve three times, which makes the emphasis that this is the word, the fight is not against flesh and blood but against those in high office who are not equitable in their dealings with other folks. As maturity took its rightful progression I was able to appreciate that even if my mother was not able to follow all the precepts of the Bible, which indeed is a very tall order, she had that sense of consciousness which placed her in a position to believe in herself in combination with a supreme being that is all powerful.

On the morning when it was announced on the radio that a hurricane was building up in the Caribbean and it was more than likely that if it continued on its path it would hit Jamaica, I received a letter from Gloria Alvarez telling me that she had settled in Miami but would rather be in Jamaica with me, or if there is any possibility of me making plans to come and live in Miami. I was flattered with the contents of her letter, which I put down to the hospitality and kindness that was extended to her family during their short stay by The Discovery Bay folks. Regarding me making plans to live in Miami it was not something that I have ever thought about; for a start any travel away from Jamaica would be to England where I would have the opportunity to play cricket, besides to travel to American at that period in time when the McCarran Walter Act, a United States Congressional Act imposing a strict quota on people from the Caribbean entering America, was a hurdle that was not easy to negotiate. That being said the biblical story of Ruth the Moabite woman who on meeting Boaz, a Hebrew, requested that he have an understanding of her feelings towards him when she said, "Entreat me not to leave thee or to return from following after thee, for where thou lodgest I will lodge, your people shall be my people, and thy God my God". For a long time these words were to strike resounding chords as we continued to correspond with each other until after we both found partners, got married, and in the process of changing addresses we lost contact with each other. Destiny decreed that we would never have been an item, yet on the other hand with a large number of Jamaicans and other Caribbean nationals settling in Miami, cricket is quite popular.

The hurricane did hit Jamaica and it was for the third time that I was to experience such disaster in the same house and whereas in the case of the first one that occurred when I was nine years old and was not fully aware of the financial and social implications that such disasters leave, seven years after the second one struck I was sixteen years old and through the process of maturity arrived at a point of understanding of how economies are being affected by natural calamities and the extent by which people find the will to survive. Yet for all the preparations against eventualities we often forget to include something that is important for our survival. I was to discover on the evening when the wind got up to a dangerous speed and plunged the house into darkness that we had no candles. Rather than submerging into despair I took some beeswax, placed it on a tin of unopened condensed milk and lit it, that simple act was a reinforcement that in this world rather that lambasting darkness it is better to light straws. It was also an object lesson that unexpected inspiration can emerge from adversity.

Seven people were in the house on the evening, my mother, her aunt Granny Edith, my sisters, Carmen, Lurline, Elaine, Lyn and myself. As a family we firmly believed in the power of prayer and like then as it is now, when I find it difficult to explain to those people who have lost their faith that given the fact at times when one prays petitions might not be granted immediately for all that prayer is about achieving an inner strength that help in dealing with difficult situations. It is about the moments when some words of kindness or encouragement from a particular song or music which moves us to that sense of awareness of the mysteries of life and death. On the night when a broken bench from a tree broke one of the windows in our living room, guided by the flicker from the home-made candle, I climbed on a table and nailed a piece of board across the broken window and I heard the words from my mother, "Whitty, you are brave like Baba"; that is what she called my father and Granny Edith's acknowledgement "like father like son" and her humming of "Guide me o thou Great Jehovah" where the still calm voices that reassured me and put into perspective the importance of the event and the extent to which it brought us together and helped in shaping our different paths in life.

As is customary, the morning after hurricanes in Jamaica fit in with the old proverb that "after a storm there must be a calm". Like the two previous hurricanes there were structural damages to our house including fruit trees and valuable timber trees, some of which would bear again and others that could not be replaced, such are the realities of hurricanes and other natural disasters in terms of how they affect the social and economic structures of countries in which they occur. Looking around at the devastation that morning I noticed that the trunk of a bread nut tree that was uprooted in the 1951 hurricane and left lying on its side was standing upright. Two theories were advanced, the first was that prior, or after, the storm there was an earthquake that affected the movement of the rock formation; the second theory was that the tree gave shelter to the entrance of a cave where Jamaicans earliest inhabitants, the Arawaks, lived and it was their spirits that caused the stump of the tree to rise. At twenty three years old at the time and with my experience in the Tourist Industry I felt that the latter theory would have boosted the industry. But the situation in as far as I was concerned was not about theories, it was about finding solutions to repair the damage that was done to the house, one thing we all agreed on as a family that whatever it takes we were prepared to face the challenges that life had to offer. It was a case of making things happen. For my part it was going back to my job at the Post Office in Kingston and to start my course at St George's Extension College on East Street. Amongst the writers recommended were W.H.D. Sprott and Emile Durkheim. My choice was Durkheim to whom R.E.K. regarded as one of the most influential.

Sixteen years after in 1974 when I was granted leave from the Post Office in Manchester, England to pursue a course in Applied Community Studies at Manchester Polytechnic, which later achieved University status to Manchester Metropolitan University, Bob Guttfreund, who lectured on the subject was equally enthusiastic about Durkheim as R.E.K Phillips. This enthusiasm was even more reinforced when in 1999 I went back to the institution to pursue a Masters Degree. By then Bob was Professor Bob Guttfreund. My dissertation was "The significance of African Caribbean Achievements through sports and its influence in the development of role models and mentors in the community".

On reflection I am convinced that I could not have chosen a better time to start the course at The St Georges Extension College in Jamaican than in 1958 when the country was rapidly moving towards self rule which ignited a new sense of national consciousness amongst Jamaicans regardless of racial origin, colour, ethnicity, or gender, than embracing aspects of the political zeal that eventually led to emancipation in 1834. The new social order was prepared to dig deeper and to lay a solid foundation that would give us, as Jamaicans, the opportunity to identify with Jamaica and to appreciate the fact that we could express ourselves in sports, arts, literature, education and in all the fields of human endeavour, with a sense of pride that underlines the best in our country's traditions. In the process of gathering data to present my first paper to my tutors on "The effects of the industrial revolution in Britain and the Caribbean" I started to have a better understanding of why things were as they were in Jamaica. For instance, the exodus from the rural areas to Kingston was borne out by falling sugar prices, Panama disease and natural disasters that ruined banana plantations, other timber producing and fruit trees and other crops on which the small farmers depended on for food and subsistence living. Out of this chaos came Norman Manley and William Alexander Bustamante. Both cousins, they were part of the British ruling class and except for their different political ideologies had a deep respect for British traditions. Manley wanted an early demise to colonial rule, whereas Bustamante felt that more could be gained by delaying the thrust forward for independence. This new sharp learning curve was to further my interest in listening to people like St William Grant, a grassroots political activist who preached a brand of Nationalist politics from the then King George the Sixth Memorial Park in Kingston. With the advent of independence the Park is now The Saint William Grant Park named in his memory.

In between the preparation of my essay I took the test at the Half-Way-Tree Police Station for entry into the Jamaican Constabulary, which I passed but at the final selection at the training school at Elleston Road, I was rejected on the grounds that I was too short; the required height was five feet eight inches and I failed by one inch. The disappointment was short-lived. At least I knew I had satisfied myself in terms of testing out my options regarding my future, as I have alluded previously it was a time when the wind of change was blowing at a tremendous pace and the entire population was in the preparation mode that come the changes which were inevitable one would find themselves in a position to reap the benefits that were promised by the people who were in the forefront of advocating the philosophy of "building a new Jamaica" that would be free of colonial domination.

The reality of the situation was that there were more dogs than bones and the gap between the haves and the have nots was getting wider. The interesting aside was that as some of the have nots made progress they became more antagonistic to the group from which they had come, a reinforcement of the poacher turned gamekeeper mentality. I recall Duckley, who was a Union Representative for the National Workers' Union lambasting one such individual as "A common privileged under-privileged". I suppose that is the way that some people wanted to be but my take is always that people can be whatever they want to be providing they are willing to let me be who or what I want to be. In other words the attention drawn by events that were taking place at the time in the Caribbean, North America and Europe in general, but in particular England, increased and influenced my own thinking on the decisions that I had to make for my advancement. A further logic to this thinking was the response of my tutors to the paper that I submitted which clearly highlighted my bias towards sports in general, but cricket in particular, and that the concept of the Industrial Revolution was born out of the desire for Britain to continue to create and maintain "an Empire so large that the sun never sets on her", in keeping with the social and economic changes and as a result of the revolution organised sports and other leisure activities were introduced as a means of social and political control and the creation of wealth for the chosen few, and the same system applied in any country or society that was under British rule.

There was an agreed consensus between my tutors that my essay was a good one and in my discussion with R.E.K. Phillips about travelling to England, where I planned to work and study towards a career teaching physical education, his response was encouraging, which prompted me to write to a cousin who was living in Moss Side, Manchester, about prospects in England. In the meantime I was quite happy with my job in the bulk section of the General Post on Orange Street, studying and weekends playing for a team from Alman Town in the football season at Race Course, or when it was cricket for a team from Constant Spring. It seemed to me that although I had the ability to hold a regular place on the Post Office team that played in the Carib Cup Competition, it was not the man in form but the man in favour. I had every reason to support my way of thinking because the team was not doing well to justify sticking to a winning team. Just as I was resigning myself to the fact that I would never be asked to play, Berry from Parcel, who captained the side, came into the Branch to tell me that I was picked to play against the Fire Brigade. Within half an hour Ed Baugh, who also worked at Parcel Post, came and asked for a loan of one pound on the understanding that he would return it on the Friday, which was pay day.

Come pay day and Baugh was as elusive as a snake in a belt factory. Suddenly it dawned on me that I had paid him to be picked to play, something that I have never ever subscribed to from the very day that I started to play as a youngster through to captaining my school and my village teams, that players on my team were there on merit and not through grace and favour. Sadly that was the case in the Jamaica of my time, that being said I still had to wait to see if my assumptions about Baugh were right.

For the match against the Fire Brigade I had match figures of 7 overs, 2 maidens, 2 wickets for 25 runs; I also took 3 catches fielding at second slip. Baugh was one of the umpires and I felt that I had done sufficient to be included in the squad for the next game. At least we had beaten the Fire

Brigade, but like the previous games that I played in the Inter-Departmental Competitions, some twelve months previous, I was surprised that very little had changed in terms of the comment about my performance to some of my detractors. My weight training technique was not important even though I tried to convince them that it was an idea that I read where Bill Nicholson, the then Manager of Tottenham Hotspurs, encouraged his players to use weights for all round physical fitness, if they did subscribe to that line of argument. My status as a country boy was deeply ingrained in their mind set, to me it was never a problem. To add insult to injury I was selected to play against Prison Officers the following week only to be made twelfth man. When I turned up on the day of the match I took the decision in the best tradition of a cricketer ,"A sportsman on and off the field", even though I knew that there were members on the team who felt that an injustice was done and would support me if I took a stand. I figured that it was best to deal with it my way, I wanted to find out who was behind denying me a place in the team; Baugh was my first target in demanding my money and it was from him that according to the grapevine I was due to be promoted, but both Mr Fox, a superintendent, and Mr Watson, a Supervisor, and who was also was a Team Selector, objected. As far as I was concerned all promotion meant was a job at the lower end of the Civil Service pushing a pen and sitting down waiting to fill dead people's chairs and as far as how things were moving, very little chance of reaching the level of playing cricket to satisfy myself that I had given the best in that area of my life.

At that time my brother, Noel, and I lived at East Race Course, across from where The National Heroes Circle now stands, and I decided that I would not discuss my plans about leaving the Post Office on the grounds that he would persuade me to stay, which indeed would be a very tall order, realising that once I decided to do something I will follow it through to completion. When I finally had the opportunity to speak to Mr Watson it was about his failure to recognise my potential to the team and not about promotion. At least I had enough street savvy not to put Baugh into the firing line, even though he still owed me a pound, but whether it was by accident or by design Mr Fox came into the office and became part of the discussion, which was certainly not in my favour. It was as if they were prepared for me and waiting for me to place the proverbial rope around my neck and jump, either from a low or high tree. That I was not going to do for the reason that up until that time I had fought so many battles and lived to tell the tale and in the process have learnt that in the heat of battle the best equipped army displays signs of weakness that can be exploited by the opposition.

The temperature of the political climate island-wide had reached an all time high, it was a time when people were willing to raise their heads above the parapet and stand up and be counted. If, for instance, you were a member of the People's National Party, which I was, my clench-fist salute and hailing my fellow party member as "comrade" was as predominant as the Labour Party member with his two finger 'V' sign. Words such as 'nationalism', 'socialism', 'colonialism', imperialism', 'political victimisation', 'the way forward for the common man' and 'communist' were everyday words used in accordance with one's political and social schools of thought. So I said to the two men that, "you and your little Shibboleth are running the cricket team like a racketeer's charter". The quotation was one I heard some years previously from F.L.B. "Slave-boy" Evans, who was a P.N.P. Member of Parliament for Hanover. I think that it was rather appropriate to the point that both men demanded that I make a written apology or else face the consequence of being suspended on the grounds of insubordination. I was prepared to give as much as I could take. That morning reiterating that they were small-minded men who enjoyed their roles as oppressors, and in as far as a letter of apology what the Department will get is a letter of my instant resignation as it was my intention to travel to England to work, play cricket, go on to University and in five years, by which time Jamaica would be an independent country, I would return and chase them out of their jobs.

For my part it was a tall order; a tremendous challenge with the onus on me to deliver. I could not afford to lose face, neither could I be a laughing stock, so my first task was to tender my resignation. Both sides agreeing that parting so mutually this was to prove financially beneficial to me as within a month of leaving there was a staff appraisal and a salary rise going back two years and my brother who worked for The Telegraph Department collected it in my absence. On the very day that I tended my resignation I went to The Victoria Mutual Building Society on Duke Street, in Kingston, took sufficient money to pay my fare of seventy five pounds, which I booked at Chin Yees Travel Service and bought my travelling case, which I still have, leaving myself with sufficient funds to tide me over for the three weeks that I spent in Discovery Bay prior to my departure to England.

Two songs were hitting the airwaves, and being sung at street corners and dances. These songs were topical and relevant to the migratory pattern of the period; one song made popular by Sugar Belly, the Jamaican Mento Singer, went like this:

> *Thousands of people are asking me*
> *How I spent my time in London City*
> *Now that's a question that I cannot answer*
> *I regret the day I leave sweet Jamaica*
> *And if I had the wings like an aeroplane*

159

I would fly back to that beautiful country again
Chorus: *Jamaica Jamaica I bound to remember*

The other verses of the song were sum totals of the climatic conditions, the struggle to find proper living accommodation and the lack of understanding and ignorance by some members of the host community, that the relationships between Jamaica and England were developed over many centuries and in essence, Jamaicans were coming to "The Motherland".

The other song which went like this

Come along everybody hear what I have to say
Listen and I will tell you what is the talk of the town today
For in every corner that you may walk
You will see a group of people park
They are not skylarking, they are only talking about Ethiopia.
Some talk about Ethiopia, and other Liberia
But no matter where I do not care
For I want to get my share
Of all the riches and delicious dishes of Ethiopia

Oh what a glorious morning Blackman
When we land on Liberia shore
Our prayers will all be over Blackman
And then we will weep no more
But if I die before that day
My duppy shall be going away to Ethiopia.

The central theme of both songs was to put into context the actual and anticipated experiences of people who had a long history of being a part of and wanted to be fully accepted. In as far as I was concerned I was aware that I had to remain conscious of the complexities and confusions arising out a history that reinforced European points of view at the expense of Africans who where the majority group in Jamaica. So implicit to my thinking as I spent the last days making my final preparations to leave Jamaica on the 12th day of August 1959 was that I was part of that long history of people where the processes of liberation theology, reconciliation, and achievement came about through education and sport. I was also to become part of that group to which some Caribbean social commentators have described as "Colonizers in Reverse". In terms of the liberation theology argument and the two songs that I have alluded to, the processes of time and events has placed me in a position to make the point that with the advent of people from the Caribbean to Britain and their children, who were born there, the whole shape and structure of British competition from Club to International level has changed for the better.

I can recall in the process of packing my case, Granny Edith and my mother were not happy that I was taking my cricket bat and cricket boots with me; they said that from what they heard it was always raining in Manchester and common sense dictated that I should not speak back to my elders, especially from the letter that I sent to my cousin Lester Gordon, who lived in Moss Side, regarding my coming to England. Instead of him replying to me he wrote to Aunt Cis, his mother, which was my mother's aunt, that England was not a bed of roses and I must be prepared to stand on my own two feet.

I knew that England was not a bed of roses, neither were the streets paved with gold. This was made clear to me not only by Colonel Blake, my supervisor in the Bulk Mail Branch, but by soldiers from the Duke of Cornwall Light Infantry (D.C.L.I), who were stationed in Jamaica at the time. I think they were the first to play football under lights. As far as accommodation was concerned they assured me that as a footballer and cricketer I would have no problems getting fixed up at the Y.M.C.A. With that bit of advice I went to see the Reverend Jethro Calvert Carriss, an English Congregational Minister at St Stephen's Congregational Church Crossroads, where I attended, who arranged a letter on my behalf from the Y.M.C.A. As far as standing on my own two feet, although many times it was on bare feet, that has always been the sum total of my experience and I would never want it any other way. Having said that I did send a cable to my cousin which read, "Leaving Jamaica 12th August, arriving London 14th". Everything was done and dusted for the take off save for my send off party, which took place at 18 East Race Coarse, and what a party it was, one that went on long and hard. It started at seven o'clock on the evening to approaching midnight and would have continued possibly until the early hours of the morning if Granny Edith did not call a halt to proceedings.

It was good that she did as I am sure that the neighbours would have called the police and have them press a charge against Al White, who was in charge of the music, for malicious destruction of records of Sam Cooke's "You send me", Bill Hayley's "Rock Around the Clock" and Wilson Picket's "Midnight Hour". Maybe they had each paid him to play those records, but as they say, all good things must come to an end. The follow on from that was time for prayers, bible-reading and the singing of hymns in keeping with the custom of goodbye until we meet again.

The Bible reading was from Psalms Chapter 12: "I will lift up mine eyes unto the hills from whence cometh my help". Prayers were said by my mother, and Granny Edith closed by reminding me to read the Bible and pray every day, to avoid the bright lights so as not to finish up like the prodigal son, find a job and send money home, show respect and manners to Lady Queen's people, make sure that I eat properly and go to Church every Sunday. Her final words were "Whitty, walk good nuh mek fowl mash you". Those words of advice meant that breaking any of them would be seen as bringing shame and disgrace on myself, my family and my country. In her eighty three years it was the second and last time that she had ever visited Kingston. I communicated with her up until her death in 1978 at the age of one hundred and two; I have always stressed that longevity is on my mothers side of the family and it could be as a result of their diets. It was from Granny Edith that I learnt the skills of making cakes for any occasion, making guava jelly, orange marmalade, tamarind balls and curing meats and fish. Her motto was, "Eat some today, and preserve some for another day". The last meal that I cooked on the morning before I left was typical of a Jamaican breakfast of ackee and saltfish, callaloo, boiled green bananas and chocolate tea.

On my way to the airport, I drove past some of my favourite places where I had many good times, places such as Bournemouth Club, the Mineral Baths, Siganay Beach, Gun Boat Beach, from where I swam two years previous in the Annual Pepsi Cola Cross the Harbour Competition, finishing at Bournemouth and then on to the airport that lends itself to a commanding view of the mountains where it seems as if they could touch the skies. I could not help but think of the poet William Cowper asking if it is a land that I will visit once more. I consoled myself to the fact that I would be away for only five years, at least that was my plan and I had to believe in myself that it would happen. Being at the airport that morning was the beginning of the process in which I as a person joined the countless thousands both before and after me who took wavering steps into the unknown where experiences gained, whether over a short or long period of time, became relevant or meaningful for the reason of the exodus and as I waved goodbye to family and friends that August morning of 1959 it was to become another defining moment in my life.

CHAPTER TEN

Steal Away Home to Blighty

STEPPING ON board The British Overseas Airways Corporation (BOAC) plane on the morning of Wednesday, 12th August, 1959 was proof, according to the Jamaican phraseology at the time, that I was "chopping out" from a homeland that was still not fully liberated from colonial rule, where the Union Jack still flew, and although I was not a Citizen of Jamaica, I was according to the stamp in my Passport signed by Governor Sir Hugh Foot, the brother of Michael Foot, a one time Leader of the British Labour Party, a "British Subject Citizen of the United Kingdom and Colonies" and I was proud of that.

I was leaving a land famed for its natural beauty with its range and diversity of peopl's and culture, people who had a zest for life expressed in their music, their dance, their sporting activities, their food, their art and their literature, yet for all that the opportunities for the thousands of us who were ambitious were few and far between, and I was prepared as best I could ever have been for my trip to "The Mother Country" where I have said before, I knew that it was neither a land of milk and honey or its street paved with gold, but by the same rule there were opportunities available and I was quite willing to take on the challenges that would help me achieve some of my ambitions. I was all geared up for the British weather, other than an overcoat I was sartorial elegance in my light grey felt hat, check jacket, blue New Yorker shirt, black pants, Three Castle shoes and blue tartan scarf. My flannel vest and long johns made by Mother, God Bless her, were packed away in my case for use in the winter months. I have never used long johns, or for that matter any such item of clothing, over the years living in England.

The flight itinerary was Kingston to New York, New York to Gander, Newfoundland, Gander to Shannon in Ireland and Shannon to London Heathrow. A very long one indeed, but it was far from boring, less than half an hour into the flight we started talking to each other, strangers we were, but we were all affected by the same cause of "push and pull" with the slight difference that some of us were "send fors" and like the students on board had someone coming to meet them, others of us were "although having an address, not sure if anybody will be coming to meets". I was one of the latter but was not worried in the least as I was confident that I would get accommodation at the YMCA.

At New York it was discovered that there was some fault with the plane, which meant that the flight would be delayed. The respite gave our little interest group of four, which was Webb from Hanover, who was going to join a cousin who lived in Harlesden and had a job lined up for him with British Rail, Cissy from St Elizabeth, who was joining an Aunt who lived in Stoke Newington and had a job lined up for her in a Lyons Tea Shop, then there was Aston from Portland, the most worldly wise and oldest of the group; he had been to the United States of America twice on the Farm Workers Programme working in places such as New Jersey and Wisconsin. He was in line to work as a chef, all arranged by his cousin, Baron Baker, who has been credited as the Jamaican responsible for making Brixton the Caribbean Centre. Then, of course, there was me, the only one going to Manchester, with no job to go to other than the possibility of getting in touch with Northampton County Cricket Club to see if they would want me to play for them.

The body language from my three acquaintances said it all, think of something else and by the time we were ready for the second leg of the journey tiredness dictated that even above the monotonous sound from the engine of the aircraft, a couple of cat naps helped to stifle conversation, and in between sleeping what I did remember about Newfoundland from my history lessons is that it was the place from where we got our beloved salt fish, which without Ackee would not have the distinction to be the National Dish of Jamaica. Other than being transferred to another plane for Shannon I remembered very little of Gander. Coming into land at Shannon flying over a number of farms, the early morning reminded me of driving through Moneague in St Ann or Luidas Vale in St Catherine in early December. I recall coming through the airport lounge where there was a battalion of soldiers going in the opposite direction when one shouted to us, "You are coming into the cold and we are going out to the warm weather"; it did cause me to think and over the years I was able to fully grasp the meaning of the weather and its impact on the "proverbial brass monkey".

The remark from the soldier was the shot in the arm that Aston needed to tell me that seeing as I had no job to go to in Manchester, why not stay in Brixton where he was sure that from the contacts that his cousin, Baron Baker, had in London, he could get me fixed up. The idea seemed a good one, especially when he mentioned that it was Baron who told a British Bobby to show respect to Chief Minister Norman Manley of Jamaica, who visited London in 1958 and was having a walkabout in Notting Hill where the riots had taken place and the police asked him to move on when he was talking to a group of Jamaicans. Aston was proud to emphasise that the ovation and sense of appreciation was more thunderous at Heathrow. One male passenger, whom I assumed to be the oldest on the flight, in praise of the pilot said, "He could land on an egg and it wouldn't mash". Aston had the final word as we walked to the terminal building when he said, "Sten boy we are in Blighty, let us make the best of it". Interestingly, I have never heard from Aston, Cissy or Webb; I figured that like a number of people from the Caribbean who stayed in London, Manchester is in the Country.

Having indicated to the porter who took my case that Rum was in it I proceeded through customs to have it declared. In the process of examining the contents of my case, which other than the bottle and quarter bottle of rum, which in those days could attract paying duty on the larger amount, my cricket bat strapped on the outside of my case, my boots and flannels inside aroused the interest of the Officer, who I was to learn in that short time was originally from Nottingham and was quite happy to talk about great cricketers such as the Gunns, Harold Larwood and Bill Voce. As far as he was concerned Gary Sobers would, over time, be the greatest player the game has ever seen, no wonder Sir Gary eventually played for Nottingham. We could have spent all day talking cricket but he had a job to do and I had to make haste to catch the waiting bus to the Rail Station in London where I would travel to Manchester. He wished me good luck with my trial at Northampton and as the Porter wheeled my case to the waiting bus he took a packet of woodbine cigarettes on which I signed my autograph 'E W W Stennett', the extra 'W' was just my way of telling the cricketing world that I had arrived in England and so far all was well.

I could not help but notice the dirt and grime caused by the heavy pall of smoke from factories as the train drove through towns like Birmingham, Walsall, Stoke on Trent, Rugby, Stockport and for the first time in my life I was beginning to put into context William Blake's vision of building of a Jerusalem, based on the green and pleasant land that I had seen from above and the dark satanic mills that I, rode past. To me it was all a part of the fast learning curve that was relative to being in a new environment. It was quite late when I arrived in Manchester, where I was now faced with the prospect of either getting a cab to the Y.M.C.A., or to the address of my cousin in Moss Side. That decision was taken away from me by a taxi driver who, without my telling him where I was going knew, that I was bound for Moss Side. In those days the assumption was that all black people go to or, rather, live in Moss Side. The cricket bat strapped to my grip once again made communication between the taxi driver and myself much easier as he waxed lyrically about the exploits of those "two little pals of mine, Ramadhin and Valetine" and the batting prowess of the three W's, Worrel, Weekes, and Walcott, whom he said that he had the pleasure of meeting in his role as a taxi driver. It was obvious that he was a West Indies cricket supporter and when I told him that I would be going to Northampton for a trial he wished me good luck, adding that one of his friends, 'a coloured lad'', who like himself was a taxi driver, played cricket in the mid-week for the taxis. The journey from the station to 174 Moss Lane East, Moss Side, was rather too short for us to have a much more in-depth discussion as is the case when connoisseurs of the game meet. I paid him his fare and thought to myself that twice in one day my cricket bat or my love for the game served as the Mission Statement that my arrival in England was to continue to re-affirm that from my own point of view sports in general and cricket, in particular, can be effective in igniting popular consciousness, political and social action and self actualisation.

What better place to have started from, in terms of following my dreams, than from 174 Moss Lane East, then a row of Victorian houses. Demolition and modernisation has altered the location and 174 can best be described as where the bus stop now stands across from the fire station. At that time my cousin had a grocers shop on the ground floor of the premises where, amongst other things, he sold yams, sweet potatoes, green bananas, plantations, bread fruit; most of these came from West Africa, hence the shop became a focal meeting place for people from the various Caribbean Islands and West African countries, from whom I learned quite a lot about their varying customs.

My arrival was greeted in true Jamaican fashion, resonating the song "long time bwoy a neva see you come mek we shake your hand". On the other hand there were those that evening who, on hearing of my intended arrival, were there for a "little drop of the thing"; in other words a drink of white Rum to have travelled from Jamaica and not taking a bottle of liquid sunshine was tantamount to committing a felony and when Tailor Stewart, who hailed from Westmoreland, tasted the Rum and declared that it was from Serge Island in St Thomas, I knew that I was in the company of a Connoisseur on Rum, in that it was part of what was left from the demijohn of John Crow Batty from Serge, which is rum taken from the still before it is refined to make the punch at my send off party.

A further explanation as to why Tailor Stewart had such unique taste on the varieties of rum revealed that he played cricket in the Crum Ewing Cricket Competition, which was designed for the Sugar Estates in Jamaica. Gilbert Barrett was equally informative with his understanding of local community affairs and the way forward for people from the Caribbean in Manchester and Britain as a whole. At the time he was one of the leading figures organising social events in Moss Side for Caribbean people. Both Tailor Stewart and Gilbert Barrett seemed to have showed some interest in me achieving my objectives, which according to them would demand a lot of sacrifice. Our discussion would have gone on much longer into the night had not Lester, my cousin, reminded them that not only was I tired but that he had to be up early to go to Smithfield Market.

My room was in the attic, very spacious, clean and fully furnished and at two pounds per week was quite reasonable. I cannot remember how long it took me to fall asleep, I was more anxious to be up early so that I could go to the market with my cousin. It was to prove a wise decision on my part in that I was offered a job working with Thirkettles. That same day I went to The Labour Exchange at Aytoun Street, signed on and received my cards ready to start work on the Monday. From my observations on the Friday morning when I went to the markets it was evident that I had no item of clothing suitable for that kind of work. I had fifty pounds in my wallet, a lot of cash in those days; interestingly. I still have the wallet as it was my twenty first birthday present from my brother, Noel, and from the fifty pounds I went to Barry's, a clothing outfitters on Princess Road, and got clothing in keeping with the job. I was itching to get started and to show my cousin that I could stand on my own two feet.

Walking on Darcy Street on the Friday evening I heard someone shouting down from the open window of a house, "Hello, are you from Jamaica? Wait there I am coming down", and within a matter of seconds the person came down to introduce himself. "I am Kenny, Kenny Williams, my father is from Trinidad, come on let me introduce you to my family". It was quite a short introduction and I felt quite at ease in the presence of his family, but Kenny was anxious to take me up to the second floor of the building where he had a gym. It was like walking into a United Nations Conference in terms of the guys who were there, Caucasians, Africans, Caribbeans and mixed race and I was not prepared for training and explained that I used weights as a means to keep fit for my favourite sport of cricket, and given that I was not in training gear I did a demonstration of my routine which consisted of standing back and front press for the shoulders and squats for stamina and power at a bodyweight of eleven stones, eight pounds. I squatted with twenty three stones two pounds, twice my body weight, it was a record for the gym and I was told some weeks later by Les Murray, who trained there, that the remarks made by some of the guys in the gym was that "it is the quiet Jamaicans who are powerful". I suppose it was quite flattering and it did something for my ego. Kenny, who at the time was a serving member of the Royal Air Force, was always encouraging. He was later to make a career in showbusiness and become a very good golfer.

The truism that things always happen in threes could not more be justified than on coming back from Kenny's house. Roy Gilchrist, the West Indian fast bowler who was playing professional cricket for Middleton in the Central League, was at the shop. It was almost four years since we had last met and it was nice to talk about the various things that happened to us during that time cricket-wise and otherwise in as far as playing in the league. He reminded me that whether you are a professional or an amateur, providing you are a West Indian clubs expect the best from us. I accepted the comment in line with the school of thought which says that, "if a job is worth doing it is worth doing well".

Within minutes of Gilchrist leaving the shop David Mumby, who I met a few times when as a youngster he came to the beach at Discovery Bay from Browns Towns, knew of my coming to Manchester through Mrs Gordon, came in to find out if I had arrived and if I was interested to play in a match on the Sunday arranged by his friend. As it happened, his friend, whose name was also David, worked for The Daily Mail in Manchester and was involved with a team called The Press Association that played friendly matches all over England. It was a case of "Pack cricket bag I'll travel". Sometimes they had a very good side, other times a quite mediocre one. It was from my observation who was available, that being said the games in which I was involved in were played in the true tradition of cricket, hard but fair, and I truly valued the experience. In as far as that match was concerned I had everything except a pullover, once again Barry's on Princess Road came in handy with a sweater, though not a cricket one. It kept the body warm even that Summer, which was a pretty good one. To go into a match just four days after travelling over five and a half thousand miles by air and no practice was indeed a tall order but I did not want to miss the opportunity of playing my first match in England. The match was played at Prestwich Cricket Club, quite a good wicket and other amenities, a far cry from what I was used to in Jamaica. The Press Association lost the toss and I was asked to open the bowling and what a baptism of fire and brimstone it proved to be against both opening batsmen, one of whom was John Kay, who wrote cricket for the Manchester Evening News. In Caribbean cricket jargon, "lay some lashes on my backside", and I suddenly reflected on what Gilchrist had said to me two days previously of the best that is expected from a West Indian cricketer. I thought to myself that I was a bit too nice, and it was time to really show the opposition that I had the ability to tickle a rib cage, or get a batsman to duck, or bob and weave, with rising balls. Would it ruin my chances of playing again?

In my sixth over, when I started having the batsmen reeling and taking evasive action the body action and hand claps started with our wicket-keeper and transferred to others of my team mates like wildfire, which boosted my confidence and placed me on a high when I had Darbyshire caught in the slips for a well deserved 35. It was my first wicket playing cricket in England and what a feeling of elation and accomplishment. Sadly, my feeling of elation was short-lived when in my next over John Kay took his eye off a rising ball which hit him on the cheek and resulted in him being taken to Crumpsall

168

Hospital for observation, which revealed nothing serious. During the tea interval he came over to reassure me that I should not be too hard on myself, and I figured that he meant well because at the end of the match, having realised that I had only been in the country just over four days, he told me about his friend who owned a warehouse and would give me a job. I politely refused, seeing that I had given my word to Thirkettles at Smithfield Market to start on the following day.

The prospect of a job to go to was to me just as important as to ascertain how I was being rated playing in my first match. With figures of twelve overs, one maiden, sixty three runs for one wicket, according to Mumby, my Agent, there was the feeling amongst the team that I had ability but could well have been suffering from stagefright and the change of weather. As far as stagefright was concerned I totally disagreed and told Mumby what I really missed was the spectator participation that cheered me on when I am doing well and jeered me when I was not doing well. So far as the weather on that day it was not bad, although I kept my sweater on throughout the game. All things being equal it was a brilliant start to my cricketing experience in England and as I confided in Mumby at the club bar, that I did not believe that I would ever get used to drinking tea or bitter, to which he replied, "You will. See, you are in England, and by the way, are you available next week?"

CHAPTER ELEVEN

One Step up a Little Higher

SIXTEEN DAYS from my visit to The Post Office Headquarters at Brown Street I received a letter asking that I come in to sit the Entrance Examination. Courtesy demanded that I informed Harry Thirkettle, who wished me good luck. Of the fourteen people who turned up, Sam Odoffin from Nigeria and myself were the only two born outside of Britain and who did not serve in any of the armed forces, to which I was to find out later though it could be an advantage, it was not an option carved out in stone. The test was by and large designed to be in keeping with a good understanding of the English language, to have the ability to decipher and accurately deal with literary and numerical miscalculations. Seven of the fourteen of us were successful, but as was explained by Personnel, until references and a positive medical report was received, there was no guarantee that we would be offered a position.

The references that I brought with me from Jamaica were sent back for authentication. That was expected anyway and it was another fortnight after taking the Entrance Examination that I received a letter from The Post Office instructing me to go for my medical examination at the surgery of Doctor Stennett Redmond off Stretford Road in Hulme. At the end of what was a very thorough examination, he said to me that in his time practising as a Doctor examining people from the various Government Departments, I was one of the fittest persons that he had ever come across; a fact that he would be putting into his report, and if my fitness was the criteria on which I would be employed then I should have no fear. I walked out of his surgery that evening feeling ten feet tall and ready to take on the world.

For all the excitement about moving on to a new job, it was with some sense of sadness that I had when the time finally came for me to leave Smithfields Market, where during the short time that I had worked there I came across real people to whom that I was willing to put in a hard day's work for my pay, one who was not a 'nark', 'a good grafter' 'not pushy', 'minds his own business', but still 'one of the boys'. As I have said they were real people who would willingly walk the last mile for me without expecting anything in return. What I was also to miss were the 'swingers', part of the market tradition where on a Saturday morning every stall would swap the goods that they dealt with which meant that every worker went home with a full supply of everything sold in the market. I liked the custom because it reminded me so much of villages in Jamaica where we shared and shared alike, but as the old saying goes 'parting is so much sweet sorrow'. A man had to do what a man has got to do. Smithfield market was beginning to be part of my own history in terms of my education at the University of Life, where I have always stressed that if the experience had to be measured in terms of taught subjects in sociology, psychology, and politics within an academic setting, the Smithfield experience meant one hundred percent pass mark at a very advanced level.

The Training School for the Post Office was in the building on Oxford Road where the Manchester Chamber Business Enterprises presently have their offices. True to form I was of a class of seven. The first to arrive was the Instructor, Mr Shepherd, the archetypal Englishman in terms of punctuality and manners, who during the formalities, without any reservation, made it clear that he expected to be referred to as Mr Shepherd and by the same rule he would be referring to us as Mister. His assessment of the Post Office as a branch of the Civil Service was that it was more than just delivering letters or telegrams but part of a British institution that gained international recognition Listening to Mr Shepherd, I harped back to the first day in Jamaica when I went in The Bulk Mail Delivery Branch of the General Post Office in Kingston and met Colonel Blake, a paragon for the expelling of British values.

By the third day at the school, given that so far Mr Shepherd was a very good instructor, questions were beginning to be asked amongst us trainees that if by his own admission he really worked with British Intelligence in Egypt during the Second World War, and if he was head hunted by the Post Office from his job as a Senior Lecturer at Sandhurst. Amongst his don'ts to us during the introduction process was that at no time during the fortnight at the school should we go to the pub for a drink; to do so meant instant dismissal from the course. His treatise to us on the evils of drinking, in which he said he had never indulged, made Mother Theresa look like a hooker! Some of my batch mates felt that what they did in their lunch time was their own business. I took the view that if it was a course requirement I had no problem. My feeling was that he had over-estimated himself; he knew every subject under the sun, there was no place that he had not visited in the world in his time. According to him he had met famous people such as King Farook of Egypt, Gracie Fields, Joe Louis, Satchmo, all the players at Lancashire county Cricket Club, Manchester United and Manchester City. He was dubbed a Romancer by members of the group, but when Fred Ludlum saw him coming out of The Salisbury at the back of the Oxford one lunchtime his credibility took a nose dive. But Mr Shepherd was a smart cookie that day, immediately after lunch he got us together and placed some stones that looked like potatoes on a table; amongst the stones were also real potatoes and when we were asked to identify from a distance what was a potato and what was a stone all seven of us made mistakes which led us to concur with him 'that things are not always what they seem to be'.

At the end of the two weeks training, after being given the opportunity to assess each other's performance, we met with him individually for a final briefing. He had no doubt that I would make it in the Post Office, citing my sense of good time-keeping, the ability to listen and to work effectively as areas of strength. In terms of weakness, he said that I was too cautious. Regarding me wanting to play cricket for Northampton, he made no bones in telling me I would need to give a lot of consideration to the long term effect of having a job in the Civil Service where I can build up a pension as opposed to one where I work seasonally. He said to me, 'Mr Stennett, if you really want to play cricket, in the Post Office you can play in The Civil Service Competitions, the inter-department competitions and in The Wednesday League. You will be playing so much cricket that you will hardly be at work'. Over time I was to appreciate that it was one of the best bits of advice that I have ever been given.

On the day of my appointment I was taken in to see Mr Dawson, Head Postmaster at Newton Street, who, after welcoming me as a new member to the organisation, informed me that after a long discussion with members of his team the conclusion that they had arrived at was seeing that I had only recently arrived from a warm country it would be in my best interest to employ me as Indoor Postman as opposed to me delivering letters on the streets in sometimes what can be atrocious weather conditions. Well, I was brought up to believe in prayer and also to understand that God don't answer them instantly, but when I heard those words coming from the Postmaster that chilly November morning in 1959 I was willing to argue the toss with any theologian that God answered my prayer overnight as I desperately wanted an indoor job where I could feel warm.

The tongue of good report relating to my prowess as a cricketer and my physical fitness had, by all accounts, preceded me as on leaving Mr Dawson's office he assured me that he would be looking forward to coming to see me play for the Post Office in the coming 1960 season. Simon Younge was the first person to greet me when I followed Bob Mack onto the floor, a far cry from the Post Office that I had left in Jamaica in terms of its operation and mechanisation. The next person I was introduced to by Simon was Roy Tomlinson, the Captain for the Post Office Team; quite an affable man who assured me that from what he heard about me as a player from Simon and one of his friends, who saw my first game at Prestwich, was that I should have no problem making the team.

On the third morning, when I went into work from the Faraday Street entrance, a shout went up, "Here comes Stan Stennett". The sobriquet was related to Stan Stennett of the Black and White Minstrel and that name was to remain with me for a very long time. In those days the majority of workers from Chief Inspectors to cleaners had a nickname, it simply went with the territory. One Inspector had the name "The Gentle Giant" as a result of the quiet and gentlemanly manner in which he handed out a letter of reprimand, called 'a skin', for a misdemeanour. Then there was "The Scarf" for the way he stayed around to make sure that the tasks were being carried out, "Night and Day" was a worker who worked all the overtime that was available; the colloquial term for overtime was 'buff'. An ex-policeman from Nevis, A H P Slack, was called 'Nutty' and a chap from Ireland was called "The Elf".

I recalled one of the things that Mr Shepherd said to me, that I would need to be able to take and give as much as I can and the thing that would shield me from any face to face confrontation as a result of my colour would largely be due to the fact that I played sports. Although I did not have the experience of having the 'N' word being voiced in my presence, it was not uncommon to see it written in the toilets; it was always quite embarrassing for the vast majority of workers who were decent and honest to come to terms with the reality that in society there were people who, for whatever reason, had hang-ups about other people, either because they were short, or of another gender, race or religion. What indeed was the case with that visible minority that they failed to have come to terms with the history of their own society that highlighted the valuable contributions of African-Caribbeans in making Britain, according to Winston Churchill, "A land fit for heroes". Over time, and with some efforts from The Post Office management, the appearance of unsavoury writings became less and less, however on a personal note I was able to draw from these situations that the environment in Jamaica in which I had been socialised created the basis on which I was sure of my African-Caribbean identity and a feeling of pride in "The castle of my skin".

Ten days after I was appointed I had my first sorting test, the required rate was five hundred letters in fifteen minutes. My Instructor was Danny Thomas, who left no stones unturned in preparing me for the test, and I did five hundred and ninety five in the allotted time and, according to Les Napper, one of my colleagues, I was "shit hot" in doing the test. Again this is another of the processes of acceptance relative to a new working environment that embraced people from a wide cross-section of social, religious, gender, political and ethnic backgrounds and experiences. It was by all accounts a steep learning curve that had to be negotiated with tact, patience and tolerance, but then as the old Jamaican saying goes, "Just when one feels there is peace and safety there is sudden destruction".

What was to happen to me was more than a destruction, it was a culture shock out of all proportions considering the circumstances and the environment in which it took place. It was on the third occasion visiting St Mary's Anglican Church in Hulme when the Minister said to me, "I don't mind you coming but some members of my congregation feel that you sing too loud, maybe you would be better to find a Church where your kind go". For the first time in my life I was stuck for words and was enveloped in a cloak of frustration and anger, that a Minister of the Church that had been established in Jamaica for over one hundred years should be so alarmed of my presence in his church. When I related this incident to Lester Gordon, my cousin, he said, "Religion is for export, The English missionaries took the Bible to Africa and The West Indies, gave it to the natives and took their riches back to England". In as far as he was concerned the only reasonable Church person he came across in England was Brother Bernard.

CHAPTER TWELVE

Playing Cricket in the Leagues

MY PREPARATION for the 1960 cricket season was at The Roy Collins Indoor Cricket School in Didsbury. It was the first time in my life that I had ever practised indoors. The school attracted both professionals and amateurs from Lancashire County Cricket Club and other clubs that played in the various leagues, Central Lancashire, Lancashire, Cheshire and in and around Manchester. It was during these sessions that I met professional players such as Gary Sobers, now Sir Garfield Sobers, who played at Radcliffe, Clairmonte DePeiza, who played at Heywood, Reg Scarlett who played at Stockport and Syl Oliver who played at Todmorden. I went to improve my bowling and felt quite flattered when players of the calibre that I have mentioned supported and encouraged me at how best to improve my game.

One person that I was quite impressed with in terms of his accuracy and consistency in bowling line and length was Jim Cumbes, who played for Lancashire County Cricket Club and who eventually finished up as Chief Executive for the same Club for many years; how he did not play for England is still a mystery because man for man he was one of the best fast bowlers around. I remembered when I played my first match for General Post Office versus Manchester Transport, Queens Road and had match figures of 7 for 113, John St John from Grenada, who was their Captain, commented on my ability to bowl good line and length; my response was, "I have been watching Jim Cumbes".

A club in The Wednesday League in 1960 was Pauldens, a large Department Store in Piccadilly. As I understand it, some members of that team were from Kendal Milne, a similar establishment to Pauldens. This I believed to be true because I got a voucher which entitled me to thirty percent discount on any purchase from both stores. Other teams were Daily Mail, Manchester Taxis, National Coal Board, Leigh Wednesday, Salford Transport, London North Eastern Railways (LNER), Oldham Transport, Stockport Transport, Manchester Transport Northenden, Manchester Transport Birchfields and Parrswood, Manchester Transport Princess Road, Failsworth Co-op and Newton Heath Locomotives. Pauldens and Daily Mail dropped out of the league in 1962, National Coal Board and Leigh Wednesday followed in 1963 and Salford Transport the following year.

The standard of cricket was quite good, the majority of clubs attracting players from the Lancashire, the Central Lancashire, Saddleworth and Cheshire Leagues and the Manchester Association. Failsworth Co-op had players such as Alex Dawson, David Herd, Nobby Stiles, and Nobby Lawton, who played football for Manchester United. They also had Colin Barlow, who played football for Manchester City. Then there was Father David Mcgarry, a Roman Catholic Priest at Newton Heath; in the seventeen years that I played against him I have never seen him get a duck, he was the complete cricketer both on and off the field.

Oldham Transport had a galaxy of players from Barbados, some of whom played at national level, such as Douggie Clark, Colin Boucher, Bridgeman Ford, Neville Critchlow and Tyrone Knight; they even had Andy Goram, who represented Scotland both at football and cricket, playing for them. Newton Heath Loco, who played at Johnson's playing fields in Moston, had the Barbadian all rounder Granville Greenidge, from Jamaica there were V Bird and Josh William,s and from Nevis was Odin Williams; Odin was the second Afro Caribbean person in the North West to drive a train for British Rail. The first was Norman Kirkland from Portland in Jamaica.

Queens Road, arguably one of the strongest teams in the league, had Hughie Douglas, who played for Frome in the West Indies Sugar Company Competition and also Nethersole Cup Cricket for Westmoreland; also from Jamaica were Harry Dean and Ken Powell, who represented Portland. Ken opened the batting with Freddie Gleave, a Yorkshireman who was as stubborn as they come, most times he would carry his bat for little over 15 runs and whenever I played against him it was always to let him be and concentrate on the strokemakers like Douglas, Dean, Storer, Powell and St John from Grenada, who captained the side successfully for many seasons. I played against Douglas for over twenty years and have never got his wicket; the nearest was when we played against them in a Cup Final at Newton Heath Cricket Club in 1968 and Calvin Palmer dropped him fielding at third man before he got off the mark. He batted on and when he was on 98 I caught him fielding at second slip off the bowling of Calvin Palmer, yes cricket is indeed a funny game.

In my view the two outstanding cricketers for Manchester Taxis were Menzies; he was 'the coloured lad' that the taxi driver who took me to my address when I arrived in Manchester in August referred to, and Harold Lewis, who played for Prestwich on weekends. Harold was a very good all-rounder who took his game seriously, but by the same rule a gentleman on and off the field. Whenever we met it was like the "gun fight at the OK Coral" , in cricket the fast bowler will always win, especially when he has the ability to bowl a good line and length and a deadly Yorker. Harold was responsible for bringing a number of cricketers over from New Zealand to get experience playing under English conditions. Playing for Northenden were Derek Bolton Ashworth, Faulkner, Cliff Gittens from Barbados, who left the buses to follow a career in acting where he appeared for many years in Granada Televisions internationally acclaimed soap opera Coronation Street; from Jamaica there was Vincent Evring, who migrated to Canada. Derek retired to Prestatyn and was responsible for the staging of the annual cricket match between Prestatyn and a select eleven organised by Hopeton Harriet, who served as Landlord at the Sea Hawk public house in Hulme for many years.

Birchfields and Parrswood had Julian from Grenada, a very hostile fast bowler and useful middle order batsman; from Barbados were Colin Hunte and Colin Harewood, both all-rounders who opened the bowling. Harewood was the quicker of the two but Hunte, who claimed that he was a cousin of Sir Conrad Hunte, the West Indian Test Player, was a better batsman. Colin opened the batting with Tommy Barrington, quite a decent batsman, to motivate himself Colin was always talking, most times to the annoyance of the other players; not so when Mr Fairhurst was umpiring, who before the start of a game would go over to Colin and say, "Mr Hunte, I don't want to hear so much as a whisper from you today". Tommy Fairhurst was both a cricket umpire and a football referee who did those duties until he was in his nineties; he did not miss a trick and as far as umpires go he was honest and was always willing to give the batsman the benefit of the doubt.

I remember Colin getting a hundred and seven against General Post Office at Mount Road; as it happened, every time he scored a boundary off my bowling he said to me, "Same ball next time Stennett let me wet you ar**". I did have the last laugh when I had his off stump out of the ground with the inswinger. On his way back he said to me, "Be Jesus Christ boy, I owe you a drink". True to his word my cold pint of Guinness was there in the bar waiting for me after the match. He retired from the buses and went back to live in Barbados.

Another outstanding personality from Barbados who played in the Wednesday League was Keith Tate; he lived in London and travelled every Wednesday come rain or shine to play for London North Eastern Railways (LNER), who played at Woodley near Stockport, always immaculately dressed in his three-piece suite. According to the cricketing grap vine he was a Law student and the two players who always travelled with him were ringers from Middlesex and Derbyshire County Cricket Clubs. When the three got going LNER was no easy nut to crack. Cricket-wise and otherwise we went our separate ways and when I went on holiday to Barbados in 1988, Keith had a thriving business as an architect and builder and the last time we met was in 1996 when he came over to the funeral of his brother, Oscar Branch, who was a member of a fraternal organisation of which I was a part.

Like Birchfields, Princess Road played at Mount Road in Levenshulme, and had in their line-up George Burton, a spin bowler from Jamaica. Also from Jamaica were Albert Clarke, Bill Reid and Lester Reid; from Barbados there was Trotty Trottman, who also represented Manchester Transport in the National Regional Cricket Competition. Bill Reid left the buses to set up his own business, The Old Trafford Bakery on Shrewsbury Street. It was at Mount Road that Rudolph Smith at age sixteen, playing in the name of his father who was employed at Princess Road as a driver, made a hundred and eight against GPO; it was a day when I just could not get it together and it seemed to me that he came especially to put lashes on my back. In one over he plundered twenty off my bowling, playing shots all round the wicket, and when finally I did bowl him by knocking his leg stump out of the ground, the grim statistics of 18 overs 3 maidens 2 wickets 143 runs did not make good reading, especially when Albert Clarke was still there at the end of the innings with 59 to his name. It gave him a lot of pleasure telling people how he carted "Stennett the G.P.O quickie all over the place". It was certainly a good match both for Rudolph and himself, but I made sure that in future games I curbed their appetites for runs. By and large Mount Road was one of my happy hunting grounds, but something happened to me there which almost made me give up playing cricket.

It was in July 1962, GPO played Oldham Transport, who won the toss and were off to a good start until I bowled Neil Parris with the Yorker; next ball I had Jump, the incoming batsman, caught by Derek Hill for a duck. Next batsman in was Scobie to face the hat-trick ball, which he dispatched to the boundary for four with Douggie Clark still there making hay in the sun. There was no way we could think that we were out of the woods. The Umpire that day was Tommy Fairhurst, officiating from the end where I was bowling; when he signalled to me to stop and started talking to Scobie I am sure that if it had anything to do with my action Tommy would have had me. Douggie got a single and Scobie was now facing me; the ball pitched on a good length reared and instead of moving away he ducked into it and he fell almost motionless on the ground. Within seconds there was a swelling almost the size of a tomato just above his eyeline. I feared the worst as Carl Garner, who skippered our team and was a qualified first aid man, tried desperately to revive him. Within a matter of minutes the ambulance came and I could not keep the tears from falling as he was driven to the hospital still unconscious.

For the number of times that batsmen have been hit off my bowling and had to be seen by a doctor, it was the first time that one had to be taken off unconscious on a stretcher and taken to hospital in an ambulance; it made me very upset to the point that I decided to stop playing, even though I was assured by players from both teams that it was an accident. Scobie was taken to Withington hospital where he was detained for observation. It was a sleepless and prayerful night for me, hoping that Scobie would pull through his ordeal. When Carl Garner and myself arrived at Withington Hospital on the following morning, Bridgeman Ford and Scobie's wife were already there, other than exchanging pleasantries we all sat in silence. It was rather uncomfortable for me knowing that I was the one responsible for a gathering of silence in a hospital corridor waiting for news that could mean life or death. There was a feeling of relief when a nurse came out to inform us that Scobie had had a fairly comfortable night but until the doctor made his rounds there is very little more she could say. The feeling of relief on my part was to linger on when Tommy Fairhurst arrived and explained to the group that his coming to the hospital was to see to what extent what Scobie said to him when he stopped me from bowling - that he was feeling dizzy - could help the doctors have an understanding of his condition, and at the same time help me to come to terms with any feelings of anxiety that it was all my fault.

It was almost like an eternity for the doctor to complete his round and the good news was that although there was severe bruising where the ball had hit him, there were no signs of any other damage that would have any long-standing effect; but by the same rule it was advisable that until the bandages were removed he stayed in hospital. For the fleeting moment that I was allowed to see him courtesy of his wife it was clear that he accepted that it was an accident that had happened out of the blue. On our way back from the hospital Carl said, "Stan, it could have been worse, and I know that you have been shaken badly but in order to get over it you need to get by playing as early as possible".

The advice was taken with a great deal of thought knowing that however much there was an expressed understanding of what had happened I was the one that had delivered the ball and the mention of my name as being a demon fast bowler was not one that I could ever feel good about.

Keith Heslop from St Mary in Jamaica and Lindsay from Queensland in Australia were the only two people to play for the Post Office in the Wednesday League that did not actually work for the organisation. Keith prayed on weekends for Flowery Field in The Saddleworth League and Lindsay played for Sale Moor in The Manchester Association, and like other clubs in the League that attracted players from clubs whose standards were far higher than that of the Wednesday League they saw it as preparation for the weekend games, and as such the competition to make and stay in the Post Office team was very high.

In the eighteen years that I played for The Post Office I played under four captains. The first was Roy Tomlinson, who also played for Middleton in the Central Lancashire League. He was an opening batsman who kept wicket occasionally, an affable man, he encouraged his players to give of their best at all times. Two of my best performances were under his captaincy in the 1963 season when GPO won the championship and I had 5 wickets for 5 runs against Salford Transport playing at Swinton, hitting the stumps every time. The follow up was 9 wickets for 31 runs against Stockport Transport playing at King George's Park, the second ball of my third over I hit the centre stump so hard it snapped in half. The article that appeared in the Post Office Newsletter telling its readers that "Stennett bowled like a man possessed" was certainly one that I could live with. I was possessed with the zeal and commitment to do well for a team that consisted of like minded players.

Derek Ayres was the first wicket-keeper when I started playing. After Derek left the job his place was taken by another Derek, Derek Hill, arguably the best in the league. He opened the batting with Roy Tomlinson, quite a dependable pair who consistently paved the way for incoming batsmen such as Calvert "Teddy Proul" Hinds, a Barbados Colts Eleven representative, his brother Ron, Euton Christian, Tony Clough, Terry Lawton, Frank Johnson and Keith Heslop to play their shots. Both Teddy and Ron were masters at cricket clichés. Teddy's famous cliché was, "Boy, I come today to bat like a dog", Ron's was, "I going hit shite off that ball". I remembered playing against the Inland Revenue in a Civil Service Competition match at Cheadle Cricket Club when I was promoted from my number ten slot to number eight, according to my team mates to use the long handle of my Gunn and Moore bat to curb the fast bowler who was making inroads into our side. The first ball he bowled to me was short on the off; I duly hit him over his head for six. The next was treated in similar fashion, only this time it was on the leg side, even the bowler was clapping. As Ron came up and said in his broad Bajan accent, "Be Jesus Christ Stan if Alex Bedser, the England Selector, was here today you does sure play for England", such was the manner of the Hinds, never a dull moment when they were around.

I opened the bowling in those days with Ron Beaman. His mode of travel to matches was on his motorbike and sidecar. Second change bowler was Tony Mills, then Ian Williams and Pete Judge. The slow bowling department was manned by Euton Christian, his famous by-word when he beat a batsman was "crickey". The all-rounders were Mick Mills, who in time developed into a very useful pace bowler, Ray Beaman, brother of Ron, Frank Coughlan, Terry Grimes, Pete Lamb, Jack Henshall, Ken Knight, who left the Post Office to pursue a career in showbusiness, and Glyn Davis, who after he left the Post Office got a job with Lancashire County Cricket Club in promotions. The next Captain after Roy Tomlinson was Carl Garner from Barbados, a very shrewd man in terms of field-placing and changing of bowlers. He studied every action of batsmen and would always pass on tips to his bowlers on how to get them out, like the time when we played Manchester Queens Road at Middleton Road and Johnny St Johns was batting superbly when Carl came up and said, "Young man, don't you bowl bouncers any more, one or two will just help him to concentrate his mind". After the second whizzed past Johnny's nose he called Carl over and complained to him that my bowling was not in the true spirit of the game and I should be taken off, to which Carl replied, "I'll take him off once you are out". Next ball Johnny gloved it into the safe hands of Derek Hill behind the stumps. Walking back to the dressing room he said to me, "Stan I like the way that you follow instructions". Two balls after that I bowled Ken Powell all ends up with the Yorker, his remark on walking back was, "Good ball, boy".

Carl relished these moments when his instructions proved successful by saying to his bowlers, "What did I tell you, he didn't have a clue". It was Carl who recommended me to Clairmonte Depeiza, who with his fellow Barbadian Denis Atkinson, who captained the West Indies against Australia in the 1954-55 Test Series, created history in their seventh wicket partnership of 348, Atkinson, 219 not out, DePeiza 112 not out, to secure a draw. DePeiza played as professional at Heywood in the 60s and was responsible for recruiting both professional and amateur cricketers to play in a series of matches all over the country during the season. On one of the tours to Cornwall we were playing at St Austell and I was fielding at long leg when I saw one of the spectators, who I recognised as an Inspector from Newton Street, slowly walking towards me. On the end of the boundary were a group of youngsters requesting my autograph. For a start I should not have been in Cornwall playing cricket as I was off work on the sick; quick thinking on my part I limped down to the square leg umpire and told him that I was suffering from cramps in my legs and would need to go off at the end of the over. Depeiza, who was captaining the team, saw what was happening and signalled for the 12th man as I limped to the safety of the dressing room to avoid Mr Collinge recognising me.

When I went back to work Mr Collinge asked me if I had a twin brother as he explained that during his holidays in Cornwall, he went to see a match and the West Indian quick bowler had a very strong resemblance to me, but before he was able to see if it was me the chap limped off and he went to the scorers and the name of the player was Bancroft - that was my ringer's name when I played for National Dock Labour Board in the South Lancashire League. Euton Christian, who took over as Captain from Carl Garner, was a man who played hard and expected the same from his players; a stickler for rules, he gave no quarter and took no quarter. I supposed that his attitude to the game was borne out from his playing for the Royal Air Force, of which he was a member during the Second World War. We referred to him as The Sergeant Major, behind his back of course. He always wore his yellow cap given to him when he played for RAF Sealand near Chester. Except for Jack Henshall, Euton Christian was the best turned out cricketer in the Wednesday League, his whites with boots even down to his studs were immaculate. Whilst Carl Garner was responsible for getting me to play with Depeiza's touring team, it was Christian who got me involved with the West Indian Sports and Social Club team, formerly The Manchester Colonials. They played in The Manchester Amateur Cricket League of the fifties and sixties, winning every division of the league, and held the Championship for ten successive years. In addition to playing on weekends they played in a number of testimonial matches for Caribbean professionals in a number of leagues as far afield as the Midlands and South West of England. It was a privilege and honour to share dressing rooms with players such as Chester Watson, Roy Gilchrist, Charlie Stayers, Sir Garfield Sobers, Rohan Khan and Cec Wright. It was in one of those matches, playing against Whitchurch on the borders of Cheshire and Shropshire, that the Chairman of Whitchurch offered me the opportunity to play for expenses. Whilst it was tempting working shifts in the Post Office put paid to the proposition, although I did turn out for one match for them playing against a team from Durham when I got 6 for 83, took two catches at second slip and batting at number 10 with the long handle style got 16 runs in one over, which included two sixes and one four. I got £20 for my expenses.

Frank Johnson, the last Captain that I played under whilst working for The Post Office, compared to Tomlinson, Garner and Christian in terms of cricketing skills. Though not a King, he was certainly not a beggar, but one thing in which he stood head and shoulders above all three was his man management skills. To the casual onlooker he could be seen as laid back, the truth of the matter is that he knew his players and what we were capable of achieving, not only as cricketers but also within the career structures of the Post Office. He was well aware of sports contributions to the good and welfare of the employees and as such it was easy to understand why efforts were made to encourage and cater for every sporting and leisure time interest in which workers were able to participate.

I remember in 1968 when John Stonehouse, who was Minister of Posts and Telecommunications under Harold Wilson, visited Newton Street Post Office. I was one of the people that was introduced to him. In our conversation he expressed his appreciation for Michael Manley, the Jamaican politician, who like himself studied at the London School of Economics and shared the belief that more opportunities should be made available for the working classes to achieve their potential. I think that he was impressed when I told him that in addition to playing cricket and studying part time, I did voluntary work within the West Indian community. His response was, 'Giving something back to your community can be quite rewarding".

Playing Cricket in the Leagues

When Keith Heslop suggested that instead of going to the Cricket School at Didsbury to prepare for the 1967 Season we should go to Lancashire, little did I know that it would see me playing for Styal Cricket Club, who played in the Cheshire Cricket Club Conference league. I was recommended to them by Charlie Hallows, who was Head Coach at Lancashire. According to Mike Horner, who captained Styal, Charlie was impressed with me as a medium fast bowler and left handed batsman.

The cricket in the Conference was of a very good standard. Some of the clubs I recall playing in the Conference were Toft, Knutsford, Mobberley and Peover. Styal had a tree, it could have been an Oak, almost on the boundary line and in a match against Toft, one of their batsmen hit a ball into the tree and I caught it on the rebound. The batsman stood his ground, making the argument that he should be awarded with a six or at least four runs. The umpires ruled against him on the grounds that I took the catch within the field of play. It was whilst playing for Styal that my all-round ability developed; it was all to do with the points system that determined outright win or a draw and whether a team was bowled out or not which meant that batting at number ten I was to occupy the crease as long as possible. Mike Horner's instructions were, "Stan, get your head down, front foot forward". Following instructions has never been a problem for me, but being the compulsive hooker that I was, balls that had hook me written all over them got the treatment to the extent that players in the Conference likened me to Roy Fredricks, the Guyanese left hander who opened for the West Indies in the 1970s.

In this life one can never be sure of what is around the corner to derail us, yet by the same rule one should be prepared just in case something happens. Cricketers more than most people have an appreciation that life like cricket is a funny old game. I was to realise the truism when I played in a friendly match for the West Indies Sports and Social Club against Norton, who played in the Staffordshire League, where I had to walk off the field and took no further part in the game as a result of hay fever. Two days after that I was admitted to Withington Hospital where it was confirmed I was suffering from an acute attack of Bronchial Asthma due to pollen in the air. It was my first experience of hay fever, which became an annual ordeal until I went to the Civil Service Sanatorium in Beneden, Kent that had a unit that specialised in the effects of allergies on the pulmonary system. Over a period of three visits lasting two weeks, then one month, and then six weeks, I had a total of three hundred and sixty six allergy tests for almost everything imaginable. The final conclusion was that I was allergic to grass pollens and cats. Cats I could steer clear of but not even wild horses could keep me away from being in the open where I was exposed to pollens of every description during the cricket season. Thanks to Doctor Houri, the leading Specialist on Allergies at Beneden, a medication was made for me which proved successful over the years.

Clunis "John" Stephens from St Mary in Jamaica was the person who got me to sign on with Manchester Dock, who played in the South Lancashire League and also in the Regional National Dock Labour Board Competitions. The South Lancashire League of the sixties was one of the best, attracting clubs from Lancashire and Cheshire; the standard of cricket was very good and with the divisions clubs played hard to achieve and maintain first division status. That I was asked to play for Manchester Docks at a time when they more or less ruled the first division roost, and had players in their second team who were equally as good to play in their first team, speaks volumes to what Harry Dean, the first team wicket-keeper said that, "Stennett is not one of the fastest bowlers around but in terms of accuracy he is almost the best". It was very reassuring and boosted my confidence no end. Sharing the new ball with Roy Gavin, who later left to play for Massey Ferguson in the same league, or with Herman Bogle and Myron "Dusty" Hull, or even being first change to any of them, was no mean feat. With a batting line up of Harry Dean, Peter Hinds, Neville Ormsby, Herman Bogle, John Brown, Carl Marriott, Gerald Essue and Clunis Stephens, it was not unusual to see three hundred runs scored in an afternoon by Manchester Dockers. Anything less was an abject failure, and cricket being the game it is, it happened more than once. The most outstanding was when British Steel, playing at their home ground in Irlam, bowled us out for 93 runs. They had a right to feel on top of the world as their openers signalled their intentions that it would be a cake walk; not so Harry Dean, our Skipper, who brought me into the attack with strict instructions to bowl a mixture of inswing, outswing and Yorkers. Bowling at the other end was Gerald Essue, the spinner. From 27 for 1 they finished up with 85 all out; I had match figures of 13 overs, 3 maidens, 7 wickets, 35 runs. I hit the stumps three times and Alvin "Cockshan" Stephens, brother of John and one of the best slip fielders that I have ever seen, took four fielding at first slip. The headline on the sports page of the Salford Reporter read, "Bancroft bowled Dock Labour to victory". It was to be my best performance playing for the Docks and no one was more appreciative that the real John Bancroft under whose name I played, not being a docker. He was more interested in Rugby than Cricket, but as time went by he started to develop an interest for the sport to the point where he started to take his family to watch the team. I think that he rather enjoyed it when the scorers enquired of the bowlers name and the response was Bancroft.

He travelled with the team to Thick Hill in Yorkshire to watch the semi final between Manchester and Grimsby docks, the winner to travel to London for The National Dock Labour Board Cricket Final. Grimsby won the toss and had the worst start imaginable when their opening batsman stepped on to his wicket off the bowling of David Page. Off the first ball in the last ball of his over he had the number two batsman caught by Alvin Stephens at first slip; the score was 2 wickets for 7 runs. To players and spectators the game was definitely won. Undeterred by the early disaster the Grimsby batsmen, especially the left-handed Morris, stood firm and took away the initiative from us. I was not introduced into the attack until after tea when Morris was on 90. My first two balls he dispatched to the boundary for fours and he was now on 98. My third ball I went around the wicket and with the inswinging Yorker I had his leg stump out of the ground to deny him of his century.

Grimsby's total of 231 was not a formidable task for Manchester, especially in light of Keith Heslop and G Gardner, quite reliable batsmen, being drafted into the side. By the time we had lost four wickets for 151 runs the feeling amongst us was that it was in the bag as things continued to run smoothly until panic stations set in when two of our lower order batsmen ran themselves out; the score was then 224 for 9 with three balls to go 8 runs to win and in strode Bancroft, the Apostle for Lost Causes.

The first ball I hit the bowler straight over his head for six runs, in those situations I have always been at my most dangerous and the next ball was a hook for four and a well deserved victory and a place in the Finals. Walking back to the dressing room I was stopped by an old gentleman, who told me that I reminded him of George Hirst, the Yorkshire cricketer. When he was told by his friends that George bowled left arm and batted right hand and I was the other way round he said to them, "Too right, but like Georgie he can hook". That was a great tribute from a man who revealed that as a player he kept wicket for Manny Martindale, the Barbadian fast bowler who played for the West Indies in the thirties and who also played professional cricket for Burnley in the Lancashire League.

Four years before I started playing for the docks they were in a similar position and players such as Roy Gavin, John Brown, Harry Dean and John Stephens were full of anticipation and delight about travelling the second time to London for the Final. I figured that from my performance I stood a chance of being selected for the match. Sadly our hopes were dashed when on the Monday the Secretary of the Club received a telephone call informing him that Manchester would not be taking part in the Final because it had been discovered that they played players who were not employed by them. I felt saddened, not so much for myself, but genuinely for John Bancroft, who was making plans to take his family to London. It was just one of those things and something that I learnt from John when we were having a discussion over a drink in the Dockers' Club at Monmouth Street, Salford across the road from where the Copthorne Hotel now stands, is when he said, "Stan, from the very day sports started, people have been pulling fast ones and it will continue until the world ends". I was never a docker and certainly on the day of the match nobody approached me and suggested that I should play bad, but from rumours there was a feeling that money could have some bearing on the outcome of the match, who knows, and in Jamaican jargon, "Mouth is made to say anything". That being said I decided that for better or for worse I was no longer prepared or wanted to play under another person's name, in the true sense of the word it was not cricket and the solution was to find another club.

The club I moved to was The Post Office Engineers, who had a team in the second division of the South Lancashire League. The captain of the team was Gordon Kingston Hamilton, a good cricketer and as a skipper an Officer and a Gentleman on and off the field, a man who inspired his players to give of their best. In my first season I shared the opening bowling with Neville "Manny" Pittersen from Race Course in Clarendon, Jamaica, who played in the Crum Ewing and West Indies Sugar Company Competitions for Monnymusk. Second change bowler was Bert Jepson and then Jag Patel from Kenya. The team was strengthened both in batting and bowling when Len Braithwaite from Barbados joined us on a special registration from Prestwich Hospital. Opening the batting were Ron Mitchell and Chris Miles, who always laid a good foundation where strokeplayers such as Jag Patel, Len Braithwaite, Alan Miles, father of Chris, Jack Greaves, Frank Stevens and his son Tony felt comfortable at playing without undue pressure. Very rarely lower order batsmen such as Barry Laslett, Frank Gittens, Neil Black and myself were asked to bat, a reflection of the strength of the team, which meant that more often than not whenever our team had to bat last I would retreat to the showers for a freshen up. It was not something that Gordon liked and to dissuade the practice he always reiterated the cricket motto that the game is never won or lost until the last ball is being bowled.

Playing in the last game of the 1976 season against Brooksbottom near Bury was to put the adage into perspective. As it happened both teams had the same amount of points and a win would decide the winner of the division. It was a low scoring match on both sides that saw the GPO Engineers bowling out Brooksbottom for 83, bowling honours going to Len Braithwaite and Jag Patel; things were to prove even more disastrous for GPO when we found ourselves on 68 for 9 when I was literally pulled from under the showers, hastily drying myself whilst at the same time retrieving the soiled cricket clothes from my bag! At the point of buckling my pads I looked at Gordon, his body language conveying defeat but the gloom in the dressing room was broken by Nev Pittersen who said, "Come on Whits, make a name for yourself". I strode to the wicket with those words ringing in my ears and the confidence that I would live up to the occasion, if for no other reason that Nev and myself had promised Gordon when earlier in the season he had announced that he would be relinquishing the captaincy that he would be going out with a winning note.

TV, the Brooksbottom bowler who had made inroads into our batting, was on his hat-trick ball, the second in his six overs; the Brooksbottom followers were jubilant and vociferous with their chants of "Come on TV" and "It's in the bag". There was even a board displaying, "Brooksbottom are the Champions". My calculation with 16 runs to win off 5 balls was, according to Jeff Anderson, a Manchester Dock Supporter, to "aim for the hills", or as Cheyney Boodie, another supporter, said, "see the woods", which meant that as far as I was concerned the long handle had to come into play. The first ball, a good length on the off was made into a decisive hook shot out of the ground and into a ravine that ran adjacent to the ground for six and a lost ball; the racist expletives and personal comments as to where I came from and why I should go back to the trees by some players and spectators was unbelievable. The second ball, a replacement, got the same treatment, third ball no score. With only two balls remaining and four to win, the Brooksbottom supporters and players were still willing TV on, the same applied to my supporters.

It was reliving the first match that I played for my first eleven in Jamaica in 1948 when I was 13 years old; then I lived up to the expectations of both my team and my supporters, this time I was seeing the ball like the size of a breadfruit. To me TV was a spent force and his fourth ball was so long of a length that I drove it past him all long the ground for four and a well earned victory that was so sweet, even more so when TV and some of his teammates in congratulating me apologised for the behaviour of the supporters and some of the mates. One of the umpires was equally apologetic whilst the others walked by as if nothing had happened; I suppose that like some members of my team their silence was out of guilt and shame, and though it may be difficult for some people to understand, in such cases I feel pity for people, who as far as they are concerned are far more educated than the black man and yet their behaviour is worse than animals. To this I believe that the only way such behaviour can be put right is through education.

Nev Pittersen, who took over from Gordon Hamilton as Captain of GPO Engineers, was from the old school of Jamaican cricketers who believed that the ball is to be hit when you are batting, and when you are bowling the idea is to hit the stumps. He was a team player who played to the highest standards of the game, as Skipper he had no favourites. An example of this is that at one time we both lived in the same house but he made it clear that I should never assume that I would automatically open the bowling; that was the measure of the man and we all respected him. It was during Nev's time as Captain that I bought my first car, a 1954 Morris Minor with the split windscreen, for £30. I called the car Jack Ruby and what a gem it was as most Saturday and Sundays both Nev's children and my own would cram into it to matches at Chloride Batteries in Swinton, ICI Blackley, Simon Carves in Stockport,

187

Bibby and Barrow in Bury, Fieldhouse in Rochdale and Chadderton St Marks. These matches were great occasions for families., getting together and the nurturing of personalities. Bibby and Barrow had Neville Neville, father of Gary and Phil who play football for England and Manchester United, and sister Tracy, who represented England at Netball. At Fieldhouse there was the Lancashire and England Fast Bowler Ken Shuttleworth, it was the Prestwich Hospital team that had the two brothers, Mal and John Tyrell, a fast bowler. Mal the wicket-keeper left and played for Ashton in the Central Lancashire League.

I played in the various leagues and later on, after my playing days were over I did umpiring, which was an extension of my experience in Jamaica where the vagaries of class, gender, needle, sledging, pride, loyalty, social political and all other agendas reflected themselves and at the end of the day it made sense as to why it is so unique as a sport. In essence, all the processes of human life in this world and the next.

CHAPTER THIRTEEN

Retracing my Steps

IN OCTOBER 1969 I decided that I would revisit Jamaica, so I flew via New York in order to see my brother, Noel, who went to live in Connecticut in 1963. It was ten years since we had last seen each other and arriving at JFK Airport on a chilly October evening I could not help but reflect on that August day in 1969 when I stopped off there for a short time on my way to England.

Driving over the Brooklyn Bridge on my way to Connecticut provided me the opportunity to appreciate the vastness of New York, of which I was very impressed, but what was even more impressive was on the following morning when I woke to see the trees in an array of colours and to be told by my sister-in-law, Minnett, that what I was looking at was Connecticut in the Fall. I have always been interested in the vagaries of nature and what came to my mind that morning was that if Heaven and the afterlife is as beautiful as the Connecticut Fall, death which is part of the process to get there is nothing to be fearful of.

The ten days that I spent in America was a twofold purpose; first to observe for myself if the suggestion from my brother that I should leave England and come to live in America was worthwhile, and secondly, I wanted to see some of the places in New York that I had read about, heard about and had seen in films. To make sure that I would be able to see as much as possible. I spent three days with my friend, Joe Daay, who had resigned from the Jamaica Constabulary Force and was living in New York. At the time he took me around on a tour of some of the places that we had heard about when we were growing up in Jamaica; places such as The Empire State Building, from where I was able to see the Statue of Liberty, and Ellis Island, from where one of the local characters of my boyhood days was deported back to Jamaica. According to the local grapevine he was involved in bootlegging and was caught smuggling alcohol across the border.

Going around Madison Square Garden brought memories back to the first time as an eleven year old youngster in 1946 when I listened to the second fight between Billy Conn and Joe Louis. The then World Heavyweight Boxing Championship was being broadcast on Radio, the transmission was almost inaudible at the time but I remembered vividly, Andy 'Admiral' Forbes, the Uncle of Lindy Forbes who was a very long time Chair of the

Discovery Bay Past Students Association in his stentorian voice shouting, "Billy Conn hook him with a left and toss him with a right. Jesus Christ is this a knockout or what?" As it happened Joe Louis won the fight and as time advanced and technology improved I listened on radio and saw many fights televised from that famous landmark for boxing.

Other places that I visited were Broadway, the New York Stock Exchange, where my friend Joe Daay worked, and the United Nations Building, where for the first time I saw the new Jamaican Flag of yellow, gold and green waving in the cool October wind. It was for me a very proud moment, a gentle reminder that however British I felt, I would forever remain a Jamaican.

The visit to Harlem was the highlight of the tour, it was so surreal walking along 138th Street and 7th Avenue, where in his heyday Marcus Garvey, the Jamaican National Hero, held sway through his United Negro Improvement Association that ignited a new consciousness amongst Africans worldwide. For me it was a step back in time to a period which I had not been a part of save from what I read about; nevertheless I was savouring the moments as I slowly and painstakingly looked at places such as Liberty Hall and the Abyssinian Baptist Church, pastured at one time by the charismatic black Congressman Adam Clayton Powell. Whilst in Harlem I met a third generation Jamaican who, although he was American as Blueberry Pie or Iced Tea, was proud to extol his heritage, going back to his grandfather who left Jamaica in the early 1900s for Costa Rica, then on to Panama where he married a Panamanian and eventually settling in Harlem. According to him his grandfather was very much involved with the Garvey Movement and was at the first UNIA International Convention held in Madison Square Garden in 1920 where, from what he was told by his grandfather, the theme of the event was "Africa for the Africans those home and abroad". Talking with Mr Taylor it became obvious, it being in 1969 when the war in Vietnam and the New Black Conscious Movement was at its height involving people like Martin Luther King Jnr, Malcolm X, Muhammad Ali, Angela Davis, Bob Dylan in America and in England, Michael X, the spokesperson for the militant Racial Adjustment Action Society or RAAS, and in Jamaica Bob Marley, Peter Tosh and to some extent the West Indian Cricket Team. That he was able to make the connection with Garvey's philosophies and its relevance to Black people in America, Europe and the Caribbean, I left Mr Taylor and Harlem with a deeper sense of self assertion and pride.

My last point of call in New York was at The Police Club on White Plains Road. As the name implied membership was strictly reserved for those who had served honourably with the Jamaican Constabulary, hence one who had not served could only be admitted when accompanied by a member. When I lived in Jamaica, as a result of some of my school friends becoming Police

Officers and through playing cricket, I visited the Police Club at Central Police Station on East Queen Street where to my observations there was always a line of demarcation based on rank. The situation at White Plains Road, though not as rigid, was still part of the status quo even though those people were thousands of miles away from Jamaica. The one great leveller was that from whatever rank they were in Jamaica, in America they were all seeking the almighty Dollar and were prepared to do any job that would help them to achieve the American Dream.

In comparison to those of us who left Jamaica to stay in England for five years, none of those that I met at the Club had such plans; some talked about leaving New York once their working life came to an end to retire to Florida or Georgia. What was also interesting and which is part of the human experience was that talking to them, whether they had left the force before Independence in 1962 or after, their political views differed with the majority having or expressing their loyalties to Britain in terms of its traditions for fair play, law and order, parliamentary procedures, pageantry and, of course, cricket, to which there was a total consensus that they would like to travel to England to watch cricket being played at Lord's, Old Trafford, Trent Bridge, The Oval, Headingley and Edgbaston. I sensed that there was a feeling of jealousy on the part of two of the people around the table where I sat when I told them that not only was I living within walking distance to Old Trafford Cricket Ground and Manchester United Football Club, but also that I had watched cricket at all the other Test Grounds. As it happened, sitting around the table was one Sergeant Gayle who did some of his training at Hendon in London during which time he went to see Test Matches at The Oval and at Lord's. In a sense I was not on my own in singing the praises for the privilege or the opportunity that had come my way in terms of my cricketing experiences and as such there was an agreement between Sergeant Gayle and myself that there was truth in Rudyard Kipling's statement that, "He knows England who only England knows".

What I found difficult was engaging anybody about present trends taking place in America - which was of world importance - such as the war in Vietnam, the Black Power Movement and Muhammad Ali's refusal to join the forces. Regarding Ali most referred to Joe Louis who as World Champion joined the Army, which did him no harm as far as Black Power was concerned. Some expressed a feeling of disquiet that it was moving across to Jamaica, especially amongst students at the University College of The West Indies, to which they hoped the Government in Jamaica would do everything within their power to stamp out what according to them was a group of agitators who were determined to bring down the United States. They were supportive of Roy Jenkins, who as Home Secretary in 1967 deported Stokeley

Carmichael when he visited England, and were surprised when I told them that not only did I join the protest march against the cricket establishment when Basil Dolivera was refused entry to play for England in South Africa in 1967, but I was also in total agreement with Tommie Smith and John Carlos, the two African-American athletes who stood on the winner's platform at the 1968 Olympic Games in Mexico and raised clenched fists with black gloves.

My argument was that far from being a group of agitators, like Marcus Garvey the new generation of visionaries were reinforcing the importance of self-determination and black identity, and in order to achieve that goal, whether in England, America or Jamaica, black voices had to come together to echo the point. I sensed that the group in which I had the dialogue was not happy, and one went as far as to suggest that I ought to consult a Psychologist because as far as he was concerned I was a very confused young man; another suggested that I should go to the barbers and get a good clean back and sides instead of my beard and afro hairstyle. Looking around the club that evening I was the only one with a beard and a distinguished afro. Far from feeling out of place I felt confident, besides I was only passing through and my thoughts were fully focused on getting the flight the following day to Jamdown.

Sitting beside me on the plane to Jamaica was an American woman, possibly in her late twenties, who was going down to work for an American company in Kingston. She was very clued up on most aspects of Jamaican life and looked forward to following her favourite pastimes of water skiing and snorkelling, which reminded me of my childhood days fishing for food and for fun and I would certainly have been failing in my duty if I did not tell her about the excellent facilities for snorkelling at Discovery Bay. I even went as far as to mention that she should, when she got to Discovery Bay, ask for Jacob Leslie who would make every arrangement for her to explore the underwater beauty of Jamaica's North Coast.

Like a number of Americans that I have had the privilege to meet, whenever I mention to them that I live in England, nine times out of ten their immediate response is always, "Is it London?" This woman was no different when she told me of her Uncle, who during the Second World War was with the American Air Force and was stationed in London during which time he visited Manchester very often. As the conversation developed it transpired that her Uncle was at Burtonwood near Warrington, almost two hundred miles away from London. I suppose that like a significant number of people who migrated from Jamaica to England it was convenient to tell people that they were from Kingston; the converse is that for most Americans, London is England. Be that as it may the flight conversation between us was quite pleasant and I needed no reminder from the pilot that we were approaching Jamaica.

At Buckingham Palace after receiving my MBE for services to the community with my eldest daughter Pat, my wife Gwen and granddaughter Nikesha.

Professor Barry Plumb of Manchester Metropolitan University (MMU) congratulates me for organising the benefit match in the memory of Charlie Headlam.

The Moss Side community team who played in the match

Mr Alan Dove of MMU presents Mrs Headlam with the trophy in honour of her husband. To the left of Mrs Headlam is Mr Oswald Smith, Chair of STEP (Strategies To Elevate People), who read a citation on behalf of Charlie.

The MMU team that played in the match.

Above: With some of my old school friends at the Discovery Bay Past Students Day in 2000 From the left: Crampy Williams, Steadman Stewart, Pushy Ward and Egbert Wisdom.

Left: Sitting out the match with Pushy Ward deciding on how much to spend on the drinks. My sitting out was due to the fact that I was not prepared to stand up to the pace of Michael "Tower" Williams's grandson in the Past v Present students game at Discovery Bay in 2000.

From the left: Vin "Uncle Money" Cover, Arthur "Comrade" Clemetson and Ernest "Castro" Cover. They are three of my old school mates who have gone abroad and returned to Discovery Bay, playing tremendous roles in giving back to the community through their philanthropy.

Mrs Cherry Byfield (left) and husband Arthur (right). In the middle is Dr Arthur Wint, who in 1948 broke the Olympic record for the 200 metres at Wembley. I learnt a lot from the Byfields about the pursuit of positive aims and objectives of Jamaicans in Manchester and the UK.

**Receiving my Degree from Manchester
Metropolitan University in 2002.**

With members of the Jamaican contingent who represented their country at Commonwealth Games in Manchester in August 2002. This event was held at the Imperial War Museum and was hosted by Trafford Borough Council.

With councillor Roy Walters at the same event where we also hosted members of the Ugandan team. Roy was Lord Mayor of Manchester whilst I was Deputy Mayor Trafford.

In the Mayor's parlour with my family on the night of my installation as Mayor of the Borough of Trafford in May 2003.

In the Mayor's parlour on the evening of my installation. Back row (from left to right): Chief Superintendant David Ryder (Trafford Divisional Commander), Mrs Ryder, Mrs Carole Hassan (CEO Trafford Borough Council), Rev. Dr David Wheeler (my chaplain) and Mrs Margaret Wheeler. Front row: Mrs Gwen Stennett (Mayoress), Me, Mrs Pam Dixon (Deputy Mayoress) and her consort Mr Ian Dixon.

People have always been fascinated by the Mayor's chain in terms of its value, its weight and how many diamonds are moulded into it. Pictured are members of the St John's Old Trafford Youth Church, looking with interest at the chain on the Sunday the Mayor's Civic Service took place at the church.

Imogen and Shanique, two of my granddaughters in my garden - check the azalea!

Left: Xavier Marshall, who I encouraged to come to play for Sale Cricket Club in 2003 when I was Mayor. He went back to Jamaica and eventually made the West Indies touring side to Australia, Sri Lanka and Bangladesh.

Right: Members of the two teams that took part in the match at Sale. The Mayor's XI was led by councillor Ian Mullings of Trafford and centre is councillor Ken Holt, mayor of Stockport, who played in the match.

Left: With councillor Ray Tully, a former Mayor of Trafford, and Mike Shaft of BBC Radio Manchester on the day when a Mayor's XI played a Mike Shaft XI at Sale CC in September 2003 to raise money for my two charities, Cancer Research and Sickle Cell Thalassemia.

Above: Receiving a cheque from Angie Smith, Events Co-ordinator for Asda in Trafford Park, who helped in raising funds for my two charities whilst I was Mayor.
Below: My wife Gwen and I opening the Tesco Express on Upper Chorlton Road

Above: Miss Mensah of the Sickle Cell Association and a
representative from Cancer Research at Christies receiving a cheque.
Below: Myself and wife Gwen with Councillor Mary Harney, left,
who was Mayor of Trafford in 2002 when I was her Deputy
Mayor, and her escort, Mr Graham Hall, right.

Largely due to the determination of my younger sister Lyn the New Harbour View has risen from the rubble left by Hurricane Gilbert in 1988. When I van struck in September 2004 I was in the house on my own. It was quite a daunting experience but I lived to tell the tale. What? Jamaica, No Problem!

Mr Arthur Clemetson, President of the Discovery Bay Community Association, Dr Vincent Riley of the St Ann's Bay Hospital, Me, the Honourable R.O. Walters, Custos of St Ann, and Mr Lynden Buchanan, CEO of the St Ann's Bay Hospital, in Jamaica at the handover ceremony of medical equipment that I made to the institution on my visit in 2004.

In November 1906 England elected its first two black councillors. John Richard Archer and Henry Sylvester Williams were elected on Labour tickets to Battersea and Marylebone Borough Councils respectively. Trafford Borough Council marked the anniversary in November 2006 when they got councillor Ejak Malik, who like myself represents the Clifford Ward for Labour, and councillor Dylan Butt, who represents Hale Barns for the Conservatives, to talk about our experiences as the only three black councillors in Trafford.

Above: Me, Roy Gavin and Nev Pittersen. Roy was a fast bowler who played in the Manchester Association, Lancs & Cheshire and South Lancashire leagues. Nev played in the South Lancs and West Manchester leagues and the Civic Service competitions for Post Office Engineers. Nev went back to live at Water Lane in Clarendon, Jamaica.

Below: Me and Kipper Lynch. As a batsman Kipper had shots all round the wicket and would square cut one to ribbons.

Me with the cricket bat and the suitcase that I brought with me from Jamaica in 1959 and some of my cricket trophies. The two mounted balls are for taking 5 for 5 against Salford Transport and 9 for 31 against Stockport in the Wednesday League in the 1963 season.

As the aeroplane started to descend and the views of the mountains and the seas became more visible my thoughts went back to ten years earlier when I was on the out-going flight to England and as the plane disappeared into the sky and I caught the last glimpse of Jamaica I harped back to the poet William Cowper, who in his poem Alexander Selkirk wrote: "My friends do they now send a wish or thought after me of a land I shall visit no more". To be truthful, although when I left Jamaica I did make a promise that I would be away for only five years, there was also a gnawing feeling that I would never live to see the country again; as time went on this feeling eventually went away. The first thing I did when I alighted from the aircraft was to bow down and kiss the ground. I was overcome with emotion and made no attempt to stop the tears rolling down. They were tears of joy, especially when I stood on Jamaican soil to watch the Jamaican flag proudly waving in the breeze, echoes of Walter Scott, poet, who wrote: "Breathes there a man with soul so dead who hath not to himself has said this is my home my native land". It was my first homecoming and as such I was buzzing with an anticipation that was difficult to explain.

What I expected to be a formality in having nothing to declare going through Customs was to turn into an irritating episode when I was pulled by an over-zealous Customs Officer and abruptly instructed to open my case and in the same breath, fielding a barrage of rapidly-fired questions as to how long I have been away from Jamaica, what I do for a living in England, the political and social organisations that I was involved with before I left Jamaica and presently in England, what was the reason for staying in America, and if during that time did I attend any political meetings that had a bias against the United States or Jamaican governments, or was I carrying into the country any firearms or literature that would constitute a danger or threat to the security of both countries.

Painstakingly I had to answer all the questions, starting from attending the local school at Dry Harbour as indicated in my Jamaican Passport where I was born, my admiration for Marcus Garvey and the Maroons, becoming a member of the People's National Party, and the National Workers Union, playing cricket for my school and village, then for the Post Office in Kingston before I eventually migrated to England. In as far as my political and social activities and the job that I did in England centred around working for the Post Office, playing cricket for them, being involved with the West Indian Sports and Social Club, which provided me the opportunity to meet Caribbean people from the various other Islands, also being a member of the Labour Party and the Union of Post Workers, I told him about the various places that I had visited whilst in New York and other than going to the Police Club on White Plains Road, where it was a natural thing that when people meet in such environment sports, politics, religion or music are always topics to be discussed. I attended no political gatherings. In the process of going through my case all he found was a bottle of Jim Beam Whisky, two Afro combs, a t-shirt with Che Guevara emblazoned on the front, three cricket balls, and two books "Black Power; the Politics of Liberation in America" by Stokely Carmichael and Charles V Hamilton. The other "Fifty Unknown Facts about the Blackman" by Gabriel Osei.

At no stage during the interrogation was I insolent to him, even though I realised that given the Officer was carrying out his duties there was a lot to be desired on his part in terms of common courtesies, again it was a case according to Jamaican parlance he had the handle and I had the blade, yet by the same rule I was willing to stand up for the things that I believed in irrespective of the consequences.

When I came out from the Departure Lounge I immediately saw the signs of anxiety on both the faces of my mother and my sister, Carmen, whom Gershom Pryce, the Brother-in-law of my brother Noel, had brought to meet me, but no way was I going to allow what transpired at Customs to rob me of the joys of homecoming and reuniting of kinship ties. Hardly had I sat down in the front passenger seat of the car when Gershom started to explain that from what he gathered from an employee at the Airport who was one of his friends the reason I was so thoroughly interrogated and searched is that with my well pronounced Afro hairstyle and beard I fitted the description of a man who had close ties with the Black Power organisation in the United States, who was recruited by Doctor Walter Rodney, the Guyanese Political Activist and Lecturer who a year previously had led the students' revolt at the University College of The West Indies Mona.

According to Gershom the ideas of Walter Rodney were getting support not only from the student body with its intellectual influence, but also from a visible majority of the country's poor and marginalized, especially young Rastafarians. Listening to Gershom talking, especially when he mentioned that among some of the earlier supporters of Doctor Rodney were men who were staunch Garveyite, although he did not mention any names I could not help but reflect on Mr Taylor, the American-Jamaican I had met in Harlem the previous day and our conversation on the philosophies of Marcus Garvey, and on the evening of the same day at the Police Club on White Plains Road. It dawned on me that someone with connections in Jamaica who I had spoken to may have taken umbrage with what I had said about the way forward for oppressed people and as a result got their friends to put me in my place.

A further explanation as to why my hairiness and the espousing of political ideas based on the importance of black awareness could be seen as a challenge to the status quo was advanced by Mother, who told us in the car of her meeting with Vernal Fairweather from Helicon, who had returned from England to tell her how surprised he was when he met me at a wedding reception in Birmingham to see me with a big mop of hair on my head, a heavy beard and preaching black power politics. My Mother said that she was relieved when he assured her that from his observations he was sure that I was not involved in drugs or drinking excessively. Interestingly, with skills as an accomplished musician, Sunday School Teacher, Choir Master, Master of Ceremonies for every occasion in the community and a cricket umpire, he was also the first person in our village, other than members of the landed gentry, to have a licence to drive a motor car. He was one of my role models, so when I met him in Birmingham I myself was rather surprised as to why he had given up a fairly comfortable lifestyle in Jamaica to come to Birmingham where he found it difficult to apply his skills. It was from that premise that I articulated my views that evening as to the inequalities in society based on race and class. However true the facts were, it would be interpreted by him to be antagonistic for the sole reason that the message of Black awareness that had linkages with Garveyism would irritate him, if for no reason than he was from that background that formed a buffer between the ruling classes and the working classes. It was seven years into Independence and a time when Jamaica was still dealing with a number of political, social, economic and cultural issues that were relative to nation building. In such an environment it was easy to understand that various groups of people were involved in the pursuing of their individual ideals as part of that process, that is why I entertained no malice towards the Customs Official, however much I felt that he was over zealous, nor to Vernal, who interpreted my stance against inequalities as that of a misguided radical. I was neither a crusader or one seeking martyrdom; I was the same Whitty Stennett, though after ten years away from Jamaica my knowledge base had expanded. The most important thing for me was that I was back home simply to reconnect with the place where my navel string was buried - and also to re-charge my batteries.

Nothing could have prepared me to fully understand the changes that had taken place in Discovery Bay, and for that matter most of Jamaica, in the ten years that I had been away. For a start there was no National Stadium when I left; it was built in time for the celebration of Jamaica's Independence in 1962. As a Jamaican I was proud to be driving on Arthur Wint Drive, named after the famous Jamaican athlete who brought international fame to his native land when in 1948 at the London Olympics he won a gold medal in the 400 metres relay. His feat reinforced the Jamaican saying of "Wi little but wi tallawah". The statute of Arthur Wint at the entrance of the Stadium summed up all the wealth of pride that I had within me on that day.

Proceeding along Tom Redcam Drive not only reminded me that the Drive was named in memory of a former Poet Laureate of Jamaica, but it was also the headquarters for the Library Service of Jamaica; there is a school of thought amongst some Jamaicans that Tom Redcam was MacDermot spelt the other way round. It was refreshing to see the Little Theatre, built in 1961 to foster the work of Henry and Greta Fowler, who founded The Little Theatre Movement in the 1940's from which grew The Jamaica School of Drama. The Theatre is used by performing groups throughout the year, two of the most famous being The Jamaican Folk Singers and The National Dance Theatre company. The first Circus that I saw was at George The Sixth Memorial Park off East Race Course in Allman Town. In addition, the Cenotaph part of the site was used as a cycle track and there were also a number of leisure activities that took place there and at any time of the day one could always get to participate in a serious game of cricket or football; it was a case of having gear or no gear you can play. I have witnessed many injuries where players had to be taken to Hospital for treatment and count myself fortunate that I have never been a casualty.

The last cricket match that I played at Race Course was in July 1959; a friendly, Parcel Post versus the Fire Brigade. Dennison, the Fire Brigade quickie, made mincemeat of us until I made my entrance at number ten, announcing to all and sundry that I was going to cool him. It was not an idle boast as I carted the last three balls of his over into cow corner for sixteen runs. The Race Course spectators went wild with excitement and when one shouted out, "Dennisonm, Stennett not only cooling you but he is schooling you", the remark was reminiscent of me reading about the cricket match at Rugby School in Thomas Hughes' Tom Brown's Schooldays when a batsman hit the bowler over the Rook Trees.

One of my great memories of the Race Course was that my desire as a youngster to play the clarinet had gone into meltdown and was suddenly being rekindled by listening to Don Drummond, who had come to live off one of the streets that ran off East Race Course and behind number 18, the last address that I lived in Kingston prior to migrating to England. Rated by George Shearing as one of the five best Trombonists in the world at the time, much to the annoyance of some residents in the neighbourhood, Don would play at anytime, morning noon or night. For me each sound conveyed a message that symbolised aspects of my past, my present, my future, and the opportunity to have a better understanding of my own mortality. At times songs such as The Re-Burial, Valley Princess and African Beat caused my spirit to soar to new heights and at other times like the fallen feather from a bird in flight the sound descends into a mystic and muffled moan. After ten years of voluntary exile I was back at Race Course, only this time it was renamed National Heroes Park.

Outside the Park on East Race Course were new buildings housing Government Ministries and other agencies all built after 1962. Sadly, Don Drummond passed away in 1969. He was one of the leading lights in The Skatalites, the band that propelled Ska Music into an accepted art form in Jamaica during the late fifties and into the sixties. As a Jamaican who in the sixties was outside of Jamaica looking in and enjoyed the transformation of Ska into Blue Beat, my visit in 1969 was to further appreciate the setting in which many of our outstanding sports people and musicians who achieved international recognition were nurtured.

My Afro hairstyle and full grown beard was not sufficient disguise from the petrol service attendant at Saint Ann's Bay to recognise me as a friend of his cousin, Atlan Forrest from Chalky Hill, whom I played cricket against in the Moulton Barrett Schools Competition some sixteen years previous. To confirm that he knew what he was talking about, the young man opened his wallet and produced a clipping from The Gleaner which carried an article which appeared in the Manchester Evening News with me blowing up a hot water bottle; according to him Atlan saw the article and hinted to him that he knew me. That was good enough for him as he asked that I come out of the car so that he could introduce me to his workmates and customers who were waiting to be served. It was quite a humbling experience, especially when a woman who was selling fruits remarked, "I like to see when my people go abroad and make good." A much younger woman chipped in: "Especially when they come back home and don't bruck style on us." I drove away promising that I would like to meet up with Atlan only to be told by his cousin that he was off the Island, which caused me to think that maybe he had joined that long line of Jamaicans who leave to seek a better way of life abroad.

Every human being needs a place to start from, a place where memories start to germinate and grow into what we carry around in our consciousness. Discovery Bay was my beginning and whatever I achieved would have to be weighed up into that beginning; my terms of reference were rooted in my family, my time at school, my love for cricket, swimming, running, getting struck by lightning, working at the hotel and at the Public Works Department. Now after ten years living in England I was back to see for myself the changes that had taken place, of which I had heard through letters from my Mother and other relatives with occasional photographs or newspaper clippings.

For a start the Discovery Bay I left was no longer a one street community. With the advent of the Kaiser Bauxite Company that attracted a huge labour force of both skilled and unskilled workers, new housing schemes with dwellings that could easily be equated with those in the suburbs of Kingston and Saint Andrew sprang up on lands where as a youngster I roamed freely shooting birds or picking fruit, and now there were two shopping plazas with

197

facilities for banking and eating. Fishing and tourism, which were the main sources of employment, were now living cheek and jowl with an industrial and shipping regime which meant shift work of earlies, lates and nights to keep the industry going. It was all in the cause of progress, a progress which on the one hand was reasonable but on the other quite stifling, as I was to find out on the first morning of my arrival when I went to have a swim and was told by a Security Guard that I had to pay to enter the beach. Immediately I harped back to the time some twenty years previous when Major Brock from England, who had a house on the other side of the road from our school, sent a letter to our Headmaster demanding that we should not swim in the sea. Hardly had the teacher finished reading the letter when Kipper Lynch and myself shouted out, "He can't stop us swimming in God's Sea". There was a loud chorus from the other boys: "A true Him can't stop Wi'", but then we were under British Rule. Even so, Major relented provided we did not make any noise that would disturb Lady Brock. It was a fair compromise and fitted in with the old Jamaican saying, "No mug no break no coffee don't throw away".

1949 was a far cry from 1969; Jamaica was now an Independent country and as far as I was concerned denying the people the right to use the beach was just not on. Given the fact that I could use the Fishermans Beach without paying was not the point, it just seemed at the time that although the country was independent and in some cases moving forward we could well be losing the vision of Norman Manley, who I as a starry-eyed schoolboy would along with my friends look forward to him talking to us about a New Jamaica on the Fishermans Beach during the Summer months when he holidayed at Mount Olivet. Incidentally, Norman Manley died in September 1969, a month before I made this first visit.

The stance that I took against paying to enter the beach was certainly not out of character in as far as some of my contemporaries were concerned, like Ephraim "Jack Ruby" Dawson, Manny Leslie and Frank Williams, who chose not to travel abroad and who remembered me as somebody who would speak out for what I believed in. Gone was the Red Seed Tree at School where under the shade as schoolboys we discussed sometimes using coded language so as to confuse younger listeners.

It was under these trees on my first visit that I was to learn at least from those at the grassroots what was taking place in the country, according to them "the Real Runnings". I was impressed with the level of discussion, even more so that some of the people involved were guys of my generation who gave up on school just after leaving Junior B, hardly able to sign their name, but now able to sustain and make valuable contributions to discussions, and in this respect they were very appreciative for the efforts of my last headmaster, the

Doyen of all headmasters who have taught in Discover Bay, Albert Spencer Sudlow, who on retirement opened the basement of The United Reformed Church at Discovery Bay for adult education classes, which proved to be very successful as some of the graduates were able to pass the written test to obtain jobs with The Bauxite Company on cruise liners and at the American Army Base in Guantanamo Bay in Cuba.

Central to the discussions under the trees and with other people in different settings during the twelve days of my stay were the extent to which popular artists and leading politicians were coming together as a unified force against oppression. In some quarters there were those who echoed misgivings about Jamaica achieving Independence from Britain, and that the rise of Black Nationalism fuelled by Marxist thinking would eventually lead to Castro having a strong hold on the country. At times commonsense dictated that I keep my thoughts to myself, especially with one Mr Terry, a man with a very interesting antecedent who according to him studied Political Science at the London School of Economics under Professor Harold Lasky. He later changed course and did Geology and came to work as a Geologist with the Kaiser Bauxite Company, and after parting company became involved with The Community College at Browns Town.

Once he established who I was he encouraged me to come home and build accommodation for tourists on the land that I owned; he even went as far as to introduce me to the manager of a bank in Browns Town regarding raising a loan to get started. It was almost like history repeating itself where an overseas person was pushing me to do the same thing, but even if I wanted to take up his offer Jacob Leslie's assessment of Mr Terry, although they both shared the same political ideal, was that he was too smart and could well be an agent for the CIA. I wasn't sure whether Jacob was being sarcastic or complimentary when he said, "Mr Terry should know that he can't fool the Englishman." The Englishman he was referring to was me, and before I left the term was being used more than once and I was not in the least bit upset.

Some things never change, and when I was invited by Mr Neville Johnson, Headmaster of the Discovery All Age, to come to the school to address pupils and staff I was following a long-standing tradition of past pupils who had done the same thing. On the morning of my visit I was introduced by Vernal Fairweather, Chair of the Parent Teacher Association, who in his introduction made mention of our meeting in Birmingham, and although he was not in agreement with some of the things that I said he was impressed with my determination to do well in a country where people from the Caribbean were in a constant battle to survive.

The questions from both pupils and teachers were varied: "Are you an Englishman or a Jamaican?" "Is it true that when you need to have a bath you have to make a fire in the house and bath in a tin bath?" "Have you ever been chased by a Teddy Boy?" "When it rains and snow is falling do children go to school?"

A majority of the school had seen the article in the newspaper of me blowing the hot water bottle. Some said that their parents have it on the wall in their house, others said their parents put it into their Bibles; others also told me that relatives of theirs talked about me being the best swimmer in school. One boy insisted on telling the school what his grandmother had told him about me, leading out the boys from top division with all the blackboards and taking them to the beach to use as surfing boards a day before school closed for the mid-term holiday. I remembered that incident very well and for the first time in my life I explained that the surfing idea came from an article that I had read along with pictures in the National Geographic magazine about surfing in Australia. For the record, I was severely reprimanded before the whole school by Spencer Sudlow, who after school took me to one side and in his stern but rather assuring voice said, "Stennett, make sure that you use your ability to lead in the right way." That is a lesson that I have never forgot.

The highlight of my visit to the school was the presentation that I made of three cricket balls, and Courtney, who received them on behalf of the school shook my hand and said, "We are proud of you." I knew that there was sincerity both in the words and the actions of Courtney by simply stepping back in time when as a schoolboy I did the same thing in recognising those people from our community who in their time made efforts to invest in themselves and their families, and by coming back to show appreciation to those who had helped to support them in their growth and development. Their individual achievement became part of the community's achievement and as such I realised that my coming back after ten years for a visit was a confirmation that nostalgia will always have its place and that I was in a unique and privileged position to appreciate that the years of independence had ushered in a number of changes. Living in England, where daily I had to face a number of challenges for my own survival, there was no conflict or contradiction in me singing some of the old songs that I sang as a child and into my twenties, such as 'God Save the Queen', 'Land of Hope and Glory', 'I vow to thee my Country' and 'Jerusalem', with the same gusto and sense of pride as when I sang 'Jamaica Land We Love', Bob Marley's 'Redemption Song', 'No Woman No Cry' and 'One Love', or listening to Byron Lee playing 'Pupa Lick' or Don Drummond playing 'Roll on Cool Don'.

On the evening before I had to leave as usual family and friends came to share in what was available. Curry goat and rice with Wray and Nephew White Rum and Red Stripe beer always take pride of place in the culinary order of things. Reminiscences ran high as Arnold "Banky" Sullivan regaled us with my days at school and as first eleven cricket captain when he was always at hand to give me the two-headed penny and insisting that I call heads. My sister, Lurline, talked about the girls at school admiring my lisp when I recited, and my mother telling all about the time when I arranged a cricket match under the mango trees; it was a cup match and, unbeknown to her, the cup we were supposed to be playing for was a Queen Victoria Coronation Mug that was given to my mother by her Aunt and had pride of place in her Whatnot.

Our send-off discussion took on board the change from pounds, shillings and pence to the Jamaican Dollar, the Quattie, which had been out of circulation for a long time and had become indelibly ingrained in popular culture in the song 'Carry mi Ackee go a Linstead Market not a Quattie wot sell', likewise the shilling engraved with the lion and for which, according to Jamaican folklore, an admiring suitor gave his female friend in return for his salacious desires. When he realised that she had no intention of heeding to his request he demanded the return of his shilling "wid de lion pon it" in time almost for the reasons the new currency led to "The Dollar Whine".

As was customary in my mother's household, on the morning prior to leaving the Bible reading before prayer was from Psalms Chapter 122 Verses 1 with the ending verse number eight, which reads: "The Lord shall preserve thy going out and thy coming in this day forth and for evermore." On the flight back to England I could not help but acknowledge that I was flying from one home to another home.

CHAPTER FOURTEEN

Through all the Changing Scenes of Life

"HERE STENNETT, I thought all you black boys carry knives." These words, uttered by an Inspector at the Newton Street Sorting Office, were synonymous with an action that I was not prepared to let go without challenging. My response was: "Mr Thomas, I resent your words and your actions, which are done out of ignorance and arrogance; for a start I am not coloured, neither am I a boy. I am a black man who has never carried a knife and I have no intention of carrying one." Mr Thomas stood almost motionless and, as if the blood flowed from every vein in his body, turned his face like a ripe tomato before he walked away saying, "Stennett, you have not heard the last of this."

The incident started when I was taken off sorting duty to join the group who were opening mail bags, which required scissors to cut through the material that sealed the bags. My scissors were stolen and it was upon requesting another pair that Mr Thomas made his remarks, which most of my colleagues said was out of order and they would be willing to support me if he took it further. Minutes after Mr Thomas walked away I was given "a skin", the then Post Office terminology for a written warning relating to any rules being breached by an employee. My "skin" stated that I was being insubordinate to my superior, and so as to avoid any drastic measures being taken against me I had to write a letter of apology to the officer concerned.

Without going into any details of what occurred, my written response was "not over my dead black body will I make an apology, verbally or written, until the officer in question is willing to do the same," signed Prince Eunice Whitfield "Red Blood" Stennett. The Prince that I used was a reminder of my Grandfather, who always talked proudly of his royal African roots. Red Blood was my own experience as a ten year old youngster in Jamaica coming from the river with a bucket of water on my head along with other boys who were eating mangoes taken from one of the landed gentry's property. On seeing the Overseer and the District Constable the boys scampered to the point that some lost the water and had to go back to the river. I stood my ground and when the Overseer and District Constable asked why I did not run I told them that I was not eating any stolen mangoes and, besides, "I am a red blood Stennett who run from no man, only when I call him a nickname."

I knew that my response to the "skin" would not be accepted, to all intents and purposes Mr Thomas was spoiling for a fight and I was up to the challenge. The next stage was that I was summoned to see the Chief, Mr Bob MacIntosh. I was allowed to take with me a Union representative and I took Fred Checkley, one of the most honest Union persons that I have ever met; one of those people of goodwill and good works to whom respect is due. In explaining to the Chief Inspector of what had transpired, Mr Thomas started from the premise that I had a chip on my shoulder and he could not understand why I was so upset. According to him I had belittled him before the staff and it is for that reason he wanted a written apology. When I asked him why he had seen fit to throw the scissors on the table instead of handing them to me, and that kind of behaviour along with his words were being disrepesectful to me, he refused to answer, even when Fred Checkley pointed out to him that my question was a legitimate one. I was asked to leave the room so that Fred Checkley, Mr MacIntosh and himself could deliberate. When I was eventually called back in to the room Mr MacIntosh applied what to me was the wisdom of Solomon that there were misunderstandings on both sides and so as to bury the hatchet we should shake hands; at first he refused but eventually or reluctantly he did.

Deep inside I carried no malice for the man, but he did not have the strength of character to forget the matter because as we walked out of the office with Fred in front, he was behind me and deliberately kicked my heels and said, "I will be gunning for you", to which Fred said to him, "I have heard that Mr Thomas". My response, in my true schoolboy fashion, was: "You will never kill this black bird". I had enough savvy to keep out of his way and according to the Good Book, "If it is at all possible live at peace with all men", something that I have always made the effort to do. All this happened within a fortnight after I had returned from Jamaica where I had gone to reacquaint myself with family and friends and to recharge my batteries, which were running low after ten years of continual struggle for survival, and the opportunity to make a valuable contribution to a society where at one time the African Caribbean presence was highlighted by the fact that had it not been for our coloured friends British industry, our Health Service and our transport system would have ground to a halt.

With the advent of the 1962 Immigration Act and other Acts curtailing migration from the Black Commonwealth Countries race became an issue and as a result racism entered the body politics of British society, as was expressed by Peter Griffiths, the Tory candidate for Smethwick in the 1964 General Election, where his election slogan was: "If you want a nigger as a neighbour

203

vote Labour". His battle cry was picked up by Enoch Powell, another Tory who in making the case for the repatriation of black people to from whence they came prophesied of over-crowding hospital maternity wards and streets being overrun with "grinning pickiness". An interesting aside is that it was the same Enoch Powell who, as Health Secretary in the 1962 Tory Government, went to the Caribbean to recruit nurses for British hospitals. With the introduction of the Act almost overnight the political agenda changed and those who earlier had been bathing us in the pool of platitudes were quite happy for us to be washed away by a tidal wave.

The twelve days that I spent in Jamaica and the five in America made me realise that, starting with the pursuing of materialism, there were other isms such as Communism, Marxism and Socialism which I would need to confine to the dustbin of history if I was to continue to follow my road map, which would eventually take me to the place where I would be able to make a difference and a valuable contribution. During my period of maturation I looked at Communism, Rastafarianism, Garveyism, Marxism and Christianity with more than a passing fancy, especially at that time in my life when I was in conflict with representatives of a Christian denomination when my faith, my humanity and my spirituality were severely tried and tested. I discovered that all ideologies have contradictions and as such it became important for me to take from those ideologies the elements that afforded me the opportunity for people of goodwill and good works, irrespective of colour, creed, class, gender or race, to come together with the commitment to rally round common causes.

Like a number of Jamaicans who migrated to England for whatever reason starting from the eighteenth century up until the introduction of the 1962 Commonwealth Immigration Act and beyond, we did not come politically alive here, neither were we guided by wishy-washy liberals as how to articulate our concerns. That sense of political awareness was born out of the spirit of resistance, a spirit tempered with caution and patience which on no account should be taken as signs of weakness but, as some elements of the various Commonwealth Immigration Acts kicked in, gave almost a no-holes-barred to immigration and police officers to challenge suspected illegal immigrants without a warrant. It was to that group of politically aware people that the black community looked to for support. The first generation people were a majority who over the years had taken their Britishness seriously and were willing to turn a blind eye and to compromise to some of the discrimination and prejudices that they were facing simply because they had an optimism that life for their children would be better. The reality was that a significant number of second generation African Caribbeans, who had gone through the British Education System, gaining only an appreciation for fish and chips, Yorkshire puddings and jelly and had no or very little understanding of the curriculum. A majority were to find themselves on the scrap heap, alienated and adding to the frustrations of their parents.

"Brother Stennett, I know that you are on nights but I would be grateful if you can come as early as possible so that we can sort something out for somebody." The voice on the phone was Aston Douglas, one of my mentors who from the first time we met in August 1959 encouraged me to follow my dreams. I will never ever forget that telephone request on a cold February morning in 1970. As it happened I was on my way to the Annexe on Chester Road where Stretford Technical College ran day courses for adults; I was determined to get the necessary qualifications that would enable me to get me into an institution of higher education. Having said that there is no way that I could have denied Douggie.

When I got to his house there were two African Caribbean women who were quite upset, even with the help of Mrs Douglas to calm them. What had happened was that the older of the two women was a nurse and she had gone down to Jamaica for her Aunt's burial and, on returning, her niece, who had already been granted permission to enter the country before the death occurred, travelled back to England with her. On arrival at Heathrow Airport they were taken into a room where they were strip-searched by a Customs Official while his colleagues came in laughing. According to her one of the Officers went as far as saying, "Look what the dog has taken in for breakfast" when she was asked to remove her bra. Her bitterness about the ordeal was summed up when she said, with tears flowing down her cheeks, "And to think that I was recruited to come here to work as a nurse through rain, snow, sleet and ice. I have never been late, never been absent and this is the thanks I get." Her nieces experience was in collaboration to hers and both wanted to go to the press to publish their ordeal, but by the same rule they wanted to remain anonymous, which in essence would defeat the objective. Moreover they felt that they could not deal with the publicity.

After a series of correspondence and a vast amount of telephone conversations by Douggie and myself with a number of government agencies, it was almost six months before a letter was sent to both women which when read between the lines could only be interpreted as Custom Officers not having enough evidence that the incident did take place, and if they did there was a regret. Throughout the period Mrs Douglas and her friends gave a lot of support in helping the women concerned keep body and soul together and they eventually migrated to Canada to start a new life.

This incident was to prove another sharp learning curve for me in that any attempt at challenging or seeking to change anti-oppressive practices or actions, either as an individual or as a collective, power relationships must be taken into consideration. It also reinforced my belief that unless one has an inborn understanding of one's culture there will always be difficulties in dispensing effective counselling or advice. In other words, hearing what one is saying and knowing what one is saying are two different things and if I was serious about making a difference by the very way in which society is structured, whether it was in England, Africa, the United States or in The Caribbean, the onus would always be on me to make every effort to widen my knowledge base through an academic discipline. It was for this reason I opted to do night duties which would give me more opportunity to attend day classes.

I have to admit that there was always the temptation to throw the towel in, especially during the winter months, when, after sometimes finishing a twelve hour shift and having to be home to take my youngest daughter, Angela, to her child minder and then go on to college, it was no fun, but what kept me going was reminding myself of the boast that I made to my Supervisor in Jamaica that I would go to England play cricket, get a University Education and then come back and kick him out of his job. In addition, I also knew about my Uncle Joshie, who migrated to the United States, worked on the Railroad Dining Cars, studied in his spare time and eventually qualified as a dentist, and the book "Up from Slaver", the Autobiography of Booker T Washington, the American Black activist who founded Tuskesee University. They all acted as stimulus for me to continue with my quest towards the achieving of my goals.

The saying that a little child shall lead them could no more be amplified in terms of my goal aspirations than one March morning in 1970, when the weather was so cold that it would have decapitated the brass monkey. As I was taking my youngest daughter, Angela, in her pushchair to Mrs Taylor her childminder she started to sing "Ata-tiga-ata-tiga". I made every effort to ascertain as to what she was singing but she completely ignored me. It was only when I got to Mrs Taylor's that she told me that Angela was singing "I am Tiger", made famous by Lulu. I think that on that cold morning it was my daughter's way of reminding me of the fighting spirit of the tiger. Years later when Esso had an advert put a tiger in your tank, it always struck a resounding chord of that morning in March. Thank you Angela for your child-like intuition which helped me to keep on keeping on.

In view of the fact that before 1938 day nurseries in England were few and far between, and but for the 1939-45 World War when both men and women were engaged in the war effort and arrangements had to be made for caring for their children, that The Child Minders Act was introduced in 1948, the very year when people from the English-speaking Caribbean countries started coming to England in large numbers. The Act made it possible for individuals to keep the children of other people for a fee providing the environment in

206

which the child or children who were being cared for was of a suitable standard. Also, the person who had the responsibility to look after the child had to be fit in mind and body.

There were cases where some African Caribbean women who became childminders took on more children than they were able to cope with and as a result came into conflict with the local authorities. This was not the case with Mrs Taylor, who cared for my daughter and another youngster in surroundings that were quite hospitable, so it was very upsetting for me one morning when I took my daughter to Mrs Taylor to hear an over-zealous social worker talking to her in a very condescending manner, using words like "you people come here and want to do as you please" and "this is England not Africa where hygiene counts for very little, and besides you need training to look after children". Having been brought up to appreciate that soft answers drive away confusion and grievous words heightens conflict, I could not contain myself as I challenged the social worker regarding her lack of respect for Mrs Taylor and her ignorance of Africa, reminding her that African Caribbean women have a long history of taking care of white people from the cradle to the grave and that what Mrs Taylor was doing is part of our tradition to look after each other, especially in a strange land where if we do not nobody else will. To her credit the social worker, whilst not apologising for her off-handedness, did say that it was a neighbour who complained that Mrs Taylor's place was over-crowded. Not long after she received a letter from the Council informing her that from the report tendered by the social worker her premises were suitable and a relieved Mrs Taylor was the first person to have suggested that I put myself forward to be in the position, according to her, to "speak up for the small people" - and such a suggesting was quite flattering.

Without people like Mrs Taylor, Annie and Winnie Walters, my wife Gwen and I would have taken a much longer time to achieve any level of success in England. Their acts of kindness as childminders could never be compensated for in pounds, shillings and pence. They were there for us as mothers and their husbands as fathers and their children as of the same family blood line willing and encouraging us to carry on regardless. It was the continuation of the part of rural Jamaican life where we encouraged and shared in each other's success. Even my two daughters Pat and Angela, who had their experiences of being looked after by childminders, if for no other reason they became aware of the importance of Jamaica's other language, Patwa. From Annie and Winnie Pat inherited 'Wan Degeh Pound' and from Mrs Taylor Angela inherited 'Lawd Mi Gawd'. In essence, as long as I live those and other friendship links will never be broken and they strike resonating chords in Bob Marley's "No Woman No Cry" in remembering the days of cooking and meeting friends along the way.

My experience of these friendship links in Manchester forged above and beyond kinship or blood lines pushed race, ethnicity, gender, class and religious affiliations into the background and working regular nights in the Post Office at Newton Street made this fact much clearer. We all had different reasons why we chose to do regular nights but there was one commonality that binded us together, which was to get the job done to the satisfaction of the supervisors, which would give us time to have more than our fair share of breaks during the night, which in my case gave me the opportunity to catch up with my course work.

As I have mentioned many genuine friendships were created and in some ways it would be no exaggeration if I make reference to ourselves as the A team, the famous television series of the 1980s when, even in the face of disagreements within the group, the iron fences that could easily have divided us were not as solid as the thin thread that bound us together. I recalled a situation where a worker was caught by Jimmy Scott, a Union Representative, writing derogatory messages about Black and Asian workers which automatically meant instant dismissal. The union - like the management - was rather surprised when the Black and Asian workers intervened on his behalf. It was a case of not only wanting him to be a martyr but to convey to him that we believed that "to err is human to forgive is divine".

The act of forgiveness was one of strength and intended to take away the stigma of guilt and shame of our Caucasian friends and was clarified by one who said to me during the break period, "Stan, I hope you don't believe that I am like that B.......d". The duty that I was on that week involved at around 3.30 in the morning taking mails on the van to Atherton, Swinton, Tyldesley, Irlam, Whitefield, and Prestwich to be sorted for delivery the same day. My driver was Tim, I never did get to know his surname. I called him Tim O'Shenko, that is behind his back of course. He served with the Irish Fusiliers in Jamaica, hence his sense of affection for Jamaica and Jamaicans, and he was always talking of the good times he had in Jamaica. On the morning following the incident with the man who scribbled obscenities about black postmen, Tim was very quiet, obviously he had heard about it and maybe was not sure how I would take it if he raised the subject. Prestwich was always the last drop and as always the guys at the loading bays were wise-cracking. This particular morning one of the guys greeted us with "Gone Fishing" in a Louis Armstrong like voice. Tim became very upset, telling him to "Cut the Crap". It was as if this was the cue that he was waiting for to tell me that as an Irishman he hated people who pick on other people on the grounds of religion, or colour, citing that the man imitating Louis Armstrong was directed at me and "Gone Fishing" was intended for him simply because he chose to be on regular nights so as to enjoy following his hobby of fishing.

In a way we were two different people making sacrifices to follow our interest and whilst I was not unduly upset by the Louis Armstrong take, to which I explained to Tim reminding him that if I had to take on board every unsavoury incident I would be paving the road to the Mental Institutions or the Prison. The discussion came to a sudden halt when, either through anger or tiredness, he jumped the lights on red driving down Bury New Road when I said to him, "Tim you have jumped the lights". He responded, "What lights, yes Stan we wont let the B.......ds get us down, providing you can play your cricket and I can do my fishing". Life does play some very funny games as within a week of Timo retiring news came that he died getting ready to go fishing.

The news could not have arrived at a worse time as within two days of receiving it I was in my back yard at Khartoum Street in Old Trafford pumping iron with my friend Les Murray, and at the back of the yard a man had a garage and more than once I had to pick up banana skins thrown over the wall but I never saw who or when it was done. Things took another step further when one of the windows in the top back room was broken by what I could only assume was a ball bearing fired from a sling shot. This incident was reported to the Police but with the lack of evidence very little could be done. On this particular day I could hear the "Eni mene mini mo" chant coming from the garage. When Les and myself opened the back gate there were two boys, possibly aged fourteen, along with the proprietor of the garage and these three people seemed engrossed in what they were doing. .There was no point asking them anything besides the old adage of sticks and stones breaking bones and not words. Hardly had we closed the gate and resumed training than there was the clunking noise of metal hitting the barbell that Les was using. This was a step too far, enough was enough. On opening the back gate we saw the two boys running away, we both gave chase on Ayres Road across Auburn Road over on to Kings Road and into Wordsworth Road where we finally caught up with them. Les shouted out, "Don't move or I'll shrink your heads into marbles. The command had its desired effect and within minutes a Panda car had arrived and on alighting from the car the police officer threatened to arrest us for harassment, threatening behaviour and breach of the peace, adding that from information we were seen chasing the boys with machetes and knives shouting out that we were going to kill them.

For a start, when the police arrived we were not holding the boys and there were no knives in our tracksuit pockets, which we were asked to turn out, neither was there any machetes around. Having explained to the officer what had happened, especially in the light of me making a report previously of my window being broken, they went to the garage to investigate. The people there saw nothing other than, according to them, these crazy coloured guys bursting through the gate with machetes threatening to do the kids in. The step ladder from which the boys climbed to fire the pellets from the sling shots, which they still had on their person, was still standing near the back gate and when I insisted on the officer finding out who owned the ladder then it was quite clear that they would have seen what had happened. The police left promising that they would come back to see me. They did not, but by the same rule I did not have any more incidents afterwards and I had to agree with Tim who said don't let them get you down.

Kingsley Smith was the man who encouraged me to look at Youth and Community work as a career option. He was born in Spanish Town, the capital of the Parish of St Catherine in Jamaica, and prior to migrating to England he played cricket for Bernard Lodge and Innswood in the Crum Ewing competitions. He developed his skills as a community activist through his involvement with the Sugar Industry Welfare Organisations. At the time when he introduced me to youth work he was involved with a voluntary youth project run under the auspices of the West Indian Organisations Co-ordinating Committee (WIOCC) at Carmoor Road, Chorlton-on-Medlock, which was formed as a response to both the Hartley and Hunt Reports of the late 1960s and early 1970s which highlighted the failure of the Department of Education and Science and the Youth Service to provide proper facilities, on the one hand that would cater for the needs of second generation African-Caribbean young people and, on the other hand, make courses available where both black and white people could be trained to work with young people either within a multi-racial environment or a single race environment. There was no getting away from the fact that the "Rivers of Blood" speech of 1968 and the Immigration Act of 1971 were a great hindrance to good race relations and equal opportunities for a significant majority of people from the Black Commonwealth countries.

Working at Carmoor Road provided me with a number of windows from which I was able to view the political, historical and social context in which young people in general, but in particular young African Caribbean, were placed and the kind of strategies that had to be put in place to meet their needs. These needs were varied, involving young people who got caught up in the judicial system. Sometimes the spin-off resulted in them finishing up in either the penal or mental institutions. There were also those who experienced exclusions from schools and those who, according to sociologists of the time, were in the "caught between two cultures" syndrome. In essence this group was seeking out their identify.

I continue to emphasise my good fortune in regards to the good people that I met along the way. The Carmoor Road experience was no different, in that people like Berry Edwards, a Pan Africanist, Ron Phillips, who was responsible for setting up the George Jackson House in Whalley Range, Hartley Hanley a dedicated youth worker, and Gus John, made an invaluable contribution in helping to shape the Youth Service in terms of how they addressed the needs of young black people. John's study, reflected in his book "In Service of Black Youth", is a testimony. Arthur and Cherry Byfield, Louise Da Cacodia, Arthur Jackson, Bob Clarke, Ed Allen and his wife Carmen, all of the Jamaica Society, all pooled their various skills, which helped to keep the bodies, souls and minds of vulnerable people together. The first Supplementary or Saturday School had its beginning at Carmoor Road. It was also the first project to have embarked on celebrating culture week in October of each year.

It should come as no surprise that, whilst we were involved in helping to make the lives of people more bearable, the racist tails were continuing to wag the racists heads both at Central and Local Government levels, although "Paki-Bashing", a prevalent pasttime enjoyed by some white youths, did not occur as often in Manchester as in other parts of the country. There are many instances when African Caribbean youngsters, including youth workers walking home from youth clubs, would experience racist comments from passing cars. There was no point reporting these incidents as they often fell on deaf ears. The sting in the tail was decision-makers seeing fit to define African Caribbean young people as rebellious and Asian young people to be docile and those of us black people who had the courage to put our heads above the parapet and demand a fair and better deal were black power agitators, empire building and anti-law and order.

The truth of the matter is that all we were asking for was the opportunity to engage with decision-makers and to explain to them that, well meaning as they believed that they were, the system as it was was not an equitable one and until positive efforts were put in place there would be misunderstandings between the various groups.

One agency that made some effort to come to terms with some of the misunderstandings that existed between them and some members of their African Caribbean client group was the Probation Service in Manchester, who under Mr Cliff Metcalfe, the Chief Probation Officer at the time, introduced a scheme that trained lay people from the African Caribbean community to be Accredited Prison Visitors. Berry Edwards and myself were the first two African Caribbean people in Manchester to have completed the course and became accredited.

My first assignment was accompanying Vivienne Philpots, a qualified probation officer, to Strangeways Prison in Manchester; that was how the system worked; an Accredited Visitor had to accompany a fully fledged officer from the Probation Service. As it happened the visit was to see a

Jamaican man who applied for parole. His reason for being incarcerated was that, from his story, there was a report of a vicious mugging that took place on Moss Lane East and he was on his way to a party when the police drove up and started to question him about the mugging. The only description that the victim had of the attacker was that he was a black man wearing a round felt hat. On that description he was taken to Platt Lane Police Station where he was subsequently arrested and finished up being sentenced to eighteen months.

I must confess that even before I was introduced to him by Vivienne, his body language and his stare conveyed to me that as far as he was concerned I could as well take a long walk off a short pier. He was just not interested and I could well understand why because at the time there were no black probation officers in Manchester and seeing me in what he assumed to be a good position would be making the case that I was part of the establishment or in other words a sell-out. What was even more interesting is that as the discussion continued I was able to understand why he was in such a predicament. To begin with, he could not read or write, he had only been in the country for six months and his command of the English language was lacking to say the least. I calculated that he was a victim of circumstances, an underdog who could neither bark nor bite for himself.

The only time that his body language changed was when I was leaving and I said, "Look now Bredda ef you want mi fi elp you leggo nex time when mi kum back". I apologised to Vivienne for talking to her client in a language that might not have been familiar to her, adding that because of his inability to have a meaningful dialogue with her, his parole would take a long time to be granted. She agreed that on our next visit she would allow me to do most of the talking. On the second visit the client was as nice as rain. His eyes lit up when I said, "You alright mi bredda". His response was, "Yeh mon". The interview went down very well and he did eventually get paroled, but I felt that he should not have been sent to prison in the first place; if his so-called victim was only able to identify him on the grounds that he was wearing a round felt hat, which a number of black men wore in those days. There was a difference with his hat as it had a bright yellow band around it; besides the offence was committed in Rusholme where he had no reason to go. He was living in Hulme and was stopped by the police on Alexandra Road on his way to a party at Yarburgh Street in Moss Side. As I have stated I was not convinced that justice was seen to be done and when after he got his parole I met him on the streets, I was quite taken aback when he started to big me up before his woman as the person who helped him to get paroled. I think that it was rather amusing coming from a man who when we first met had completely dissed me. By his account he said that I reminded him of "A

Topanarris from one of the big schools in Jamaica". It was a confirmation of my assumption about him that he had created a gap between us as a result of seeing me as a Black probation officer, who, as far as he was concerned, would forget where I was coming from. His encouragement for me to train to be a solicitor was borne out of the fact that he realised that he was not properly represented in court and hence his incarceration.

Cliff Metcalfe, Vivienne Phillpotts and Bob Mathers were many light years ahead of their times when they not only talked the talk but also walked the walk when, in the late sixties and seventies, they rolled back the frontiers of the Probation Service in Manchester that contained isms that negated not only against their African Caribbean client group but also against members of the community who had the ability and the wherewithal to make their valuable contributions to the Service. Thank God that over time the status quo changed and the Service reflected the diverse community in which they served.

The visits that I made to institutions such as Hindley and Risley as an Accredited Visitor were with Both Mathers. Even though I resisted the encouragement of Cliff, Vivienne and Bob to avail myself of the opportunity to train for the service I will always remain grateful for their support and sincerity in helping to shape the service in line with their caring ethos. Retirement took Cliff out of the frame and I have no idea what became of Vivienne, but Bob stayed with the Service and the last time I heard of him he was in charge of the Service in Lancashire.

Whereas it was Kingsley Smith who pointed me in the direction of Youth Work it was Mick Mannion Jnr, whose father played cricket for The Post Office, who encouraged me to do the Cricket Coaching Course conducted annually at Blackpool under the auspices of the North West Federation of Physical Education Teachers. The year was 1971 and the person in charge of the coaching was Ray Morris, who played cricket for Essex. It was quite an intensive course which attracted not only teachers but people from other disciplines. One of the people on the course was John Lyon, who kept wicket for Lancashire county prior to him going to live in South Africa.

Not being a teacher, and for that matter being an unqualified voluntary youth worker I was not entitled to a grant, so I paid my own way, which meant that I made every effort to pass, but that was not to be as I was to realise that although I had been playing cricket for as long as I could remember there were aspects of the game to which I was still ignorant. It was to become another sharp learning curve for me. In actual fact, going on the course proved to be a blessing in disguise in more ways than one; for a start, when Ray Morris realised that I was embarking on a career in Youth and Community Work he gave me all the information relating to the National Association of

Youth Clubs (NAYC), who ran courses in youth work, which would put me in good stead when I went on to do the full time course at university.

Ray was a true Ambassador for cricket, placing it as one of the most powerful agents for affecting positive changes; listening to him I came to the conclusion that if it was left to him every village throughout the length and breadth of England would have a cricket ground, be compulsory that it is taught in every school, and during the winter months it would be played indoors. The idea of indoor cricket struck me as rather interesting and I was determined that in time I would introduce it to the Moss Side community. Participants to the Federation Eight Day event, which started on Good Friday, were encouraged to use as many of the facilities that Blackpool offered. I opted to go to Brian London's Club and to Blackpool Football Club, yet it is rather uncanny that in this life some things never go as planned, as I was to discover when on the Saturday afternoon I bumped into Cliff Patterson, who lived in Moss Side and was down in Blackpool with Honey Boy Zimba, the Jamaican born wrestler who was doing a show. Cliff had done some boxing, in his time sparring with boxers such as Randy Turpin, Joe Erskine, Brian London and Joe Bygraves.

Arrangements were made that after the wrestling was over we should meet at Brian London's place. Always the showman, Cliff introduced me to Brian London as a relative of Ezzard Charles, the former World Heavyweight Boxing Champion, in the same breath telling Brian of my ability to blow up a hot water bottle to the size of a balloon, and as my agent he would be pleased if Brian booked me as an act, to which Brian agreed. Brian was completely different from the way in which he was portrayed on television; as a bruiser, which of course goes with the territory of his profession. He displayed courtesy and dignity during our discussion on many aspects of a variety of sports and sports people. In as far as cricket was concerned his favourite Caribbean cricketers were Clive Lloyd, Gary Sobers and Rohan Kanhai, who played professional cricket for Blackpool.

In my experience, whenever there is a discussion about sporting achievements the question is always asked why black people do not excel at swimming and golf. That evening at Brian London's was no exception as the caucasians in the group advanced the theory that black people's inability to compete successfully at swimming was due to our body density and bone structure; both Zimba and Cliff kept quiet on this point but my take was that in Jamaica where I was born I can't remember at what age I started to swim, not only for fun but also for food. If and when the opportunities became available, I suggested, black people will excel at both sports. My explanation was cut short when I was asked to get ready to appear on stage to the tune of "I'm forever blowing bubbles in the sky". On stage I was given a brand new hot water bottle still in cellophane, which I asked two people to examine and open, and as I took a deep breath and started to blow I could hear Cliff shouting, "Come on Ezzard, blow it man, blow it". That evening something happened that had never happened before, the bottle exploded at one of the seams and the crowd went wild as Honey Boy Zimba came on stage and lifted me off with the applause deafening. When I told my friends what had happened on stage that evening one mentioned that the hot water bottle was made on the late Friday shift. In this world one cannot do right for everyone yet by the same rule two of the caucasian guys who were talking sports with us were avid golfers who invited me to come along with them the following day to the golf course to have a go. I did make several excuses, which were legitimate, to avoid taking up the offer, starting with I did not have the proper attire. They did not fall for that one as my tracksuit bottoms and cricket pullover were good enough; likewise they would supply me with shoes. My last line of excuse was that as a cricketer I bowl right-handed and bat left-handed; again, to them that was not a problem as one played right-handed and the other played left-hand golf.

On reflection I would have been the loser if I did not accept the offer of Tommy Taylor and Bill Jackson, who turned up at eight o'clock on the Sunday morning, to play at a course on the way to Southport. It was my first time on a golf course and holding a golf club in my hand. Bill, who played left-handed, proved to be an excellent coach as he explained the right way to hold the club and to strike the ball, which should not be too difficult, he explained, for somebody who had played cricket and had ball sense and eye coordination. As a youngster growing up in Jamaica the men referred to this asset as "having eye sight" which was a result of boys eating raw carrots to enhance our eye sight; that being said, it was easier said than done on that Sunday morning to have club hitting ball that would at least suggest that I had the slightest idea of what I was doing, but Bill had a lot of patience and I was determined to prove to myself that I could at least hit the ball in the air like I did in cricket. Eventually, when I did make contact and saw the ball soaring into the air, it was one of the best moments that I have ever had in my life. I equated it to the first time that I made love under the sea grape on Kennedy's Beach at Discovery Bay in Jamaica on a full moon night.

Bill expressed the feeling that with proper coaching I would make a good player, which I was quite pleased to hear. At the end of the eight days I left Blackpool with a feeling of disappointment because I had failed the course, but with one of optimism because I knew exactly what I needed to do so as to achieve my goal. The road map had been in place for a very long time and as I travelled along it I was coming across people who were willing to help me realise that my efforts would not be in vain. That being said there was one road that I was definitely not prepared to go down, as was hinted by Cliff Patterson, who suggested that I should include arm wrestling along with the hot water bottle blowing and make it into a strength act. He was confident that I would do well to the point where he wanted me to become a member of the Actors' Union. According to him the money that he received from Brian London for my appearance would go towards paying my Union fees. The bottom line is I was not interested in appearing in smoke-filled clubs blowing my lungs out and having my arms twisted; having said that, Cliff was not easily put off and was indeed a determined Jamaican and when he produced his card as a car salesman insisting that as a sportsman I needed my own wheels I could not help but see what he had on offer. It was a 1957 Morris Minor with the split windscreen. He assured me that he would never sell me a bum steer and I took his word and bought the car for the princely sum of £25. It was the first car that I bought and I was as proud as punch, not so Gwen and her Uncle Charles, who reminded me of the British Market in Boroughbridge in Saint Ann Jamaica, where animals including cats can be bought or sold and where on several occasions people purchased animals and before they reached home they died, or in other cases the animals were either lame or blind. I must admit that the pressure did get to me that I had been duped and when I went to see if I could get my money back I was made to understand that Cliff had gone away with Honey Boy Zimba, who was involved in a series of wrestling shows in France.

My black 1957 Morris Minor turned out to be one of the best buys that I had ever made. It was purchased in May 1971 and kept going until September 1974, during which time, except for replacing the exhaust, it gave me no trouble. I called it Jack Ruby, the name of the man who shot Lee Harvey Oswald, who was supposed to have assassinated President John F Kennedy. Cliff, who was always well dressed down to his felt hat worn at a rakish angle, reminded me of Jack Ruby.

Having decided against going into showbusiness I felt that I ought to check out what Tommy Taylor and Bill Jackson said when we went playing golf in Southport, that I had the potential to be a good player. I went to see Roland West from Trinidad, who at the time was the only Caribbean professional golfer in Europe and was also professional at Altrincham. I was immediately struck with his outgoing personality as he discussed the intricacies of the sport, even more so when he took me onto the driving range showing me what to do. I will never forget what he said to me at the end of the half hour that he had given free; that the two people who told me that I had the ability to play at a high standard were not leading me on and he would be prepared to help me to achieve that goal. Of course, there would be a cost involved, of which I was well aware, and I knew that he appreciated my honesty when I explained to him that as a result of many other commitments I would find it difficult to avail myself of the opportunity to put the time in for training, so we parted company on the understanding that it is a sport that can easily take over one's life.

There was no doubt in my mind that I would eventually take up golf, but there was also the gnawing feeling that I ought to go back to do the Cricket Coaching Course so as to get the certificate, and the opportunity presented itself again through Mick Mannion Jnr, who informed me about a course that was being conducted at the William Timpson Sporting Centre in Liverpool under the auspices of the Lancashire Cricket Federation.

The course started in January 1972 and finished in May of that year involving every Sunday. It was a bit of a strain, especially when I finished a night shift on a Sunday morning and had to drive to Liverpool to start training at nine o'clock until three o'clock in the afternoon, but it was all worth it when on the final day I had to demonstrate all that I had learnt in the previous five months. One of the adjudicators on the day was Ossie Wheatley from Glamorgan, who wanted to know if I was related to Roy Fredericks, the Guyanese and West Indian Test Player who played for Glamorgan. I don't believe that he was very charitable when he said, "I have been watching you bowling and would have no hesitation in putting you on my side, but except for the hook shot your batting leaves a lot to be desired and I suggest that you demonstrate that shot to the toffy-nosed b......ds today." With this in mind, after I did all the necessary requirements in terms of net safety, fielding, catching, bowling, wicket-keeping, umpiring signals and so on, I said, "Today I am going to demonstrate the hook shot". It was as if providence had decreed that the first chap that bowled pitched the ball on a fairly good length on middle stump and I duly executed the shot, to which he ran down facing me shouting, "That shot is not in the rule book you should have played straight". Not to be outdone I said to him, "Young man, when you are batting what are your aims and objectives?" For a number of seconds he was dumbstruck before he asked me what I meant. I was in my element when I said to him, "When I am batting my aim and objective is to put runs on the board and entertain the crowd". Almost theatrical-like, Ossie Wheatley entered the stage and in his best Welsh accent said, "Laddie, don't argue with him, he is a West Indian who will hook them off his nose and if needs be sitting on his back side". The gymnasium erupted in handclaps as the dejected bowler walked back to his position and the next bolwer pitched the ball right on the penny to which I got in line and played it with the kind of stroke that was well in keeping with the manual.

More and more my confidence started to rise as I got in line and played each ball on its merit, much to the annoyance of the fast men who I could only guess were riled when I faced up to one of their counterparts and explained to him what batting meant to me. As a fast bowler myself I should have known better to keep my mouth shut, which was always my style because at the end of the day the fast bowler will always win. There again I was reacting to what Ossie Wheatley had said regarding my batting and immediately the session finished I told him that I felt that his remarks could well be the reason why the bowlers gave me such a baptism of fire. His response was that he expressed what he saw but I rose to the occasion and proved to him that I was not only a very good bowler, especially in the application of the Yorker, but a more than useful batsman and in as far as he was concerned I was good enough to be a coach. Those words were music to my ears and confirmed one of the things that I have always believed in, which is that honest criticism will always outweigh wishy-washy praise.

CHAPTER FIFTEEN

One Never Walks Alone

ON THE 19th May 1972, when I received my certificate from the Lancashire Cricket Association acknowledging that I had satisfied the examiners of my competence to teach the fundamentals of cricket, I was a happy man. At least it gave me the confidence that I could go on to Lilleshall to do the Advanced Course and if successful follow up the offer made to me by Tony Enharu, a Nigerian who was doing a postgraduate degree in Medicine at Manchester University, to coach cricket at one of the prestigious colleges in Nigeria. Sadly this did not happen and I have never questioned why; suffice to say that whatever will be will be.

I dedicated the certificate to the memory of my father who, during the sugar-shipping season, would find employment as a winchman loading sugar on the ships from abroad. Three weeks before he died in May 1946, the last boat that he loaded from Rio Bueno was the SS Lombardy, whose destination was Liverpool. During the course many discussions took place on the importance of the port in terms of the trans-Atlantic slave trade, and the line between Empire-building through the cultivation of sugar cane and the manufacturing of rum and molasses in the Caribbean by which the white planters made handsome profits which helped in the sustaining of capitalism in England on the one hand, and the other hand the spreading of cricket in the Caribbean. As the only African-Caribbean on the Liverpool course I was, metaphorically speaking, batting for the Caribbean historically, politically and culturally. I vividly remember McConnell, a third generation Irishman who as a course participant, asking me why was it when West Indian cricket was in its ascendancy Ireland bowled them out for 69 runs? He answered the question suggesting that the West Indies were swept away by the tide of Irish hospitality where Guinness could well have been a contributing factor.

Reflecting on McConnell's analysis was to hark back to the days when I was captain for my village team and when teams, especially from Kingston, who had players that played a higher standard of cricket than us, came to play, how racketeer Leach, one of my Mentors, would go out of his way to encourage the City players to refresh themselves before play started; his philosophy was based on the fact that a full belly does not help mobility, how right he was. By the same rule, all that McConnell, who was well read and had a wide world view of the over-powering effects of colonialism, was trying to remind me of was that all human beings carry that sense of national pride, the instinct and the single-mindedness to excel in sport at whatever level of completion.

The Reverend Anthony Durrans, an Anglican priest who served at St John's the Evangelist Parish Church in Old Trafford from 1961 to 1982, was another person from a recognised list of people who in the process of my journey helped me to realise that one never walked alone. A quiet and unassuming man he was born and brought up in the East Lancashire town of Burnley, which like a number of other towns in that area prospered from around the nineteenth century from coal mining, manufacturing, especially cotton, and later chemical industries. Tony had a deep understanding of how the established churches mining companies, mill owners, and other industrial agencies created the opportunity for their workers to be involved in leisure time pursuits both as spectators and participants, organised sports like football and cricket with their subtle forms of exclusiveness and inclusiveness not dissimilar to the situation in the English speaking Caribbean countries of the same period. They attracted large followings from the working classes which resulted in Clubs coming together to form leagues such as the Lancashire League, of which Burnley became a member, and had the distinction of West Indian Test players such as Manny Martindale, and Charlie Griffiths from Barbados, and from Jamaica Collie Smith playing as professional cricketers.

One of my lasting memories of Tony Durrans, who also had a passion and more than a saintly dedication to watching cricket at Lancashire's Old Trafford, the Mecca of Test grounds in England, and football at the other Old Trafford, Manchester United's Theatre of Dreams, was the invaluable contributions that he made in the founding of the St Johns Youth Cricket Club that played in the North West Lancashire Under 18 Cricket League in the 1970s until it disbanded. To talk of such contribution is to talk about the extent to which paternalism or patronisation had no place in the way he prepared George Blissett, Robbie 'Pinch' Burton and myself to take up leadership roles, and as time went on other people such as John Stevens, Nev Pittersen, Vernon Powell and Tim Ellis, curate at St John's, came on board with their various skills that saw the club becoming a beacon of hope for youngsters and parents in the community.

Other than the seventeen youngsters, namely Trevor Barclay, Cleveland Blissett, Junior Binns, Jarvis Brown, Ricky Coleman, Trevor Coleman, Terry Pittersen, Dennis Pittersen, Cedric Powell, Earl Stevens, Claude Stevens, Sam Leader and Dave Thomas, who had raw talent and wanted to identify with the successful West Indian cricketers of the period, the club started with nothing; no funds, no ground, which at the same time seemed almost ridiculous that we should have approached the North Western League seeking admission. The comments from certain members of the community were in keeping with Jamaican man who went out and bought a saddle before he had the horse. George Blisset's response, to which I totally agreed, was that "one is entitled to dream".

True, there were organised clubs not far from the Old Trafford community who when we approached them regarding renting their grounds to play on the Thursday evenings when the League played, who in as far as the game was concerned, showed some kind of sympathy, but that was as far as it went. Others wanted our youngsters to join their clubs, which was not a bad idea as the aims and objectives in addition to playing cricket was to foster some of the old core values such as pride, confidence, respect and hard work that we brought with us from the Caribbean. In other words we felt that the onus was on us to concur with the Jamaican adage of learning to dance at home before we ventured out.

There was to be a kind of psychic news when Tony rang me at home one evening in late August 1972, just as I was getting ready to go out to start my night duty at Newton Street Sorting Office, that after a series of discussions with the officials of the League there was a majority consensus that in the light of St John's not having proper facilities, the clubs were willing that we play both away and home matches on their grounds providing we could get to the grounds on time. I figured to myself that they might have heard about Jamaican time and I decided that no way, come rain or sunshine, would we ever be late. Like myself, George Blissett was also on the night shift, at Dunlop's Rubber Factory on Cambridge Street, Manchester, and would have to wait along with Robbie Burton to hear the good news on the following morning. To say that I was on cloud nine throughout the night was more than an over-statement as I conveyed to all and sundry on duty that night that the youth team that I had been working with would be entering the League for the 1973 season. I couldn't believe that there would have been so much interest shown relating to a group of young people, who were immediately referred to as "Stan's lads", who wanted to play cricket and were given the opportunity to play in a league. The interest was not only amongst the people that I worked with in the Post Office but also in the Old Trafford and Moss Side community. It spoke volumes of the extent to which it was acknowledge not only as a first but also as a testimony to what George Blissett said in response to those people who felt that in the light of us having no facilities we would not be accepted in a league, i.e. that "people should have dreams".

When I contacted George and Robbie Burton the following morning they both agreed that I made arrangements to meet up with Tony at the earliest possible time. We met at The Rectory on Lindum Avenue on the afternoon of

Thursday 24th August 1972 to discuss the criteria of the league and the strategies that we needed to fulfil them. Our first task was deciding our roles, which resulted in Tony taking on that of Chairman, George Blissett, Treasurer, Robbie Burton, Vice Chair, and myself as Secretary. Collectively and individually we had embarked on a journey that was to take us in several directions and saw us finishing at the same destination.

For me it was a time when there was no longer a gap but a chasm of misunderstanding between a vast majority of statutory and voluntary agencies and the African Caribbean community in general, but in particular those who were sent for by their guardians or were born here and it was difficult for those of us who were aware of what were some of the root causes of the problems to keep quiet.

Doctor Bernard Coard, a Grenadian educationalist who did some work in Manchester, published his book, "How the British Educational System Has Made The West Indian Child Educationally Subnormal", which highlighted a number of key issues that were allied to some of the concerns that were being openly expressed in the community.

In addition to those problems were the vast numbers of researchers that descended on the community. Whilst some of these researchers were genuine people, others came into the community under a number of guises spouting a series of philosophies from Marxism to Free Love; in other words they were wolves in sheep's clothing pretending that they could empathise and sympathise with the Black community and furnishing them with the tools of empowerment.

Two such people that I came across acting in the role of apostle for those of us African Caribbean people who they perceived as victims were Dan and Ann Scrivens, who according to them were from the California State University of Los Angeles doing postgraduate work at Manchester University, he in Mathematics and she in Anthropology. I met Ann at Tarvin in Chester, where I had gone for the weekend for a residential stay as part of the course that I was doing for the Certificate in Youth and Community Work run under the auspices of The National Association of Youth Clubs (NAYC). She was invited as guest speaker for the weekend and to a large extent acted out her role with a degree of satisfaction, but like in every life situation, however much one is qualified in whatever vocation or profession, there will always be grey areas that will give rise to criticism or clarification and it was in this very context that both of us collided when I made the statement that history has not recorded the Black experience in a positive light and until that situation is resolved there would always be conflicts and misunderstandings between the two races and for that matter, any other minority groups that were being defined by the majority thinking that their contributions to society were not important.

The resistance on the part of Ann Scrivens to deny me of my experience was to play itself more clearer when a member of staff at one of the Trafford schools to which I eventually became a Governor when I was elected a Councillor in 1993, and which in the 70s and up to the late 80s had a track record of expelling African Caribbean pupils (It was so bad that even dinner ladies words were accepted as Gospel in the expelling process) made a remark that she was not prepared to have any dialogue with anyone who had connections with that mob from Moss Side and who was bent on bucking the system in as far as she was concerned. From what my informant told me, she said: "Mr Stennett and that lot can pack their bags and go 'home'". Whilst the Bible said, "Judge not so that he shall not be judged", I could not get rid of the gnawing feeling within me that Ann Scrivens was the root cause of the teacher making the negative comments about people like myself who were genuinely making efforts to create an atmosphere where those people at the sharp end of sad experiences could feel better about themselves.

I based my assumptions that from her own account she was in dialogue with people in Manchester who were involved with education, so when I went to The Nello James Centre on Withington Road in Whalley Range, Manchester, which caters for the cultural, social and educational needs of young people, and is a legacy to C.L.R. James, the well-known Trinidadian, writer, political activist and cricket raconteur for his invaluable contribution in the formation of the African-Caribbean community in Britain, to listen to a lecture by the man himself. I was quite pleased to share my experiences at the weekend course at Tarvin in conflict with Trafford schools where their children were attending regarding the inequalities that existed within the 11 plus process and how those inequalities negated against children from the south of the Borough, either on the grounds of ethnicity, class or race.

Ahead of us waiting in the queue to go into the hall where the lecture was were the Scrivens, and even above the voices of the anticipating audience waiting to get in it was not difficult to pick up that both Teddy and Ossie were contemptuous regarding to what I had conveyed them about my experience at Tarvin. That being said the consensus amongst all three of us what that if and when the issues of inequalities raise their ugly heads we should refrain from challenging them, even if there were people both from within our own or outside of the community who may be planning to sabotage our efforts. Teddy had the last word when he said in his Bajan accent: "Stan, boy, looking at those two people there is something that I don't like about them and if they are who they say they are then I am prepared to use my jock strap as an umbrella."

Sharing the platform on the evening with C.L.R. James was Darcus Howe, a Trinidadian like C.L.R. and a leading light in Race Today Collective, who was later to become a television personality on Channel Four's Devil's Advocate.

Hardly had we taken our seats, with the Scrivens noticeably sitting in opposite directions to each other, when one of the people who had travelled in from London with C.L.R. went over and spoke to Ann Scrivens and within minutes they were ushered out of the hall and off the premises in an orderly fashion that kicked any assumptions that African Caribbeans are aggressive and arrogant.

The lecture was one of the best that I had ever heard and as was expected there were a number of people who at the end fielded questions. My question was, "Comrade James, thanks for a very enlightening input, my question is a very long one: I have read 'Beyond a Boundary', which to me is one of the most powerful pieces of work that has placed cricket within a historical, political, social and cultural context within and outside of the Caribbean, especially as it relates to black recognition and awareness. Do you believe that present and future generations of non-white successful sportspeople will need to continue to be delegates in helping to challenge the inequalities that prevent black people moving forward?"

"You are perfectly right young man. Starting from the Greeks and Trojans, Jack Johnson, Joe Louis, down through to Learie Constantine, George Hedley, Gary Sobers, Clive Lloyd, Arthur Wint, Muhammad Ali and Allan Wharton, the first non-white footballer to play football in this country; all were representatives of their race, and given that the canvas will change, the frame will always remain for future generations to know and understand who they are" was his response, which attracted thunderous applause.

Given that there were a number of white people in the audience on the evening, it made it important for me to ascertain from the person who had escorted the Scrivens from the premises. His reasons for doing so he informed me were that they gained the confidence of the two community groups in the Brixton areas on the pretext that they were from the University of Syracuse in New York doing postgraduate courses in African and Oriental Studies at the London School of Economics. According to my informant they talk the talk of right on and we shall overcome politics and by the time the groups started to realise that their presence were giving rising to a number of disagreements and the failure on the part of the groups to achieve their aims and objectives, they informed the groups that their studies had come to an end and they had to go back to America.

From what my informant told me he was given the task to ascertain who they were and in the process came to realise that although they were on the register of the London School of Economics they were operating under a different names in the community; in other words they had done what they were sent to do in London and it was in Manchester that their attention was now focused. My informant said, "No way would I allow them to take root down here". It was the last I was to see of the Scrivens.

Whether what Pryce, who came to the Norman Manley Airport to pick me up in 1969 when I made my first visit to Jamaica after ten years in England, said to me was real or imagined, that the reason why the Customs Officer interrogated me so thoroughly as to my reasons for coming to Jamaica was because they were informed that I was part of a group of people who had sympathies to the Black Consciousness Movement in America and which was gaining momentum in Britain and in Jamaica, left me no option that as well as concurring with the saying, "The old age of an eagle is better than the youthful age of a sparrow", but also to have a re-think that events and incidents that had taken place in the community, some in which I was personally involved, should not be taken for granted.

I was to have a better understanding that there were people who mattered, or to put it the other way decision-makers who were willing to define and confine people like myself who were working in the community towards the upliftment of those of those who lacked the confidence and wherewithal to articulate their concerns, when I went to Manchester Polytechnic in 1974 and did my first placement with Abdul Querishi, a Race Relations officer, at the time for the Metropolitan Borough of Trafford. He gave me permission to look at files in his cabinet that would be in keeping with the extension of my knowledge base in as far as youth and community work was concerned. I needed no further proof that I had attracted the attention of people, who for whatever reason wanted to find out what made me tick, when I opened a folder with all the community organisations, including the Black-led churches and the people who were promoting them, to discover how both statutory and voluntary organisations felt about us and the expectations that they had for us. Even the Black churches interpreted it as the better of the two evils in their efforts to meet the spiritual and secular needs of its members and did not escape negating put downs such as Pentecostalism gone crazy with no sense of theology.

The take on people was over-punctuated with metaphors from Uncle Tom, aggressive, arrogant, self-seeking, social climber, dangerous to be curbed at all cost, waste of space. I was described as having a passion for cricket, loyal and trustworthy foot solder, embracer of philosophy of his Jamaican compatriot Marcus Garvey, which gives him that self confidence bordering on arrogance. Common sense dictated, and drawing on two Jamaican schools of thought, that "What is good for eating, is not wise to talk about" and that "seeing and staying blind, hearing and remaining both deaf and dumb are precepts that are worth living by". There was no need to raise any discussion with my placement supervisor that would give him ideas that I had seen the dossiers on people who were actively involved in the community. Interestingly, two days after I saw the papers he asked me to accompany him to meet a group of people who he was helping to obtain a building for community use; amongst the group were two people who were reflected in the dossiers. I was totally convinced that the opportunity to look at those papers was a deliberate action to create a reaction. I am sure that whoever was behind the act underrated my intelligence i.e. that as a cricketer I had the ability to read a Chinaman from a bouncer and, as such, I applied the technique that warranted the situation. It was well that I did because I did not get the opportunity to open the filing cabinet again and halfway through my placement, when Ann Rose, my tutor at The Polytechnic, came to enquire how I was coping, Abdul Querishi made reference relating to my high regards for confidentiality. The point was reinforced in his final placement report in as far as my weaknesses were concerned, cautiousness was an outstanding factor. Personally I did not see it as a weakness for the sole reason that growing up in a rural Jamaican community in the forties and fifties when the status quo was more robustly challenged by the majority of Blacks who were at the bottom of the pile, cautiousness and daring travelled on the same ship and in the same berth.

There was no stopping the enthusiasm of the St John's lads as they availed themselves at every opportunity to practice on any spare bit of land that could be found in the area, including a concrete wicket that was in Seymour Park which was open to all and sundry and was always being used, a devil of a strip that provided more casualties for the then Park Hospital, later Trafford General, than it encouraged players to enjoy a game without a sense of fear or anxiety of what the ball is going to do. I recall an elderly Caribbean man remarking after two players were rushed to the hospital within the space of fifteen minutes of each other, one sustaining a broken wrist and the other with a suspected fracture to the ribs, that there were demons in the wicket that need to be exorcised by Reverend Tony Durrans if members from the youth team continued to play on it. Fortunately none of the youngsters suffered any injuries; it was a situation of playing on the wings of a prayer as opposed to exorcism in its highest form.

When Clairemonte DePeiza suggested that we pick a team of under 20s to play against an over 40s I jumped at the idea. It being in September when a majority of clubs would be in the final states of their league commitments, I figured that it would not be difficult to hire a club with proper facilities to stage the match. I approached the very same clubs whom we had talked to earlier about sharing their grounds when the idea came about regarding forming a youth cricket team and they responded negatively. I can't say that I was really surprised second time round with the same response, only that this time we were put off by the fact that with it being the end of the season grounds were in the process of being seeded and, in some cases, being re-laid for the next season. Such were, and still are, the vagaries of cricket what I was able to do at that time was to put into context the Jamaican proverb that "it is a foolish man who would want to fight an obeah man for his own bush". That being said all was not lost in terms of our proposed match when Vinny Gratrix, who played for the General Post Office in the Wednesday League and on weekends for a club in the South Lancashire League whose home ground was near Jackson's Boat Hotel on the banks of the River Mersey near Sale, where they also did model aeroplane flying, made a deal with me that providing I could guarantee him a game he would get us the use of the ground at no cost. I was no wheeler-dealer but it was an offer that I could not refuse and I honoured the deal with a handshake.

Playing for the under 20s were Dave Thomas (Captain), Junior Powell, Cedric Powell, Junior Binns, Cleve Blissettt, Trevor Barclay, Ricky Coleman, Cedric Edwards (Wicket), Glen Pitterson, Jarvis Brown, Earl Stevens, Carl Duncan (12th Man); and the over 40s were Clairemonte DePeiza (Captain), John Stevens, Vinny Gratrix, Hermon Bogle, Neville Pitterson, Myron Hull, Gerald Essue, Roy Gavin, Ken Hamilton, Teddy Hinds, Carl Garner. The Umpires were Phillip Burton and myself.

The square, which facilitated three decent pitches, and the outfield were quite good, which more than compensated for the changing room and other facilities which were in a concrete-type bunker-like hut with a large metal-cum-concrete fireplace in the middle and a metal chimney going through the roof. There was no running water and lighting was provided by an old gas lamp. It was as dressing rooms are concerned a far cry form others in the leagues in which I played. Nevertthelessm, it served its purpose and for good measure with it being on the banks of the River Mersey, surrounded with very tall grass, it was a haven for young lovers and I dare say for some people who one could assume as passing that stage, sometimes being over-amorous on a nice summer's day.

I recalled playing a match there for National Dock Labour Board when Kenny Hamilton, fielding at long off, failed to take a catch, his excuse being that he was distracted by a grunting sound in the long grass. When asked if the sound was from a pig, Kenny said "Don't ask me". The truth of the matter was that Kenny was not blessed with safe hands, having said that he was one of the most immaculate players ever to grace a cricket field. That was the surroundings, minus the grunting sound, that St John's had their first competitive match dubbed a friendly, which was far from the truth when DePeiza won the toss and opted to bat and in his stentorian Bajan voice made it known to all and sundry that he had come to play cricket and not to mess about. That was the measure of the man, a seasoned professional who knew exactly how to motivate or wind people up.

My advice to the under 20s was that it was a situation of experience versus youthfulness and that they should go out and play hard, play fair and instead of playing for a draw, fight down to the last man. I guessed that it was about one of the best pep talks that I had ever given as the youngsters walked out with a confidence as if their hearts and souls were on fire, and that was exactly how it was when Cleve Blissett had DePeiza caught by Trevor Barclay fielding at second slip the second ball of his opening over for a duck; in all my years of playing and watching cricket I had never seen so much back-slapping, hand-shaking, cart-wheeling and high fives, which was a new phenomenon which eventually got rooted in the sport. Junior Binns, bowling from the other end, and Dave Thomas, the first change bowler, were equally impressive as they contained the over 40s for 130 runs in the allotted 25 overs. Opening the batting for the Under 20s were Junior Powell and Jarvis Brown, who even with the pace of Gavin and Pittersen, and DePeiza bowling a mixture of fast leg cutters, Yorkers, in and out swingers, gave more than a good account of themselves. Brown was`bowled by Gavin when the score was 15, whilst Dave Thomas, Cedric Powell, Earl Stevens and Cedric Edwards, applying the long handle technique, all made their contribution.

Given that they lost six wickets at the end of their 25 overs, they amassed 132 runs and I felt pleased when Dave Thomas said to me, "Whit, thanks for what you said to us before we walked out on the field that we should go down fighting instead of playing to draw." DePeiza was equally congratulatory and was full of praise for the ball that Blissett bowled to him which resulted in Barclay taking the catch. He said, "Boys, I am proud of you and I will let Clive Lloyd know about you." As people say, talk can be cheap, but in my view words can be said that inspire and set the soul on fire; this was certainly the case when I was encouraged by players and spectators at the match that when my playing days are over I should take up umpiring, which I eventually did, given the fact that I have always been mindful of that day I made two glaring umpiring gaffes. First, standing at square leg I took a beautiful catch hit by Hermon Bogle off the bowling of Dave Thomas and in the process of looking for members of the team to celebrate saw them looking at me in bewilderment, by which time the batsmen ran five. The second was standing at the bowling end when Binns hit Nev Pittersen playing forward to a ball that was pitched off sump and I appealed for a LBW. "Get on with the game umpire you silly moo" coming from George Blissett, the treasurer of the club, a man from the same part of Jamaica as myself and a fellow member at St John's was a bit rich, but at least he was speaking the truth, which can cause an offence but is not a sin.

By the time the 1973 cricket season started St John's was as ready as they could ever be to start playing in the Under 18 North Western League bearing in mind that there were hardly any funding agencies where we could apply for grants in those days. All the monies raised to get the club off the ground were through dances, name cards, raffles, outings and cash contributions from members of the community, every donation gratefully received.

The Manchester Post Office Sports and Social Club at Quay Street, where I was made an Honorary Life Member in 1976, was very generous with their contribution of brand new kit from Tyldsley and Hollbrook sports goods store on Deansgate. Likewise was the availability of a 17-seater minibus by Mr Martin White, Director of Youth Services for the Metropolitan Borough of Trafford, the only stipulation was to have a named driver who was qualified to drive a vehicle of that make and size. We were never short of drivers, people like Vinny Powell, Ralph Cole, Sonny Burton, Alva King, who all worked for Greater Manchester Transport. At one stage we had Inspector Kellett, Community Relations Officer at Stretford Police Station, doing driving duties for us. Jams of all descriptions and marmalade were supplied free of charge by Duerrs Jam on Prestage Street and Jamaican Hard Dough Bread, which some of the members from clubs in the league, such as Ramsbottom, Norden, Cheetham, Newton Health and Thornham, eventually took a liking to was given by Old Trafford Bakery on Shrewsbury Street.

As they say, fortune favours the brave and as already mentioned when the idea came about regarding the forming of a team to play in the league it was based on youngsters in the community who had the talent and who saw people like Clive Lloyd, Andy Roberts, Larry Gomes, Gary Sobers, Viv Richards, Malcolm Marshall, Michael Holding, Joel Garner, Lawrence Rowe and many more West Indian Test players as role models. In this respect it was of no surprise that they won the league the very first time that they entered. It was a great achievement and the lads were being recognised as ambassadors. As one of my work colleagues at Newton Street who lived in Ramsbottom remarked, "Stan, your lads are a credit to their race". As was originally intended when the idea was first mooted about forming a team that had no strong tradition or culture in league cricket but nevertheless would provide the opportunity, even in the light of spartan surroundings, to inspire youngsters to play at a decent level and then move on to better things, almost overnight after three years in the league it was disbanded and players moved on to a number of clubs in the various leagues within Lancashire, Central Lancashire, Lancashire and Cheshire, Saddleworth and Huddersfield.

Dave Thomas, for example, made a tour of Pakistan with the Sheik Hussain team, and later had a distinguished career in the Saddleworth League, Cleve Blissett had trials for Lancashire, who showed more than a passing interest to sign him, but he opted to play football following in the wake of his illustrious cousin Luther. Junior Binns went into the British Army and served overseas, Ricky Coleman moved to London and became a manager for a Wine Merchants, Junior Powell finished up with a responsible position with British Airways in London, Earle Stephens found his calling in the production of films and videos. In the meantime the small group of worshippers at St John's who were resisting every effort to affect changes that would go towards making the Church an inclusive one where African-Caribbean people would feel at ease to sing "The Lord's Song in a strange land" was still of great concern to those of us who wanted to move forward in a positive way.

One of the people from that minority group that I personally had some kind of respect for, if for no other reason than he had the conviction to say things before one's face as opposed to behind their backs, was Mr Wild, a Church Warden of many years standing, who located himself in the glorious days of a British Empire that ruled the world, when children were seen and not heard. On the subject of cricket he made no apologies that it was a game invented by the English for the English, citing Neville Cardus, who wrote that 'none except the people of English speaking countries has excelled at cricket'. Whilst he was happy to see Clive Lloyd or other West Indian players of similar status playing for Lancashire he could not see the day when according to him "a coloured man could be a Church Warden, a Curate or a Vicar at St John's".

Prayer, gentle persuasion or diplomacy, call it what we will on the part of Tony Durrans, eventually brought about the desired changes, and one Sunday after Church Mr Wild said to me, "Whit, I have come to realise that changes have to come and since I cannot fight them I might as well join them". To me it was a case that the scale had fallen off his eyes and he was in a position to sing to his hearts content two of Tony's famous hymns, "Sing Hosanna" and "Dance Dance wherever you maybe".

I had put everything into place in readiness to move on to Manchester Polytechnic, the three years of permanent night work during which time I gained 'O' level passes in English and Sociology, did the Manchester Education Committee and the National Association of Youth Clubs courses for Part-time Youth and Community Workers, and St John's Ambulance Brigade Course in First Aid were well and truly behind me; it was now a case of moving on to the next stage in keeping with my goal aspiration. Almost overnight my ambition went and I started to have some serious reservations as to whether leaving the Post Office was the best thing to do. It seemed almost strange at the time that some of the issues that were clouding my vision were ones that I dealt with and kicked into touch many years previously, the most over-riding was whether I should up stakes and return to Jamaica, which was rather absurd to say the least for the reason that I still had not lived up to my boast regarding obtaining a university education whereby I would be able to go back to kick arses. Failing that to continue with the process of applying to the United States Department of Immigration in London to relocate to America, as I have already stated those issues were dealt with and laid to rest and with them resurfacing at a time when it was in forward mode was very frustrating to my wife, Gwen, who had made so many sacrifices to see me getting this far.

The situation was to resolve itself when my brother, Noel, and his wife visited us from America in June 1974, two weeks after I had attended the Manchester Polytechnic building at Bracken House, off Oxford Road in Manchester, for the interview to be admitted as a mature student for the Certificate Course in Applied Community Studies. Sitting on the interviewing panel were course director, Reverend Brian Cramp, tutor in Groupwork Practice, Steve Potter, tutor in Sociology Bob Gutteruend and tutors in Youth and Community Work, Ann Rose and Rosemary Tolland. My entire family, likewise my friends, were pleased to know that I was given a place on the course to start in September 1974.

The Post Office was more than generous; they suggested that instead of handing in my notice they would keep me on their books during the duration of the two years of the course and although I would not be paid, all I needed to do during holidays was to ring the Duties Officer and arrangements would be made for me to come in to work. There were a number of positives to this arrangement, which had the blessings of the Union of Post Office Workers (UPWU), the most important being that if for some reason I was not successful with the course my job, which by then was that of a Postman Higher Grade (PHG), was still safe.

Two of the people who were instrumental in getting the Post Office to agree to the arrangements were Jean Jacques, the first Jamaican to become a chairman for the Union of Post Office Workers, and Ivor Zott, who was also union representative at Newton Street. When I became Mayor of the Borough of Trafford in 2003 I received a letter of congratulation from Jean which made me feel quite humble. Ivor Zott was heavily involved in Labour Party politics in Salford, serving as a local councillor and eventually Lord Mayor of Salford; he was equally congratulatory of my progress, as were Cyril Hughes, his wife Edwina and Alf Bates, who served as a councillor in Trafford and a Labour Member of Parliament on The Wirral and gave me a lot of encouragement and support to become involved in local representational politics. The same was true of Tony Lloyd, who was MP for Stretford and Urmston.

Leaving the Post Office to go on to university did give rise to its fair amount of speculation as to whether I was a genuine student or whether I was being recruited to work for the Investigation Branch (IB). This was easy to understand, especially in the light that I started the course in September and was on duty in December for the Christmas holidays when several colleagues enquired in tongue-in-cheek fashion in regards my new role as an IB man and how I coped with the rigours of travelling from one part of the country to the other.

One colleague went as far as to inform me that a friend of his whose brother worked at Mount Pleasant, the largest sorting office in London, had seen me working as a cleaner. According to him, his brother said, "One day I was there, the other day I was gone and the following a postman was picked up for stealing." Such were the kind of speculations, which I took in my stride without feeling in any way offended. I think the classic was Vinnie Orizu from Nigeria, whose cousin ran a night club in Moss Side that was losing a lot of revenue due to staff pilfering, who suggested that I do some work for his cousin. However much I tried to convince him that I had nothing to do with Investigations, the more determined he was that I was the man for the job, so as they say so as, to preserve a quiet life I eventually gave in and went along, taking my friend Vibert Rodney, the Guyanese born cricketer who played professional cricket in the Huddersfield and Bradford League and who was also doing Applied Community Studies at The Polytechnic.

Standing at the bar when Vinnie, Vibert and myself walked in were Sonny, the owner of the club, Roy Gilchrist and Ernest Bowen, a Trade Union activist and cricket and boxing raconteur who was born in Guyana and came to live in Manchester in 1943 after fleeing from Trinidad as a result of the persecution meted out against him by the aristocracy because he formed a union of print workers, the first of its kind in Trinidad, that challenged the injustices and inequalities that were the everyday experience of Black workers in the industry. From the level of discussion within the group, which was centred around sports and where for instance cricket had opened another avenue for people like Vibert and myself and many more to further self development, I figured that Vinnie Orizu was by then convinced that I was a genuine student and not an IB man for the Post Office. The penny finally dropped when Vibert, who was noted for his Freudian slips, remarked: "Stan, without Students' Union card we could drink twice as much at the All Saints Club". That being said I politely excused myself from the company on the pretext that I had an assignment to complete.

In addition to the intellectual challenge as a mature student with a mortgage to pay, a wife and two children to keep and a mother in Jamaica to support, Bracken House off Charles Street in Manchester where the faculty of Applied Community Studies was sited when I started the course in 1974 was a world away from all the previous places that I have worked in. The power supply was not always reliable, hence sometimes it could be cold in the

Summer and less warm in the Winter. It was not the ideal in terms of amenities yet by the same rule it was in the environment where an amalgamation of students representing the various strands of the society in terms of gender, ethnicity, race, religious and political persuasions, class and disabilities met to seriously look at how would-be Youth and Community workers in our roles as agents of change could be better qualified to help young people take on the challenges of an ever-changing society.

They say that all good things must come to an end, in my particular case the truism is that bad things will need to be challenged before good things come to an end and this was reflected when African Caribbean students on the course came together and brought to the attention of the teaching faculty that there were some aspects of the course that reflected a bias as to the aspirations and contributions of African Caribbean people to British society. To their credit course directors took our concerns seriously and provided modules that were reflective of how in the process of seeking to change anti-oppressive practice, whether on a personal or professional basis or in a wider social or political setting, power relationships must be taken into consideration.

There were a number of complex issues that had to be dealt with, oftentimes not to the agreement of everyone, and when I went on national television to speak out against 'The Black and White Minstrel Show', which I argued was a throwback to the old days when they were used as agents for social control and the reinforcing of white supremacy, the response from a majority of my caucasian colleagues on the course, whom I felt should or would be more progressive in their thinking, left a lot to be desired.

A further explanation to my logic was when as part of the course requirement we went for a ten day field trip at the YMCA Outdoor Training facility in Cumbria, when on the fourth evening a group of us went out for a drink at a hotel. During the course of the evening we were joined by a group of four women and three men who in the main seemed pleasant enough to have a discussion which was mainly to do with the beauty of the place. It still remained a mystery to me how immigration came into the discussion to the point when one of the seven people who had joined us made a derogatory remark about black people from Liverpool, to which when Vibert, Rodney, Colin Mascol and myself, as African Caribbeans, challenged our colleagues on the course, they alluded that we had taken things out of context. It later transpired that the seven people were members of a far right organisation with extremist views who patronised that particular hotel, yet throughout the remainder of the time that we stayed in Cumbria members of our group continued to visit the place. To me it was a case like in UB40's song, "They were proud to be British but they carried the burden of shame".

Helping me to master the theories and practices of youth and community work in a real world situation where racial, gender and sexual orientation and disabilities were part and parcel of the status quo were outsiders, who were invited to come and address us students, people such as Claire Short, Paul Boateng, and David Blunkett, who were later to become government ministers in the Labour-controlled government under Prime Minister Tony Blair. Their input was further reinforced through a series of on-going discussions that I was having with a wide cross-section of community groups and individuals regarding the way forward for African Caribbean people in Manchester.

One of the groups that I became quite interested in was the Star of Manchester Lodge No 6, conducted under the auspices of the Independent United Order of Mechanics, which was quite prominent in the Caribbean but had very little impact in England in 1950 when one George Wright arrived in London from Jamaica, and after a series of enquiries regarding Caribbean people who were actively involved in the movement back home, he got like-minded people together and before long lodges and later chapters came into being in several cities and towns in England that had a Caribbean population of note.

As it happened, the Star of Manchester Lodge No 6, which was founded in 1968 and had its official inauguration on the second floor of The Co-Op Store at 139 Princess Road, Moss Side, was one of the organisations that was reflected in the confidential documents that I had privy to when I did my first placement with Abdul Querishi as part of my course requirements. The organisation was defined as a "Group of Militant Blacks parading under the guise of Masons but whose aims and objectives are similar to the Black Panthers of The United States". Nothing could be further from the truth, as I was to discover when I joined the organisation in 1975, that far from being anti-establishment they embraced a strong sense of loyalty to Queen and Country and the promoting of self-esteem through the processes of education, thriftiness and an appreciation of the liberal arts. I was particularly impressed by their concept of brotherly love, relief and truth and taking care of their members and their families from the cradle to the grave.

My first job after finishing the course at Manchester Polytechnic and subsequently leaving the Post Office in 1976 after seventeen years service was with Trafford Metropolitan Borough as a Community Centre Warden at the Old Trafford Community Centre at Shrewsbury Street. I was the first person to hold that post ,which was basically to encourage community groups to use the building for a number of activities. I was answerable to the Leisure Service Department of the Council, but with my long experience of living in the community and doing voluntary and part-time paid youth work it did not take long before a number of activities taking place within the centre were youth orientated, a particular aspect of this work was that with the close proximity of the centre to Hulme and Moss Side it was not unusual for youngsters from those communities to use the facilities. I recall Carl Ince and Chet Alexander, who introduced Wu Shu Kwan, an aspect of Martial Arts, to Manchester, having weekly training sessions that attracted participants of all ages and gender from as far afield as Oldham. It was an example that service users will never be confined by boundaries. Carl eventually relocated back to Guyana and in the process of giving something back to his community became a leading figure n the developing of squash; the last I heard of Chet Alexander he was living in Florida.

Working at this Centre was not without its challenges of what was real or what was imagined in terms of what I was to experience, starting from the third day of the first week when I started on the job. The arrangements were that the caretaker who lived on the premises would open up at eight in the morning for the cleaner who lived opposite the centre on Shrewsbury Street to prepare for the day prior to me starting work at nine. On that particular morning it was about nine-thirty when George, the caretaker, told me that he was going over to his flat to make his breakfast. Doris, the cleaner, was in the main hall cleaning and I was sitting at my desk glancing through the papers when suddenly I looked up to see what appeared to be a person passing the window and moving in the direction of the main hall. My immediate reaction was to get up from my desk thinking that the person had come to see me. I went into the main hall where Doris was still working but there was no one except her there, but on going back into my office there was a strong odour of Yardley aftershave lotion, which I had never used. Interestingly, I did not feel afraid and I plucked up the courage to say, "You stay in your world in peace and leave me in my world in peace". It was the first and last time that I saw an apparition in the Centre, but by the same token I was to experience presences, odours sometimes of fresh flowers and more than once the radio being switched off. Enquiries as to who occupied the houses before they were being demolished failed to make any connections until six months before I left the job. A woman in her seventies who was born and brought up in the area and was evacuated to Shropshire during the war and had come back for a function at St Brides Church dropped in to have a look around the centre. In the process of her reminiscence she made mention of her childhood friend who lived in a house where the centre was built, according to her he was always immaculately dressed, he joined the forces and was killed in Belgium and from time to time she would dream of him bringing flowers to her. All things being equal I came to the conclusion, and Rose who manages the centre and who has had similar experiences to mine, has also agreed that it was a friendly spirit who she refers to as George.

George certainly had nothing to do with my decision to leave the centre in 1979 to take up the position of Youth Leader in Charge of the Greenhill Youth Centre at Glodwick in the Metropolitan Borough of Oldham. Even before I went for the interview for the job the expressed view by some of the people who I met as a result of playing cricket was to steer clear of the area, which had attracted a negative reputation due to the result of a murder that had taken place on Waterloo Street some months previously. Yet for all that not even wild horses could stop me from rising to the challenges of working in a community that was so diverse with a population of English people, first, second and third generation of people from Ireland, Scotland and Wales, who were came to work in the cotton factories and mines. There was also a population of Eastern Europeans from Poland, Czechoslovia, Hungary and the Ukraine, who settled after the war and to a large extent lived their separate lives.

The largest concentration of Caribbean people were from Barbados, followed by Jamaicans and a sprinkling of others from the Windward and Leeward Islands, who came pre- and after the arrival of the Windrush in 1948. There was a shared solidarity within this group and names that were almost household when I went there were from Barbados: Ivan Padmore, who had the distinction of being the first black magistrate in the Borough, the Marshalls, whose son Wayne became an international musical icon, Sassy Nurse and Mrs Violet Griffiths Drummond, two of the most loyal and dedicated grass roots community workers that I have ever come across. It was not a surprise to me when in 2005 Mrs Griffiths Drummond was awarded the Member of the British Empire (MBE) medal for her contributions and services to the community of Oldham.

Jamaicans who were household names when I went to Oldham in 1979 were Granville Lawrence, a man who embraced the philosophies of Marcus Garvey until his dying day; he was an active trade unionist championing the cause of workers without fear or favour at Vitofoam, which had a large African Caribbean workforce. Like Sassy Nurse, Granville served on a number of committees both voluntary and statutory in Oldham; they were members of my Youth Committee at Greenhill Youth Centre.

Ernie and Veronica Campbell, the Findlaters, the Mears, the Coleys, the Pryces were also Jamaican background people actively involved. Almost the latest in line of immigrants from overseas settled in Oldham in the time I was there were people from the Indian sub-continent, the majority Pakistanis, and then there were people from the newly independent countries of East African, Kenya and Uganda, who at the time were not as actively involved in community work save concentrating on building up small businesses. Mr Siddique, a Pakistani, was well known as a TV repair man and almost anything to do with electrics. Mrs Munchi, from Kenya, was an Educational Welfare officer who worked for the Borough when I went there. I learnt a great deal from her in terms of how to avoid the pitfalls that would create any misunderstandings between the various groups within the Asian communities, these lessons for my part were well learnt.

What proved to be more than a blessing in disguise is that when I was appointed to start work in September 1979 the two storey building which was intended to be the Youth Centre and which was originally the science block when Greenhill School was operational was still being refurbished and would not be ready for occupation until mid-October. In addition to practicing the skill of engaging with young people outside of a youth club setting I also had the opportunity to meet with the builders and convey to them my concerns that their plans for where they intended to site the coffee bar and the toilets for males and females and no provision for a quiet room would hinder my effectiveness as a Leader.

These discussions did not go down well with construction professionals, who felt that they were being dictated to by a layman. The final outcome was that further discussions with other officers of the Council, including the Youth Adviser, Mrs Nancy Brierley, agreed to the points that I was making and the situation was resolved amicably to the extent where one of the builders, who was the most stubborn in his view to what I was suggesting, said, "I will have to hold my hand up now that the plans have changed when everything is completed the place will look much better".

The opportunity had also presented itself whereby I was able to persuade Nancy Brierley to put on a three months in-house part-time course for the staff who would help in running the club. They were all local people who in their spare time had voluntarily worked for community groups in the area. The course was designed for those people such as Wes Coley, Jean Grindley, Doreen Biggs, Gwen Findlater, Val Mears, Susan Ayub, Sabir "Bruce" Mamood, and Veronica Campbell who were already involved in various aspects of voluntary work within the community but who needed to refine their skills that could be effectively applied within a statutory youth work environment. All the course participants were successful and in time people like Veronica Campbell and Susan Ayub went on to do the full course in Youth and Community Work, Val Mears opted for the course in Probation Work and went to work for the Greater Manchester Probation Service.

Val was straight-talking and whilst at the beginning we did not get along like a house on fire I admired his what I called rough and ready kind of honesty, loyalty and commitment which was then and now still a rare commodity amongst a lot of people. That was the measure of the man and when within two years Greenhill won the Borough's Sporting Competition organised by Greater

Manchester Youth Association, it was a testimony to his dedication and a fulfilment of what we asked the members of the club to do by believing in themselves that they could achieve. The highlight of the year was wrestling the Victor Loudorum Cup from Fitton Hill Youth Centre, who had held it for years. Graham Gibson, the Senior Youth Worker in Oldham at the time and Worker in Charge at Fitton Hill had been known to criticise my approach to youth work, but on the night when the cup was being presented to Gay Coley, who received it on behalf of Greenhill, he was manly enough to acknowledge that this assessment of me was wrong and that the Youth Service in Oldham could benefit from talking on board some of my strategies that would be reflective in working in a multi-cultural, multi-racial and multi-faith community.

Like longevity, success one way or the other has got a price to pay, and with the gradual rise of the BNP in Britain at the time. I can't say that I was totally surprised when one evening I answered the telephone to hear a male voice at the other end telling me to "F .....g leave Oldham and go back to work with the N....s in Moss Side". I kept it to myself on the grounds that sharing it could cause undue anxiety to members of staff and members of the club. The follow up to the telephone call was that three days after, on my way home to Manchester, I stopped off as I always did to pick up my fish and chips at Mother Hubbard's when three men came out of a car and started to chant, 'mene mini mo.......'. I certainly was not going to run away and what could well develop into a hostile situation was averted by two men who had driven up and anticipated that something was not right and told the three men in no uncertain terms where to get off.

Hughie Haggerty, the Police Community Relations Officer, who was well respected in the Glodwick community, later informed me that the two men who intervened on my behalf were firemen from Werneth who had a long association of playing cricket with and against Caribbean people within the various leagues in and around Greater Manchester, needless to say I was never molested again neither on the phone or in person.

I have always alluded that in terms of my youth and community work both in theory and in practice, especially as it related to working in a multi-racial, multi-cultural and multi-faith community, I matured in Oldham and as such it was a case of grabbing the opportunity with both hands when it presented itself to work with the Manchester Council for Community Relations as their Youth Officer. It was leaving Oldham on the one hand with a feeling of sorrow but on the other hand knowing that the two years that I had worked there I had made a difference to a number of young people and adults alike, at how together we could be inspirers and aspirers in terms of achieving our goals and it has been with a sense of great satisfaction that people such as Colin Price, and his brother Danny, Nigel Braithwaite, the Coleys, Bing Findlater, The

Bouchers and many others accepted the challenges that had made them role models for a younger generation.

Prior to leaving Oldham, in a discussion with a group of decision-makers I told them that from my experience working in the Borough if they were not prepared to bring about and implement policies that would create more opportunities for working class white boys who were beginning to become an underclass recipes for disaster were in the making which would result in riots within the next fifteen or twenty years involving Asians, who were rapidly becoming a majority group and whose presence and needs were not being adequately addressed, and for which the Commission for Racial Equality with the best will in the world and for all its good intentions was still at the time struggling to put words into actions that would reflect a level playing field in terms of better housing, more opportunities for better education and less discriminatory practices in employment. As they related to ethnic minorities it came as no surprise to me when most of the people that I spoke to on the matter located their responses as "hearing what you are saying Whit". To me hearing what I was saying and knowing what I was saying were two different things. I saw myself as a lone voice in the wilderness whose message was relevant and when the community grapevine conveyed to me that I had left some people with fleas in their ears, there was also a veiled hint that if I was not going of my own accord sooner or later I would have to jump. That could well have been the case but the bottom line was that like in Desiderata I spoke the truth calmly and given that in 2002, when there were uprisings in Oldham and other towns in the North West of England that had large Asian populations, some of the decision makers that I spoke with in 1981 would have either retired to other parts of the country or to either the South of France, Spain, Portugal, or were pushing up daisies. I guess that wherever they were when news reached them of what was taking place in those communities some would remember that Whit told them so.

Coming back to work in Manchester as a Youth Officer with a city-wide brief was indeed a very tall order and as such common sense decreed that if I was going to be effective then I would need to concentrate my energies in areas such as Hulme, Moss Side, Whalley Range and Trafford, where there were more needs.

Whilst there was general agreement from my employers as to work in Hulme, Moss Side and Whalley Range were concerned, to involve myself with Trafford was totally unacceptable on the grounds that the funding for my job was part City Council, which dictated that working across boundaries was simply not on. My argument was based on the history of African Caribbean migration to Manchester: when Moss Side became the central point of location, and over time as the new arrivals became more settled, they moved to places like Trafford, Longsight and Whalley Range. Demolition and re-housing on the part of the City Council also saw large numbers of African-Caribbean people being sent to Hattersley in Hyde and on the Racecourse Estate in Sale, which justified working with their children, and for that matter, parents who through the processes of revolution and evolution has proven to providers of services that issues know no boundaries. The Scarman Report, similar to that of the Benet Hytner Report conducted in Manchester as responses to the riots in 1981 where in Moss Side over 1000 youngsters, both black and white, were in confrontation with the police, highlighted the importance of both central and local government encouraging more inter-agency involvement in helping organisations and in some cases individuals to address the various issues that were affecting large numbers of people who were being disenfranchised and excluded from society.

To be effective and to hit the ground running I figured that the best thing that I could do was to resort to doing what I could do well, and that was to organise cricket matches, so when Clayton Goodwin, who wrote 'Caribbean Cricketers from the Pioneers to Packer' and who was also writing for the Jamaican Overseas Gleaner, telephoned me in my capacity as the Manchester correspondent for the same publication to inform me that the advertisers for Dry Cane Rum had some money that they wanted to spend on a community project either to do with sports or music, I immediately opted for sports in the form of a six-a-side indoor cricket competition at Moss Side Leisure Centre.

The competition was referred to in an article that appeared in the Caribbean Times in 1982: "When the competition started as the brainchild of Whit Stennett, Youth Officer with Manchester Council for Community Relations, it attracted players from various clubs around Greater Manchester. The winning team received a case of Dry Can Rum and £500, first runners up received six bottles and £250 and third runners up got £125 plus three bottles of rum and there were five consolation prizes of £25 plus a bottle of rum each." Dry Cane sponsored the competition for another two seasons when it was taken over by Abbey Life, the Insurance giant, whose local representative was Clairemonte DePeiza, the West Indian Test cricketer. Central to the success of the competition was the strategy that I adopted in forming a committee of people such as Aston Douglas and Aston Gore from the West Indian Sports and Social Club, Mike Bisson, who at the time worked for the Manchester Careers Service, Wallen Matthie, who was the Employment Officer with Manchester Council for Community Relations, and Charlie Moore, who was Leader in Charge at Moss Side Youth Club. This style of collaborative work was to gain momentum and helped to clear up some of the misconceptions that some committee members of my employers had regarding my role as Youth Officer and whether my job description entitled me to work with adults, in particular with the African Caribbean Care Group, which was in its embryonic stage under the guidance of Raphael Phipps, with support from people like Gus John, Hartley Hanley, Wally Brown, Elouise Edwards and Louise DaCacoddia. For me it was not a case of staying with the confines of a job description but rather to remain conscious that the prevailing themes of self-help, race, crime community and race relations were relevant to the struggles of African-Caribbean people from the cradle to the grave. In this respect I stayed with the group until it was properly established; I was to become its first chairperson and I look back at those people working from the 8411 Centre in Moss Side with a great sense of pride and a worthwhile part of the journey.

An invitation by Chet Alexander, a near white upper middle class Jamaican, to meet him to discuss the possibility of helping him to get funding to run his martial arts project from an upstairs building at the corner of Princess Road and Claremont Road in Moss Side, was another turning point in my life. Present at the first meeting that I had with Chet was Phil Martin, a local boxer who had a fairly successful career both as an amateur and as a professional, who on being retired from the sport wanted to give something back to the community by setting up a gymnasium to train youngsters from the community.

Like Chet, Phil was aware of the history of the West Indian Centre at Carmoor Road, the George Jackson Trust and the Manchester Black Women's Co-Operative, who all received funding from the Community Relations Council (CRC) under the heading of self-help with an emphasis on the African-Caribbean community, and except for the Black Women's Co-Operative, which had achieved a certain level of success, it was the other two groups which the community felt could have done better in involving more people in the operation of their activities. Phil and Chet expressed their doubts as to whether I had the ability to persuade my organisation to make the case for funding their projects.

I liked the aims and objectives of both projects and was quite impressed with the high degree of passion and enthusiasm that both men showed at that first meeting in terms of how through boxing and martial arts they could help to change the mindset of negativity and low self-esteem that young people had of themselves, which gave rise to the disturbances in the community a year previous. I felt so confident that I could get the Manpower Services Committee to fund their projects that I threw modesty out of the window with a wager that if I was unsuccessful I would go down on my knees and use my nose to push a peanut across Piccadilly; some bet indeed and had they taken me on they certainly would have lost.

241

Wallen Matthie had by then left M.C.C.R. to work for Granada Television and the task of writing up the application forms and making the case that the Moss Side Boxing Club was not only intended for recreation but also to provide opportunities for young people to be trained for jobs within the leisure industry fell on the shoulders of Hugh McWilliams, who took over from Wallen as Employment Officer. Within six months of my first meeting with Chet and Phil the Co-Op Store at 139 Princess Road, Moss Side was acquired and the second floor was refurbished and made into a gymnasium. This was a testimony of a labour of love where youngsters who eventually became members of the Club joined with adults from the community, myself included, and worked with tradesmen to make the gym one of the best in the North West of England. My abiding memory of the place: "When the going gets tough the touch gets going" written in a prominent position on the wall over the ring.

Success was almost immediate as within a short time the club started turning out boxers who were winning medals at amateur level locally, nationally and internationally. Some boxers, like Ensley Bingham, Maurice Coore, John Grant, Ossie Maddix and Tony Ekubia eventually went into the professional ranks where they made names for themselves and the name changed to The Champs' Camp. As I have always maintained, success has its price to pay and when I was invited by the club to attend a Dinner and Fight Evening organised by the North West ABC to raise money for charity at a prestigious club in Bredbury near Stockport, the evening was marred by a comedian who made derogatory remarks about Moss Side Boxing Club, its members and for that matter the entire community of Moss Side. No way was I prepared to sit in that audience that evening and not challenge the comedian, I knew and was prepared to be forcefully ejected by bouncers but when more than half of the patrons dressed to the nines in their dinner suits joined with Basil Gumbs, an African Caribbean businessman who operated in Moss Side, and myself in a peaceful walk-out, I guess that management had the savvy to avert what could have been a distasteful situation.

As far as I was concerned that was not the end of the matter as on the following day, when I went into work and reported to Saeed Ahmed, the Principal Community Relations Officer of what transpired the previous evening, he agreed that I should write to the Commission for Racial Equality and lodge a complaint, both to the ABC and the proprietors of the club. An answer from both organisations was not long in coming, both apologising for what happened, as was the case when I attended a football match at Manchester City Football Club with a friend who was a long time member and heard the Millwall supporters shouting racist abuse. I had to do something about it and on the following morning I rang from work and requested a meeting with Billy McNeil, who was manager at City, who agreed when we met that racism should not be tolerated in sport, and in keeping with his beliefs all future programmes printed by Manchester City Football Club emphasised the point. My working with Phil Martin was far above and beyond what some of my detractors alluded to as "Whit Stennett is concentrating too much on encouraging young people to participate in sports". We worked form the premise and the reality that how society was at the time sport was one of the only available tools that could be used for motivating young people. The bottom line at the time was not that I was too involved with sports but that there were a number of decision-makers who did not agree with boxing per se, but as someone who was at the grassroots and listening to those opinions youngsters had the intelligence to know what they were going into and when a parent said to me in praise of what the club was doing for youngsters in the community, that she would rather her son die in the boxing ring than being beaten up in a police station, it was a clear message to those decision-makers that people should be allowed to make choices.

Phil's passing left a tremendous gap and a rather difficult act to have followed in terms of excellent youth and community work practice and the Phil Martin Centre, where the boxing club started from humble beginnings, is a lasting memory to a man who helped so many young people to follow their dreams and who gave me a lot of support in helping the Strategies to Elevate People (STEP) Project to become a reality. STEP was the first mentoring organisation in Manchester whose aims were to raise the self-esteem of young people in general, and young black people in particular, by exposing them to black achievement in the arts, business, commerce, politics, literature, music, sports and for that matter black success in all walks of life, by taking black success stories into inner city schools to talk and share their experiences with young people whose expectations were in a number of cases quite low.

STEP was piloted at Ducie High School in Moss Side, whose head Dawn Peters and senior teacher, Dave Birtwhistle, along with other members of staff fine-tuned every aspect of its aims and objectives, which made it easy for other schools such as Oakwood High, Ellen Wilkinson High, Thomas Aquinas and St Vincent De Paul to become participants. The official launch of STEP was in November 1989 at Manchester Town Hall when Councillor Yomi Mambu was Lord Mayor of Manchester, the first black woman in the history of the City of Manchester to be so honoured. I must confess that I felt hurt when some of the very people who criticised me for encouraging young people to participate in sports were now some of the same people who expressed their concerns that although STEP placed an emphasis on the importance of young black people acquiring an education that would help them to address their adolescent identity and self-esteem, and to understand how these factors influence their aesthetic, political, social, and economic values, for all that my detractors felt that the project was intended to create an elitist group of black people. Some even went as far as to suggest that my appointment to the Manchester City Magistrates Bench as a lay magistrate was an example of my own elitism. As I said, it was hurtful, especially when people became personal, yet for all that there were many more people who believed in what I was trying to do for the community as opposed to my detractors and that in itself was quite reassuring. There was no question in my mind that STEP would have made an impact within and outside of the school community. This was reflected in the introduction of an annual Summer School at Bangor University in North Wales aimed at exploding the myth that a university education was beyond the reach of young black people from inner city areas. It was also aimed at helping to motivate young people, especially from minority ethnic backgrounds, to use the process of education as a positive route to success.

In the three years that the summer school was conducted over sixty young people participated and it continues to be a great source of inspiration when I meet doctors, pharmacists, social scientists, teachers, advertising executives and people who run their own business who hark back to the days when they were involved with the summer school. The STEP spelling bee competition, similar to the one initiated by the Daily Gleaner in Jamaica around the late 1940s, was another good example of young people aspiring together and achieving together. This project was sponsored by Victoria Mutual, one of the Jamaican financial institutions that operates in the United Kingdom. Again one of the highlights of this competition was at one of the finals at the Barn Hill Studios in Moss Side when Ramsey McDonald, the local representative for Victoria Mutual, invited Mr Ronald Graham, the Company's Chairman, to fly up from Jamaica to make the presentation to Reach Out, an education project that operates in Manchester. The runners-up were from the St John's Saturday School from Old Trafford.

Inadequate funding has always been the bane of many community projects, STEP has been no exception, and other than the Saturday School, which has lurched from step to step, the project went into decline, but certainly not its aims and objectives as year on year statistics prove that under-achievement, especially amongst African-Caribbean boys, continues to be of concern in the UK. That I should mention funding is to highlight the conflict I had with my organisation, to whom I had given thirteen years of loyal and dedicated service. It was a case of going into work and being handed a letter, the contents speaking volumes of my contribution to the organisation, but the bottom line was that the section eleven funding that paid part of my salary had come to an end. It simply meant that within a month of receiving the letter it was the end of the road for me. No compensation or redundancy packet, it was sweet Fanny Adams, take it or leave it. I felt angry at the way in which I was treated and took legal advice, which resulted in an Industrial Tribunal which I lost on a technicality. That period in my life was quite frustrating; as I have already stated I was angry but never bitter. If anything the experience made me much stronger, especially when a number of my detractors were able to acknowledge that over time they had come to realise that we might differ with each other on certain issues but I have always remained consistent.

On a cold December morning in 1993 I answered the telephone and heard the voice at the other end say, "Hi Whit, good morning, sorry to be ringing so early with a bit of bad news, but Shaun passed away last night and we, the members of the Clifford Ward group, have already selected you to be our candidate for the by-election which will be taking place in the next few weeks." It was Phil Morgan, the then secretary of the group conveying the message. I have always seen Phil as the Mike Brearley of the Labour Party, sharpness of brain, clear thinking, consideration for other people, and fair-minded to a fault. That being said I accepted the decision with a great sense of humility.

It was not the first time that I was standing as a Labour Party candidate. I had already had two bites of the cherry when I stood at Brooklands the first time and I came second to the winning Conservative candidate, a first for the Labour Party in that ward. The second time I came third in a race with four candidates - that was the way the cookie crumbled and as far as I was concerned the experiences were sharp learning curves in terms of what representational politics are about. Running in my own neck of the woods was a great challenge and was to confirm what people like Cyril Hughes, his wife Edwina, the late Ernie Bowen, Aston and Angel Douglas, Busta Clarke, Joyce Spencer, Janet McLoughlin and Ossie Smith have always said, that sooner or later my time would come to answer the call in my own ward. Their words of encouragement were similar to what the majority of people in the ward were saying as we went out canvassing in what was a very cold and wet December. I recall members of the host community, especially those living around Wordsworth Road, Coleridge Road, and Ruskin Road, aptly called Poets' Corner, said to me: "Whit, we have never voted Labour but we will be voting for you the man." From the Sikh community were the words, "Don't worry Whit, you will win it walking barefooted." The Islamic community's words of encouragement were, "Whit, you are our man, we are fully behind you." The African Caribbean community located themselves with a calypso cum reggae genre with the words, "Gwaan Whit, you can't loose."

I have always said, and drawing from the old Jamaican school of thought that "mouth mek to say anyting" and "What people sey and what people do are two different things", on the night of the election count at Trafford Town

Hall when Allan Lewis, Chief Executive of the Borough, announced the results, it was a confirmation that the residents of the Clifford Ward were absolutely sincere in what they were saying for in the history of the Labour Party at that time, I had the distinction of polling the highest percentage of votes both at a local and national level. The occasion was indeed of historical significance, but as I said to a newspaper representative at the time, "I leave historians to deal with history and asked God to keep me focussed."

Both Chris Ford and George Blissett suggested that I need to be quick on the uptake in terms of how I dealt with the media who were chasing me for interviews; their accepted wisdom was that some could ask loaded questions more about my ethnicity as opposed to my ability. George suggested that I fly to America to spend Christmas and chill out with my mother. Spending Christmas in Connecticut was great, but chilling out was just something else, as I was to find out on Boxing Day morning when I had to put on extra levels of thick clothing to help my sister, Lorna, clear the driveway that was well under two feet of snow. All together it was a Christmas and New Year well spent with relatives and friends and what I brought away with me was the idea of placing outdoor lights in the garden during the festive season. I was the first person in and around where I live to start the custom, which has now been taken on.

Amongst some of the letters of congratulations that I received when I arrived back from American in January 1994 were also some whose contents were rather distasteful. One had crude pictures depicting a tree and someone hanging from it with the words, "This is what happens to uppity n……. like you", and another was smeared with excreta. As is the case, senders of these letters never put their addresses or their names to what they write. There was an exception to the rule as one of the letters sent to me had an address and the contents were:

> *"Coon Councillor*
> *People like you make me and a lot of white people sick, you come over here from Jamaica, take our jobs and our houses, rape our women, and then bring your Yardie friends over to sell drugs on our streets and live off the State. I have served in the Army and lived in Old Trafford when I came out but things got so bad that is why we had to leave. Enoch Powell was right in wanting to send you f.....g lot packing. What he failed to do I know that in time the BNP will deliver".*
> *The letter was signed "we are the nigger hunters and chasers".*

I have always contended that I am neither a crusader or martyr, but by the same rule I like to stand up and support a cause that I believe in so with that in mind I responded to the writer of the letter requesting that we meet at any of the locals that they would have known in Old Trafford to as far as the Lord Nelson in Urmston, from where according to the address on the letter he was not living far away. In my letter I assured them that I would be coming to meet them on my own with peace and love in my heart, but they could take along with them his friends if they so wished. As far as I was concerned it was a case of believing totally in Psalm 21, which states that "The Lord is my light and my salvation whom shall I fear", and as I was to discover that having visited all the pubs, other than patrons involving me in their discussions about football, cricket, music or an episode from a soap opera, the only time that a discussion developed that had a racial overtone was in The Shrewsbury when the majority of white patrons expressed the view that Jamaicans were responsible for importing the majority of drugs into Britain. At the end of two weeks, after spending a great deal of time and money buying drinks and hoping that I could meet with someone to put my point of view forward, I got a letter pushed through my letterbox. There was no address or name attached and the contents were:

"Councillor Stennett you are a better man that us, Good Luck.

The first full Council Meeting that I attended in January 1994 convinced me that, irrespective of party political persuasions, elected representatives are committed in their efforts in helping to enhance the lives of residents in our wards and for the Borough of Trafford as a whole. At the time I went on Planning two of the most important subjects for discussion were the demolition of Longford Hall and the proposals for the development of Dumplington into what is now the Trafford Centre. These discussions evoked a high degree of passion from all sections of the political divide and I recall at one meeting a leading member of the Conservative group remarked that "the sooner that place is bulldozed to a pile of rubble that will be the better". Longford Hall is now history.

It was not unusual for officers of the Council with responsibilities for Planning and Building Control and members of the Planning Committee to visit the site at Dumplington during the construction of the Trafford Centre; it was on one of these visits that I suggested to an Engineer that with so much glass being used in the construction if any consideration had been given to solar heating. I guess that the jury is still out on that suggestion, but what I never fail to do is that when friends or relatives, whether living in England or from abroad, visit Manchester, I insist that they visit The Trafford Centre and

247

as part of my claim to fame as a Trafford councillor I never fail to remind them that I sat on the Planning Committee that resulted in the construction of one of the best shopping centres in the United Kingdom, and in a funny sort of way, which I think has something to do with that part of human nature where people from time to time play games on many occasions, I have been introduced by acquaintances to other people as Councillor Stennett who helped in planning the Trafford Centre, which reminds me that when some Jamaicans say something if it is not so, it is almost so!

On the morning of Saturday the 14th of June 1998, when both the print and electronic media conveyed the news that I would be receiving the MBE, it started a chain reaction of congratulatory messages by way of cards, letters, telephone calls and face to face acknowledgement.

My mother was ninety seven years old and, according to my sister, Lurline, being the royalist that has always been immediately had I finished talking to her on the telephone she started telling anyone who came within earshot of her that her son would be going to Buckingham Palace to be honoured. It was six months after the announcement that I attended the Investiture on the 8th of December 1998 at Buckingham Palace by her Royal Highness Her Majesty The Queen. I was accompanied by my wife, Gwen, my eldest daughter Patricia and my first granddaughter Nikesha Stennett-Bussue.

I must say that they were dressed for the occasion. On the train Gwen had three cases plus two boxes for her hats. I can wager a bet that she has a hat for the three hundred and sixty five days of the year and, of course, the extra one for the leap year. The idea of me walking down the Mall with top hat and tails was not something that I cherished, even though in one of my fortnightly telephone talks with my mother in Jamaica she did suggest that it would be the proper way for me to dress, reminding me that my shoes should be so shiny that I must be able to see my face in them. In the final analysis I decided that a lounge suit would be better.

The enormity of the occasion did not really hit me until I was in the large hall of the Palace and heard the announcement, "Eunice Whitfield Stennett for services to the African Caribbean Community in Greater Manchester", and then I had to walk up and do my bow to the Queen, who before she invested me with the medal enquired of aspects of my involvement in the community. It was a great opportunity for me to put into context my love of cricket and how it has been central to the contributions that I make in the community. I will never forget picking out from the hundreds of spectators in the gallery, my wife, my daughter and grand daughter looking down at me with a sense of admiration and pride. For a moment I felt sad that my two brothers and George Blissett, who was one of the people who had supported my nomination for the honour, were not alive to share in the celebrations.

Freddie "Punny" Essor, my brother-in-law from Blackness in Westmoreland, Jamaica, who had trials to represent the West Indies as a left arm spin bowler and was prevented to do so because he was the man in form but not the man in favour, came over from America in May 1999 after he had been away from England for over twenty years to watch the 1999 Cricket World Cup and to re-connect with his friends, many of whom had played cricket with and against him in the various leagues in Greater Manchester. Two of his closest friends were Angel and Aston Douglas, also from Westmoreland. It was at Aston's house that we talked about the sadness on hearing the news that Malcolm Marshall, the talented and much admired West Indian Test fast bowler, was admitted to hospital in Birmingham and the results from the tests carried out were not favourable. Always the optimist, Aston felt that with Marshall's age and the determination that he had as a successful pace bowler would pull him through. I had the good fortune of meeting Marshall through Bully Williams, who in his younger days as a cricketer in Barbados bowled against Patsy Hendrew in the nets; Bully was the first man to see me as a look-a-like to Viv Richards.

I was quite impressed with Malcolm, who called me Whip, and when I went to Barbados for a holiday, he took my wife and myself to lunch at Cave Shepherd, the largest Department Store, managed then by Grantley Taylor, the brother of the late Pat Taylor, who was a curate at St John's, Old Trafford. Two days after our meeting at Aston's house, where in addition to talking of past experiences we also talked of the future in terms of year 2000, The Millennium, when we would meet in Jamaica to celebrate my mother's 100th birthday and play a cricket match, Westmoreland against St Ann. When Aston and Freddie were on their way to meet with some of their friends, Aston collapsed on the street and was taken to hospital where he passed away in the early hours of the 30th May 1999, the very day that West Indies played Australia at Old Trafford where I saw Glenn McGrath bowl Brian Lara with about one of the best balls that I have ever seen bowled by a fast bowler. I was overcome with emotion and could not stop the tears from flowing as I hastily left Old Trafford thinking of the state of play with no Malcolm Marshall to retaliate and no Aston Douglas to talk with about that particular ball. My only consolation was that on the following day, thanks to Air Jamaica, I was a courtesy passenger on the Inaugural A340 Airbus flight, Heathrow to Jamaica, where I stayed at Sandals Negril for seven days, which was excellent to say the least, and a welcome respite from the outpouring of grief that was taking place in Manchester with the passing of Aston.

I spent a day with my mother and other relatives whilst in Jamaica for the seven days and prior to leaving she called me into her bedroom and told me that for the fact no man has a list on his life, there is a strong possibility that either of us could die before each other, but just in case that she should go before me she would not want to be buried in Montego Bay, she wanted to be buried beside Baba - that's what she called my father - and her final words were, "Whitty, I know that you will carry out my wishes". With that as is customary, we read from Psalms Chapter 121: "I will lift up mine eyes unto the hills from whence cometh my help". We always placed great emphasis on verse eight, "The Lord shall preserve thy going out and thy coming in from this time forth and for evermore". The older generation of Stennetts never say goodbye, it is always "take care until such time", and that was how we parted on the 7th June 1999. I came back to Manchester and picked up the pieces and moved on. One of my most pressing pieces of work was to finish the part-time Masters degree course which I started in 1998 at Manchester Metropolitan University in time for the year 2000. Things were back on an even keel in every sense of the word, until on the morning of the 5th November when Pat Taylor, who was also on the course, rang to inform me that Malcolm Marshall had passed away in Barbados. All I can remember saying to Pat was, "Thanks for telling me, they say that the good die young". I can't say that we were great friends - and he wasn't a relative - he was just a great fast bowler whom I admired and his passing was sad.

Two weeks after Malcolm's passing Gwen received a telephone call informing her that her father was seriously ill in hospital; a day after there was another call to say that he had passed away. On the day we arrived in Jamaica, Gwen, her sister Myrtle and I went to see my mother, who wanted to know what all three of us were doing in Jamaica in mid-November. I told her that we had some extra days off to travel out to Jamaica but even at ninety nine years old her head was still good. She was as sharp as a tack and when she enquired after Mr Knight, who was Gwen's father, so as not to alarm her of his passing I told her that he was in the process of making his will and he wanted his children to be present; I figured that by then she would have guessed that either my father-in-law was seriously ill or was dead.

From the very first time that I met Mr Knight, popularly known as "Masa Butty" in Jamaican language, "Mi spirit tek im". He was from that long line of Jamaican farmers who the late Prime Minister of Jamaica, Michael Manley, referred to as the backbone of Jamaica. Up in the hills of McNie near Kellits in Clarendon he cultivated sugar cane, bananas, ginger, cabbage, lettuce, yams and sweet potatoes and once when I asked him why some people in the village referred to him as a capitalist, he told me that as a result of his thriftiness, and as land which was cheap in his time became available, he bought it, put it under cultivation and in the process gave employment to people in the community.

We shared the same passion for cricket and history and on the many occasions when Gwen and I visited him we would spend many hours sitting on his veranda sipping J Wray and Nephew White Rum or Teachers Whiskey, which I introduced him to, whilst talking about cricket or history, especially about the Maroons. The day of his funeral I recalled sitting with him on the veranda in May 1991 when his wife, Imogene, died, and after pointing up and showing me the beauty of The Bull Head Mountains, he opened his bible and produced from it a bit of paper and asked me to read what was written on it, which was: "A wife is essential to great longevity; she is the receptacle of half a man's cares and two thirds of his ill humour". he said it was given to him by Reverend Harris, who incidentally was one of the ministers who officiated at his funeral and who spoke of Hubert "Butty" Knight as a good farmer, husband and father - to me he was a great father-in-law.

Two days after my father-in-law's funeral, I rang my sister, Lurline, who on picking up the telephone immediately recognised my voice and I heard when she said, "Mother it's Whitty". Her voice sounded very weak as she enquired after Gwen and I assured her that we would be coming to see her on the Monday; before retiring to bed at around 10.30pm the telephone rang and when Ken Simpson, my brother-in-law, answered and said it is for you Whit I said to the people sitting in the living room, "Mother is gone"; this was confirmed by my sister Lurline.

I understand that on the morning of the day when I rang she told her granddaughter, Christine, that I am in Jamaica and she had finished her work; she was ready to go home to rest. The last reading from the bible that Christine did for her was from Second Timothy, Chapter four, verse seven: "I have fought a good fight, I have finished my race, I have kept the faith". She was lucid to the end and it was during making the preparations for her funeral that it occurred to me that her radio was always turned on and she would have heard my father-in-law's death being announced and she would have known why Gwen, her sister and myself were in Jamaica when it was so close to Christmas and we should have been in England with our families. It was a reminder of what she said many times to me when I was growing up and tried to pull a fast one on her: "Whitty, I was not born yesterday, I am trying my best to live at peace with myself and others, I hope you are." From what those who were around her passing said, it was as peaceful as one could hope for.

With the advent of the Millennium and the various predictions of what was expected to happen, travelling by air was not one of the easiest options to contemplate, plus with it coming up to Christmas, chances of relatives living overseas who would want to come down to Jamaica to pay their last respects seemed rather bleak, but thanks to Tony Coles and Yvonne Watkins-Knight of Air Jamaica in London, arrangements were made so that both my daughters, my two grand-daughters and my nephew Paul were able to be in Jamaica two days before the funeral; for other relatives who had to travel from Canada and from various cities in the United States, listening to their experiences of how they arrived in Jamaica some on the very day, in some cases literally a couple of hours before the event, was almost Herculean.

From an early age I became aware that death is as commonplace as life, but when Pastor Alvin Francis of The New Testament Church of God, where my mother served as Secretary for over fifty years, said in his sermon: "Whit like myself you are the only surviving son, I believe that I have an understanding of what you are going through". I knew then that her passing left a new thought process in my mind in that in her lifetime she buried her eldest son, Noel, her eldest daughter, Carmen, and her eldest stepson, Egbert; now I was burying her, which according to the general order of things it is usual for children to bury parents and not the other way round, and the fact that I carried out her wishes I can't say that it was rewarding, endearing or dramatic. I think that the best way I can describe it is that the way that she brought us up was to be prepared for the inevitable; my nephew, David Stennett, in paying tribute to her remembered her for many things that she did in her lifetime that made his sisters and himself happy when they would travel from Kingston to spend the summer holidays with her and on their arrival they would be greeted with a tall glass of an ice cold drink made from the Seville orange which had segments that could either be sweet or bitter; for him it did not matter, it was always refreshing.

Two days after we had laid her to rest was Christmas Day, which is also my sister Lurline's birthday. We all figured that if mother was around she would want us to celebrate; it made it even more pressing that we did. To begin with all or most of the family who were planning to travel down to Jamaica to celebrate her 100th birthday in year 2000, that was if the world lasted that long, were already there, so why not celebrate! It started with a gathering at the beach at seven o'clock on Christmas morning. There were children, grandchildren, great grand and great great grandchildren, and friends running close to the number of sands on the shore. Deep in the recesses of my mind was that it would be the last time that we would meet. In other words, I was convinced that the Millennium would put paid, or drastically alter, the way of life in the year 2000.

If that was the way that I felt it certainly was not the way that Livingston Green, Chair, and Ernest Cover, Treasurer, of the Discovery Bay Past Students' Association felt when, during the celebrations, they invited me to come down to Jamaica in the July of 2000 to be their guest speaker at the Annual Dinner Dance; I accepted the invitation with an air of reservation but I did eventually make it and it turned out to be a wonderful experience.

The reality that over the years my mother was living for me did not really kick in until when I arrived back in Manchester and reflected on the fortnightly telephone calls on a Sunday evening, which always ended with "Whitty I am praying for you", which would no longer happen, neither would the birthday cards, the Easter cards or the Christmas cards. One of the first things that suffered was the lack of interest that I was showing in my coursework, which so far had been going well and which I hoped would be completed in 2000. Not surprisingly, what I presented to my course tutor, Janet Batsleer, as my final piece of work was well below par; the ball was now in my court as to whether I re-submit or call it a day. When I started the course I was near retirement age so it was not part of a career enlistment, it definitely was an intellectual challenge and except that I paid for it from my savings I just could not find the energy to re-submit. If the truth needs to be told I was spending a lot of time playing and enjoying my golf, besides, in 2002 we were due to celebrate our 40th wedding anniversary and how best to celebrate the event than going on a Caribbean cruise.

As they say it is always good to talk and life's journey takes more than one person to walk it, so when I mentioned to Ossie and Rudolph Smith, no relation as far as I know, and Jay Hamilton, the reason why I decided not to complete the course, all three were of the same opinion that I would be letting down a lot of people who up to that point saw me as someone in the community who possessed the ability and the determination to finish a task. Rudolph was the most forceful, either in his criticism or his sense of motivation, when he said to me, "Look Whit, you coming to discuss your intentions with me is an absolute waste of my time, at least if you don't want to complete the course. For yourself you owe it to your father and mother to finish it as a legacy to their memory." I left the Proctor's Youth Project where Rudolph Smith worked in two or several states of mind, but even if I wanted to I could not shut out, or for that matter suppress, the words "you owe to your father and mother". I knew that I had the answers in terms of what to do; the first was to spend less time on the golf course and concentrate more on my dissertation, the theme "The Significance of African Caribbean Achievements through Sports and its influence in the Community". Dedicated to the memory of my father, Joseph William Stennett, who departed from this planet on the 31st May 1946, and to my mother, Maud Elizabeth Stennett, who has gone on to higher service on the 11th of December 1999. They instilled in us the notion that victory is part of the struggle.

It would seem to me that the idea of going on a cruise to celebrate our 40th Wedding Anniversary was mine alone because as late as December 2001 I noticed that Gwen had not been doing any shopping for the occasion; the fact of the matter was she cannot swim and feels uncomfortable with being on the water. I am the opposite and would rather sail than fly, but there we have it. It takes all sorts to make the world. Gwen's change of mind was due to my sister, Lyn, who sensitised her on the glories of being on a cruise, likening it to taking your hotel around with you to a number of interesting places. That is exactly the way it was on the Costa Victoria that took us on our Caribbean Cruise; a wonderful and never to be forgotten experience, and since then Gwen is completely sold on cruises.

In April 2002 I received a letter from the Manchester Metropolitan University informing me that I was successful with my project. I was very pleased with myself and remembered that when I passed my second Jamaica Local Examination for dinner that evening we had Escovietched fish, so I persuaded Gwen, which was not easy, that I would do the cooking on the day of hearing from the University.

Recipe for Escovietched Fish
2lbs sliced fish
2 limes
1 tablespoon black pepper
1 teaspoon salt
1 medium sized carrot
½ cup cooking oil
1 large onion
2 hot peppers
1 dozen pimento seeds
1 cup vinegar.

Method
Clean fish by washing with limes. Dry fish slices and season with salt and pepper. Fry in a skillet with cooking oil. Fry until brown on all sides. Drain oil and arrange fish on platter. Cut carrots in long strips and cook lightly. Slice onions and pepper in rings. Add 1 cup vinegar, 2 tablespoons oil and pimento seed in skillet. Simmer for 10 minutes then pour over brown fried fish and leave for 4 hours.

For dessert it was Banana Delight and the recipe is as follows:
6 large ripe bananas
Lime juice
1 ½ cups dark sugar
1 cup grated coconut
¼ cup dark rum

Method.

Peel the bananas then split them in halves. Arrange the halves on a buttered baking dish and sprinkle with lime juice then wish sugar. Bake for 30 minutes in a pre-heated oven then sprinkle baked bananas with grated coconut and pour rum all over.

In terms of recipes whenever I am being asked how to make a rum punch my answer is always:

3 strong, 2 sweet, 1 sour and 4 weak which adds up to 3 parts white rum (I always use Wray and Nephew over proof)
2 parts syrup, always red,
1 part of sour lime juice,
4 parts of water

Method

Mix all ingredients together and shake well. Serve chilled.

I certainly would have liked to show more of my culinary skills but time was not in my favour, especially in the light that on the night when I was sworn in as Deputy Mayor to Councillor Marie Harney she told me that she would be making every effort to involve me in the process. Her generosity and sincerity in this respect was overwhelming, to which my wife and myself will always be grateful.

Walking on to the podium of The Bridgewater Hall at the Graduation Ceremony of the Manchester Metropolitan University was another high point in my life. My family and some of my friends were there to support me and I had this fantastic feeling that somewhere in the great beyond my father, mother, brothers and friends who have given of whatever they could afford during their lifetime were looking down at me with some sense of admiration.

With it being the year of The Manchester Commonwealth Games I was kept quite busy, but between those periods when time became available I went back playing golf, did my gardening and a little cricket umpiring and also went on a strict diet programme. The reality was that I was doing too much, which I was to discover when I collapsed at home and was admitted to Trafford General Hospital, and from the tests that were conducted it showed that at some time previously I had suffered a mild heart attack which over time had healed itself; according to the Cardiologist it happens fairly often and in layman's language it is when the heart skips a beat. I could only assume that the previous occurrence relating to a mild heart-attack was in July 1994 when I umpired a cricket match, Romiley versus Zeneca, when I collapsed and had to be taken into the dressing room for over half an hour before I was able to continue with the match. As it happened it was in the middle of the hay fever season and medical opinion suggested that the Trilludan tablets that I was taking, in addition to those that I was on for blood pressure, could well have contributed to my collapsing; be that as it may, both symptoms were identical and I survived to tell the tales.

According to Winston "Chawfine" Campbell, a serving officer with the Jamaican Constabulary who was on vacation in England and was present when I fainted and accompanied me to Trafford General, the great Council in the sky was not in need of a Deputy Mayor, besides, St Peter would rather see me making history on earth.

CHAPTER SIXTEEN

Lord Mayor of Trafford

ONE OF the most defining moments of my life was on the 21st May 2003 when I stood up in the Council Chamber at Trafford Town Hall to be invested with all of the necessary requirements befitting the office of Mayor of The Borough of Trafford. It was my tenth year as a councillor and I had witnessed nine ceremonies and now it was my turn. The hours running up to the event were beginning to get very tense and my two attendants, Stuart Mann and Peter Garde, were and have always been very supportive and reassuring to Gwen and myself that everything would go as planned, and when the Reverend Dr David Wheeler prayed with us in the Mayor's Parlour prior to going into the Chamber the anxieties disappeared. I have always believed in the power of prayer because it definitely works. Amongst the sea of faces in the gallery, where there was standing room only, were relatives and friends from as far afield as America, Canada, Jamaica and various cities and towns in England and in my acceptance speech I stuck to my cricket analogy by reminding the gathering that I would endeavour to follow in the tradition of previous Mayors who like a committed cricketer kept their eyes on the ball, bowled a good line and length, took their catches either as fielders or wicket-keepers and walked off the field of play to the applause of spectators for a well deserved performance.

The Mayor's Parlour that evening was a hotbed of activity as well-wishers heaped congratulations and cameras flashed from every conceivable angle. It was just overwhelming and when my youngest sister, Lyn, said to me, "Whitty, can you imagine father, mother, brother Eggie, Noel, Carmen and so many friends who have passed on before, what they are doing and saying in that great beyond?" It was well worth thinking about, especially in the light that the gathering was a reflection of a unity of appreciation. It was also a reminder that on the following day, my first civic duty was to attend the funeral of Councillor John Golding, a former Mayor of the Borough. It was at this occasion that words came back to me that I bear some resemblance to the United Nations Secretary, General Kofi Annan. It was for me another interesting line of look-a-likes that has been part of my life experiences to which in some cases the jury is still out on some of them. Suffice to say, people see what they want to see, the bottom line is there is only one Whit Stennett.

Two days after the annual formalities in the Town Hall there was a public celebration of the new Mayor, the first of its kind in the history of the Borough, at Lancashire County Cricket Club. It started with a tremendous welcome by children from Seymour Park Community Primary School, where I have served for many years as a Governor under the Headship of Jenny Dunn. It was quite moving as Gwen and I walked into the large hall of the Cricket Club to receive a standing ovation from the over 200 attendees as the Tony James Orchestra played "Chariots of Fire". There was pageantry, pomp and a sense of history, put into context by my niece, Marilyn Stennett, who lives in America and who said: "When it comes to pageantry no one can do it better than the British."

To a large extent fame is built on outstanding deeds, coupled with a personality where those people who have become well known are admired for their courage and their commitment for the cause in which they believe in, so on the evening of the public celebrations I used the opportunity to honour local people for the contributions that they have made in helping to enhance and improve the life of others in the community. It was the first time Trafford was making awards in this fashion, and as the Chairperson on the independent panel to choose six awardees, it was for me quite a humbling experience realising that there are hundreds of people in the Borough who give so much of their time voluntarily to help other people. The point was made by Jo Blakeway of Century Radio, who presented the awards to Elise Auden for her work with the over 60s Club at Hartford Community Centre in Urmston, the Service to the Community Award to Eileen McDonald of Friends of Old Trafford and Murial Parker, who won The Business Contribution Award for helping people who were affected by the closure of the Carborundum factory. The Young Person's Award went to Kirsty Peterson for helping her deaf mother, translating British Sign Language when out shopping and the Sporting Achievement Award went to David Poyner, who became blind after an illness that made it difficult for him to participate in aerobics, but despite that he became British Blind Sports Indoor Champion. For "Triumph through Adversity" Edgar Roberts, who suffered a stroke and was told that he would never walk again, kicked that advice into touch and resumed walking again.

My long-standing involvement within the community and my passion for cricket was acknowledged that evening when Carol Hassan, Chief Executive Officer for the Borough of Trafford, presented me with a framed poem extolling the life of the illustrious Caribbean cricketer Sir Vivian Richards. The transcript of the speech I made at the public celebrations on Friday 23rd May 2003 was as follows:

Master of Ceremonies, Mrs Delores Cooper Community Relations officer at The Jamaican Embassy in London, Honourable Tony Lloyd, Member of Parliament for Central Manchester, Honourable Beverley Hughes, Member of Parliament for Urmston and Stretford, Deputy Mayor Councillor Mrs Pamela Dixon and her Consort, Mr Ian Dixon, former Mayor Councillor Mrs Marie Harney and her Consort Mr Graham Hall, My Chaplain, Reverend Dr David Wheeler and his wife, Mrs Margaret Wheeler, Distinguished guests, ladies and gentlemen.

This evening marks a defining moment in my life and with everything that this appointment represents it is imperative that I start by first and foremost thanking and acknowledging God for his direction, inspiration and strength for without his help I would not be here this evening. I would like to extend my utmost gratitude to my immediate family most particularly my friend, partner and devoted wife, Gwen Stennett, the Mayoress. She has been a treasured blessing to me since we met in 1960. She has encouraged, supported and participated in every step of my progress. We share two beautiful daughters, Patricia and Angela and three wonderful grand-children, Nikesha, Shanique and Imogen; they have all been tools of inspiration and in a number of ways the things that I do are not only for them but also for the betterment of the wider community.

To my relatives and friends from Jamaica, Canada and the United States of America who are here to share in this most memorable occasion a much hearty thank you; equally important are those from London, Birmingham, Leeds, Oldham, and Sheffield, like the friends from Manchester our links have been forged in a variety of ways and as such I know that our lives have been enriched because we strive to dwell together in unity.

I would also like to acknowledge my parents, who although they have passed on, instilled in us brothers and sisters that any task however lowly or lofty involves prayer, patience, preparation and perseverance in addition to these virtues they have left me with a number of sayings some of which I will share with you this evening such as;

"a closed hand lets nothing in"

"The more one gives the more one gets"

"In giving you can never be used because the act of giving creates blessings from God"

For me the saying that fits me most is "De patient man ride donkey". I have learnt these lessons well and they have helped make me the man you see here this evening.

Other influences in my life worthy of acknowledgement are the people of Discovery Bay in St Ann, Jamaica. My earliest socialising skills were learnt in this rural fishing and farming village, unlike now there were no amenities like running water, telephones, electricity or supermarkets, walking to school barefooted was the norm and on many occasions even when "De rain was falling dutty was till tough" and "although de pot was boiling de food no nuff". These experiences were mere blips and could not destroy a community spirit that was built on the solid foundation of caring from the cradle to the grave. These situations have been influential in my early decision to work in a setting where people become central especially those at grass roots level.

I value the concepts of resourcefulness, resilience, patience and thriftiness as characteristics that are evident within the Jamaican working class. Overtime they have become necessary working tools in the overcoming of obstacles turning them into stepping stones to success and the realisation of a better tomorrow.

I am constantly being reminded of the following words etched in the stained glass window of the Alexandra Medical Practice on Wilbraham Road, in Whalley Range, Manchester. "Traveller there is no path. Footsteps make path"

Being a Jamaican, it is vital that I am mindful of the journeys made by previous African Caribbean people who made their contributions and have become part of a lasting history. To ignore the historical links would be to continue along the highways of ignorance and to reinforce what The Honourable Marcus Garvey said "A race who has no understanding of themselves or their history is like a tree without roots or branches". Therefore I make mention of a few mentors and role models, Marcus Garvey, Nelson Mandela, Martin Luther King Jnr, Malcolm X, Berry Edwards, Clive Lloyd, Viv Richards, Michael Holding, Sir Garfield Soberts, Louise DaCacodia, Diane Modhall, Paula, Dunn, Thomas, Elouise Edwards; their contributions have been indelibly woven into our history. Needless to say there are countless heroes and heroines who have crossed all the divides and have stood against oppression and tyranny. It would be rather remiss of me if I did not take time out to mention some of my mentors past and present in Old

Lord Mayor of Trafford

Trafford such as Aston Douglas, George Blissett, Cyril Hughes, Reverend Tony Durrans and Chris Ford, Andrea Jones, Bashir Choudry, Lilian Munday, Polly Williams, Nev Bygrave, Cleveland Williams, Frank Weekes, Joe Richards, Dan Dunbar. Well it would take me all night to name them all. Guards lock the doors these people are mine. Let us play ball nobody does it like we do. Of course I am talking about my beloved sport, cricket,. If it was not for the British teaching us we would not know how to play the sport. Now we have taught them how to play and enjoy it who can forget those little pals of mine, Ramhdin and Valentine, and of course two Lancastrians Jim Cumbes and Brian Statham. It was from both bowlers that I perfected the art of Line and Length and it is with this sense of accuracy and precision that I intend to represent the community.

Residents of the Borough of Trafford it has been my privilege living with you for the past forty years. Now you have chosen me to represent you as your Mayor, the First Citizen of The Borough. I am truly honoured and tonight I reflect on when I was elected in 1993 to represent the Clifford Ward where residents showed their willingness to look above and beyond the narrow confines of race, ethnicity, class and religious affiliations. This has also been amply reflected in the Council Chamber, where my colleagues from all sides have always been supportive and encouraging. Being here tonight is a testimony of that support.

I would also like to "Big up" and say "Nuff Respect" to my secretary, Sharon Campbell, my Attendants, Stuart Mann and Peter Garde, and general Factotums Pat Dickens and Sue Hewitt, who have all worked tirelessly behind the scenes to make this event be well worth remembering and of course Master of Ceremonies, Councillor Bernard Selby.

Master of Ceremonies, Distinguished Guests, ladies and gentlemen I began this speech by alluding to tonight being a defining moment in my life as First Citizen for the Borough of Trafford. With your support and with God's help, my wife and myself will remain steadfast in our commitment to carry out the duties that are required of us for the coming year.

Once again thank you for joining us we hope that you have enjoyed the occasion we certainly have. I bid you a very good night and a safe journey home and remember to "walk good nu mek fowl mash you".

The language of aspiration and achievement in as far as the Mayoralty was concerned were well documented in the Jamaica Overseas Gleaner, the Urmston Messenger, the Borough's Newspaper, Trafford Today, and in addition there was an interview by Mike Shaft on BBC GMR. All four conveyed to their readers and listeners of me being cast into the mould of a role model and that of a symbolic representative for African Caribbean people, which on the whole was quite flattering, but I was to remind myself of Paul's letter to the Ephesians where he stressed upon the importance of believers to walk with lowliness, meekness, and long-suffering in the task that they were called to perform and by the same rule making every effort to maintain the spirit of unity and peace. I realised that in an ever-changing society it can be a very tall order and at times a difficult act to follow. However, it was important that I stick to my game plan by keeping my eye on the ball.

But for the European elections and the all out Local Government elections in June 2004 my term of office as Mayor would have finished in May of the same year, the extra month was another case which historians would not allow to go unnoticed as during the thirteen months my wife and myself did a total of nine hundred and eight engagements. At times five engagements in one day was not unusual and it was a great experience meeting people from all walks of life locally, nationally and internationally. Some of my most memorable engagements were meeting children in schools and when they visited the Council Chamber and the Mayor's Parlour. I recalled opening a fair in Altrincham when a woman and her husband came up to us and said, "You two are like a breath of fresh air to the Borough". The tongue of good report like that of bad report travels far and wide and when Gwen and I went to Jamaica in our capacity as Mayor and Mayoress, where protocol was observed as in keeping with the office of a visiting Mayor, as we walked to our waiting car an escort said to me, "Mr Mayor, there is an entourage waiting to greet you". On reflection I could well have over-stepped the rules of protocol when I left the two escorts standing to acknowledge over fifty people headed by Arthur Clemetson, Chair of the Discovery Bay Citizens Association. It was a very humbling experience as I was greeted with handshakes amidst a wave of placards bearing, "Welcome Mr Mayor, Son of the Soil".

Unconsciously, I might have kept the official car waiting for about ten minutes as a number of folks from the welcome party requested that I pose with them for photographs. I was quite apologetic to the waiting driver, who said, "Cool running Mr Mayor, no problems, you are home with your people". Being home with my people became much clearer as the car followed by the bus came through from Old Folly up to Top Bay and there were groups of people at the roadside waving at the passing car. The bus followed us to The

Sandals Dunn River Hotel, where we stayed during the visit. On the following morning we were officially introduced to the General Manager, Mr Louis Grant. It turned out that our paths had crossed many years previously when we worked at Tower Isle Hotel; he as an accountant and I in charge of the stationery room. The ten day programme whilst in Jamaica was arranged by Mrs Delores Cooper OD, Community Relations Officer with the Jamaican Embassy in London and Miss Paulette Simpson, United Kingdom Representative in London for the Jamaica National Building Society. It was an opportunity to meet with Mrs Aloun Ndombet-Assamba, Minister of Industry and Tourism, Mr R O Walters, Custos of the Parish of St Ann; interesting Jamaica is the only English-speaking Caribbean country that has Custoses of Parishes, which is similar to a District Lieutenant in England. We also met Mr Emile Spence and other representatives of Jamaica National Building Society, Chief Superintendent Ray Palmer of the Jamaica Constabulary Force, representatives from service clubs, the medical profession, educators and local community groups. These meetings were mainly in keeping with how the Trafford community and the Jamaican community in general, but in particular, the St Ann Community, could develop friendship links that would be of mutual benefit to both communities.

In 2004, when I finished my term as Mayor, I received an award for being first runner-up in the National Co-Operative Bank Mayor of the Year Competition for 2004. The experiences overall were noteworthy and like everything else we do I know that no man is an island and that no man walks alone.

CHAPTER SEVENTEEN

Reflections

I FIRMLY believe that the general order of life, time and space dictates that longevity is solely in the hands of God, who from an early age I was taught to cultivate a closeness by making efforts to obey his law as laid down in the Bible beginning with the Ten Commandments.

It is no idle joke, neither do I intend to flaunt a holier than thou attitude, when I say that I am truly blessed as a result of God's guidance and his pouring out of goodwill upon me.

God has a plan for all of us and to me it is up to the individual in the way he or she chooses to live their lives which in most cases determines the road in which we take for the journey. In my case I have had failures, and where at times it seemed that there was not a shard of light at the end of the tunnel, then I came to the realisation that through failures and rejections our faith in God is being tested; remember what the Bible says that, "Weeping may endure for the night but joy cometh in the morning".

One of my abiding loves is that of families and I start from the premise that families are the backbone of communities; they are like my first cricket team that I captained when I was at Discovery Bay Elementary School in Jamaica. We were successful and we stuck together. Families look out for each other, protect each other, and in the process we learn to understand each other's strengths and weaknesses. The bottom line is sticking to the old adage that "The family who prays together stays together".

Prayer has always been central to me; it is tied in with hope, faith and the inner conviction that dreams can be achieved. Timbo Williams, one of the finest stonemasons in my village, who died when he was over a hundred years old, always said, "Prayer climb the Blue Mountain". In other words, with prayer God can make all things possible, and it is for this reason why as a product of the old school I support the practice of prayer in schools. It should come as no surprise that when I played cricket before each match I would always say a word of prayer.

Presently there seems to be an ambivalence about marriage in our society. Here I would argue that the key to any successful marriage starts with fidelity and respect for each other, which has played an important role in the lives of Gwen and myself since we met in 1960. Of course, there were those who said that it wouldn't last but after almost fifty years we are still together and blessed with Patricia and Angela, our two daughters, and Nikesha, Shanique and Imogen, our granddaughters.

I am conscious that the world is changing in many ways which affects traditional values, mores and norms and I sometimes carry the feeling of hurt and despair when I see that a minority of our young people, sometimes through no fault of their own, have fallen by the wayside and as a result have no belief in themselves, no self-esteem, no regard for their families or for their communities; the upshot of all this is despair, frustration, hopelessness and anger, which manifests itself in ways which sometimes has an adverse effect on the communities in which they live. Yet for all the sadness and anxieties that their behaviour might cause, we all have a responsibility to walk that extra mile in helping them to re-discover themselves and by the same token give as much recognition to the majority who are working hard and are paying their dues in the enhancing of themselves and their communities.

From the day I set foot on British soil I decided that the option to give something back to Jamaica would never be negotiable and as the years rolled on this resolve has become unstoppable and the act of giving something back has moved beyond family blood lines to projects such as donating books to schools and libraries, sports equipment to local clubs, medical and surgical equipment to the St Ann's Bay Hospital and bicycles to the Discovery Bay Police Station. I do this through Jamaican Diaspora UK, a Jamaican Government-backed organisation, which amongst some of its objectives is to utilise the variety of skills and experiences that Jamaicans abroad have acquired and how those skills can be taken to Jamaica and used towards the development of the social, economic and spiritual life of the country. As an active member of the UK Diaspora the giving something back concept is even more deeply entrenched.

I was at Sabina Park in 1958 when Sir Garfield Sobers made 365 not out against Pakistan and created a world record; I was also at Lords in 1975 when in the first Cricket World Cup Clive Lloyd, batting with panache and power, took on two of the best bowlers that Australia has ever produced, Lillee and Thompson, and posted 102 on the board giving Australia a total of 292 to make for victory. They got 274 amidst great adulations; we, the Caribbean spectators, lifted the roof with voices, music and sounds of every description when Clive was presented with the cup by Prince Philip, Duke of Edinburgh. Clive was made "Man of the Match". In 1976 I was at Trent Bridge in Nottingham when Sir Vivian, "The Master Blaster", Richards hit the likes of John Snow, Mike Hendricks, Chris Old, Tony Greig, Bob Woolmer, and Derek Underwood all over the park for 232. In 2002 when Manchester staged the Commonwealth Games I was at the closing ceremony when Councillor Roy Walters, the then Lord Mayor of Manchester, stood in the pouring rain as Her Royal Highness Her Majesty The Queen officiated. There were many other occasions of note that fits into the "I was there" scenario, so when the idea was first mooted that the ninth Cricket World Cup would take place in the Caribbean I vowed that by the hooks or the crooks, and provided I was alive and healthy, I would be going.

Other than the Olympic Games and the football World Cup, the third biggest sporting event in the world is the Cricket World Cup and to have it staged in the Caribbean made it the largest sporting event ever to take place in the region. Previous events such as the World Netball Championships, the Sunshine Showdown, the fight between Joe Frazier and George Foreman for the Heavyweight Championship of the World and the Central American and Caribbean Games have all taken place in Jamaica. I have seen none of them live other than on television or reading about them; in other words, "I wuz not dere". This time round I was in Jamaica to hear the argument conveyed through the print and electronic media and the man on the street regarding the merits or demerits of staging the event in the Caribbean.

In Discovery Bay at the St Ann Bauxite Sporting Complex, now vastly improved out of all proportions form the days of when I was a youngster as a spectator and later as a player, I participated in a number of matches for my village team and I watched some of the World Cup teams who were based in Jamaica practising in the nets. It was also a great opportunity for me to reconnect with school friends who are both living in Jamaica and abroad who have not seen each other from since we left school. In between watching we touched on our past, our present and what lies ahead.

The first warm-up game at the Trelawny Stadium, where West Indies played Kenya and won, answered a number of questions that we were all asking, chief of which was has the West Indies got back to winning ways? My whole world turned upside down when the following morning word reached me that one of my nieces who lived in Montego Bay had died on her way to work. She was thirty one years old and my questions following the news had nothing to do with cricket.

The cricket question as to whether West Indies had got back to winning ways was answered with a resounding "NO" when at their next game India bowled them out for 85 runs. What with the mourning of my niece I was plunged into despair, leaving the ground with a group of friends hoping to find a place where we could drown our reasons. The place we found was Yow's Restaurant and Jerk Centre not far from The Grand Lido, Braco and where in my schooldays Rio Bueno had their cricket ground. It is near to the sea and it was every schoolboys' dream to hit the ball into it.

As would be expected our conversation was about cricket and when Rio Bueno was mentioned it was difficult not to harp back to the old days when Benji Fairclough, who was a son of Rio Bueno, played tenor saxophone and would take solo, playing "Everytime we say goodbye", and Kenneth Edwards from Standfast near Brown Town took solo playing "Stardust Melody". I left feeling much better; at least the chicken was excellent and the festival very good, not to mention the Red Stripe beer. Under the circumstances I had the official opening ceremony of The Cricket World Cup to look forward to and what a success it turned out to be. From a political perspective it brought into focus what Michael Manley, a former Prime Minister of Jamaica, and Sir Frank Worrell, the first African Caribbean to captain the West Indies, have always advocated: the importance of cricket to the political life of the Caribbean. The point was reinforced at the opening ceremony by Prime Minister Portia Simpson-Miller of Jamaica, Prime Minister Keith Mitchell of Grenada and Mr Chris Dehring, CEO of the WICBC.

Culturally-speaking all the negatives regarding to Jamaica were kicked into touch. For example, the long-standing concept of Jamaican time which over the years has gained currency was buried into the dustbin of history when exactly on time the Jamaica Military Band marched out playing a medley of tunes. For me the most poignant was "Sammy Plant Piece A Corn Dung a Gully". As things progressed, and amidst the spontaneity of thousands of people from all over the world who were at ease with themselves through the game of cricket, I asked my friend, Ernest Cover, who sat beside me, if he believed that heaven is like the atmosphere we all were enjoying; the question was answered by a woman who sat in the row before us that if it is she would like to be there. Her accent confirmed that she was from Barbados and without being partisan it was reasonable to make the argument that Jamaica delivered all that was asked of them by the World Cricket authorities regarding its ability to put on an event of that magnitude. The country did just that as the millions who watched it from all the corners of the world have to agree.

The West Indies beating Pakistan, one of the teams tipped to go far into the competition, was just out of this world and confirmed the old cricket clichés that "cricket is a funny old game", and at least the West Indies were back to winning ways and I started to feel better inside.

The death of Bob Woolmer, the Pakistan Cricket Coach, following his team's defeat by Ireland, coupled with the death of my niece a week previously, did have its downside to me going to watch the world cup. My recollection of Bob Woolmer was when in the 1976 Test Match at Trent Bridge in Nottingham, where Viv Richards made his 232, he made 82 valuable runs for England and David Steele made 106. The match was drawn but as the old adage goes, "In the midst of life there is death". The truism is also that "In the midst of death there is also life" and as such I have consoled myself to the reality that without being boastful in any way I can say that "I was at the Opening Ceremony of The World Cup 2007 and saw some of the matches", which is just another extension of the sojourn pending me placing my feet on the soil of Ghana, my ancestral home, and just in case it does not happen, I sincerely hope that when the great master in the sky calls me up for higher service, those who are left behind will see it fit to grant my wishes by having my body cremated and the ashes taken to Discovery Bay in Jamaica, given to a fisherman who will take them and sprinkle them beyond the reef outside of channel mouth, west of the sea lane of the ships that come in to transport the bauxite ore to various parts of the world. It was beyond that reef that as a boy I swam for food and fun and from where I could see my house on the hill and way beyond where it seems that the land is always touching the clouds.

I returned to Jamaica once more in late Summer 2007. Obviously, I was happy once again to be amongst old friends and contrary to popular belief that cricket is dying in the Caribbean, I was amazed at the interest that youngsters at grassroots level still had for the sport. In this context no praise is too high for the St Ann Jamaica Bauxite Company, who sponsor the mini league competition involving boys and girls from the ages of eight to 18. Over the years the mini leagues have produced players such as Xavier Marshall and Leon Garrick, who have represented the West Indies. Other players, such as Rashard Marshall, Chris Green and Orville Pennant have played for St Ann in the senior league competitions. Watching the youngsters playing reminded me of when many many moons ago I played on the same ground at Discovery Bay, now developed out of all proportions, first by the Kaiser Bauxite Company and now by the St Ann Bauxite Company.

If I was swept away by nostalgia I put it down to part and parcel of the human condition and experience - and speaking of experience, whilst on this last visit to my home island yet another hurricane took place. Hurricane Dean did not do as much damge as Ivan in 2004, Charlie in 1958 and the first one in 1951, but it was symbolic of my journey. It has been a bittersweet journey and one that I would not want to change if I had to live my life all over again.